Nut Country

Nut Country

Right-Wing Dallas and the
Birth of the Southern Strategy

Edward H. Miller

THE UNIVERSITY OF CHICAGO PRESS
Chicago and London

Edward H. Miller is assistant teaching professor at Northeastern University Global.

The University of Chicago Press, Chicago 60637
The University of Chicago Press, Ltd., London
© 2015 by The University of Chicago
All rights reserved. Published 2015.
Printed in the United States of America

24 23 22 21 20 19 18 17 16 15   1 2 3 4 5

ISBN-13: 978-0-226-20538-0   (cloth)
ISBN-13: 978-0-226-20541-0   (e-book)
DOI: 10.7208/chicago/ 9780226205410.001.0001

Library of Congress Cataloging-in-Publication Data

Miller, Edward H. (Edward Herbert), author.
    Nut country : right-wing Dallas and the birth of the Southern strategy /
Edward H. Miller.
        pages ;   cm
    Includes bibliographical references and index.
    ISBN 978-0-226-20538-0 (cloth : alk. paper)
    ISBN 978-0-226-20541-0 (ebook)
        1. Republican Party (Tex.)—History—20th century. 2. Right-wing extremists—
Texas—Dallas. 3. Conservatism—Texas—Dallas. 4. Dallas (Tex.)—Politics and
government—20th century. 5. Southern States—Politics and government—
1951–. I. Title.
    JK2359.D35M55 2015
    324.273409'045—dc23

                                                                          2015010761

Contents

Introduction

President Kennedy's exploded head was a Mark of the Beast, some said, even during Kennedy's televised state funeral throughout the long, gray weekend of November 23 to 25, 1963.[1]

On Saturday, an honor guard kept vigil over Kennedy's body, which lay in state in the East Room of the White House. On Sunday, amid muted drumbeats, a horse-drawn caisson slowly moved the president's body up Pennsylvania Avenue to the Capitol rotunda. Kneeling beside the casket, the president's thirty-four-year-old widow kissed the flag draped over her husband's coffin. A quarter of a million strong—many crying or holding back tears—shuffled by. On Monday, six white horses drew the carriage containing the casket to its final resting place in Arlington National Cemetery. A riderless horse named Black Jack restlessly followed and John F. Kennedy Jr., on his third birthday, saluted his father one last time. President Kennedy's body lay motionless in the coffin.

But some were convinced it would not be there long: Kennedy was going to rise from the grave and become the Antichrist. Those who believed this tended to be devout premillennial dispensationalists who held that the Bible foretold in detail the chronology of the end of the world, and that the Antichrist's arrival marks the Rapture, the beginning of the Tribulation, a seven-year period that ends with the final battle of Armageddon. For them, the setting was perfect for the advent of the Antichrist. Via the still new medium of television, the world seemed to be watching, and many heads of state were present in Washington, DC. Many signs suggested that Kennedy was the "beast" described in the book of Revelation. Beyond his head wound, Kennedy had been a member of the Catholic church—the "Whore of Babylon" according to some Protestant readings of Revelation, an institution destined to play a crucial role during the Antichrist's rule and reign.[2]

Dallas resident H. L. Hunt was one such premillennial dispensationalist, embodying what historian Kim Phillips-Fein has called the "baroque strangeness" of the far right. The richest man in the world by the 1950s, oilman Hunt represented the ultraconservative wing of the Dallas Republican Party. He peddled conspiracy theories, employed apocalyptic rhetoric, and thought in absolutist terms. He was also intransigent in his belief that liberalism was equivalent to Communism. A friend once commented that Hunt "thought that Communism began in this country when the government took over the distribution of mail."[3] Rejecting ideological compromise of any kind, Hunt demanded absolute victory over a collection of enemies that included not only Communists, fellow travelers, and Democrats but also the Republican Eisenhower administration. The oil tycoon used his fortune to spread his message, parlaying his great wealth into Facts Forum, a veritable media empire that extended into radio, television, and print.[4] Hunt was an eccentric who had nursed at his mother's breast till age seven. He liked to engage in a type of exercise that he called "creeping." On the carpet of his office suite, he would crawl like an infant in order to develop what he believed to be a form of higher brain function. He was convinced that he could live forever and believed that he possessed a sixth sense.[5]

On the other end of the Dallas Republican Party from Hunt was Henry Neil Mallon, the quintessential Dallas moderate conservative Republican.[6] Molded by conservatism in his native Ohio, which he left in 1950 to become president of Dresser Industries, Mallon typified the political leanings of his adopted hometown. An active, lifelong member of the GOP, he concentrated on building the party's institutional structure in Dallas in accordance with his straightforward views: he embraced small government and hailed tax cuts; he assailed Communism and believed in a global Communist conspiracy but rejected as nonsense the idea that high-level American officials colluded with the Kremlin; and he espoused a soft segregationist stance but avoided abject racial demagoguery.[7]

During the early 1950s, Mallon became deeply concerned about Hunt and his burgeoning media empire. In 1953, Mallon wrote about Hunt to his best friend—a Yale classmate, fellow member of the Skull and Bones secret society, and US senator—Prescott Bush, the father of George H. W.

Bush. A "situation is developing here in Dallas," he wrote, that could "render sterile the Conservative viewpoint." H. L. Hunt and Facts Forum were setting out to "stigmatize honest dissent, . . . destroy the machinery for objective consideration of honest problems," and introduce "authoritarianism, absolutism and thought-control." "This movement," Mallon wrote, "is no small, localized affair. . . . It is growing daily, in terms of money expended" and "propaganda expounded."[8]

Mallon saw the need to counterbalance Hunt's message and, as a result, became more involved in local politics. He established the Dallas Council on World Affairs, a local center-right group that scheduled speakers and discussions. He attended Republican Party events, making generous contributions to moderate conservative Republican candidates and throwing his support behind Barry Goldwater. In his public pronouncements, Mallon advocated the importance of home ownership and lowering tax rates to 25 percent for the most affluent Americans. He shaped the corporate culture at Dresser Industries (which would later become part of Halliburton), hiring many moderate conservative Republicans, including George H. W. Bush, who named his third son, Henry Neil Bush, after Mallon. At Dresser, Mallon created a corporate culture that spoke reverentially of the ability of the free market to allocate wealth efficiently and fairly without government interference.[9]

The example of H. N. Mallon—a Republican stalwart who felt threatened by the rise of ultraconservative Republican activity in Dallas between 1953 and 1963 and was motivated to pursue a brand of relative centrism—illustrates the main argument of *Nut Country*. This book focuses on relationships and ideological exchanges between the ultraconservative and moderate conservative Republicans of Dallas, Texas, and shows how ultraconservatives like H. L. Hunt, who received widespread national media attention in the 1950s and 1960s, served as important catalysts for the diffusion of conservative ideas across the entire right wing of the American political spectrum. Hunt and other ultraconservatives provided the impetus behind much of the conservative activism of the era, among both moderate and ultraconservative Republicans. They not only pushed moderate conservatives into an increasingly active role in 1950s and 1960s Dallas Republican politics, they also radicalized the right wing of the national party and forced the mainstream to embrace some of their "fringe" ideas.

Ultraconservative Republicans offered moderate conservative Republicans cover in constructing political identities: by labeling ultraconservative doctrines "extremist," the moderate conservatives could position themselves at the local and national levels as comparatively respectable and credible. Ultraconservatives like Hunt received the lion's share of the brickbats and catcalls from the American national media. By comparison, more moderate conservative activists, intellectuals, and politicians like H. N. Mallon, Congressman Bruce Alger of Dallas, Senator John Tower of Texas, and Senator Barry Goldwater of Arizona often remained shielded from attacks and could develop policies and political styles that mirrored, albeit subtly, those of the "fringe."

Nut Country shows that ultraconservative Republicans were more essential to the rise of the Right than recent historians have appreciated. Many of the original scholars studying American conservatism acknowledged ultraconservatives but largely dismissed the Right as suffering from status anxiety, burdened by irrationality, possessing a "paranoid style," or simply reacting to social or political backlash.[10] Beginning in the 1990s, a wave of historians concluded that the committed and persuasive conservative activists of the 1960s and 1970s were not a paranoid group on the wane but mainstream, rational, educated, upwardly mobile "suburban warriors" motivated by ideas gleaned from the books they read. In abandoning a narrative that dismissed and disparaged the Right, scholars made a welcome and salubrious corrective. Yet much as the Right was largely *written off* in the older scholarship, ultraconservatives and extremists were largely *written out* of the newer story, with its emphasis on a milder-mannered conservatism.[11] *Nut Country* highlights ultraconservatives' decisive role in reconfiguring the American Right at the dawn of the civil rights era. Ultraconservatives here take their place alongside the moderate conservatives—those pragmatic, middle-class professionals and housewives enjoying upward mobility and embodying mainstream values. This book examines the influence of ultraconservative Republicans in Dallas who did not completely jettison their predilections for apocalyptic fantasies, overheated rhetoric, conspiracy theories, and assertions of white supremacy, and argues that these ultraconservatives were even more important than the moderate conservatives.

This book also presents a novel interpretation of the Republican Southern Strategy. As many scholars have shown, Republican leaders like Barry Goldwater, Richard Nixon, and Ronald Reagan broke the Democratic Party's hegemony in the Solid South and segments of the North by capitalizing on the reactions of white voters to events of the 1960s, when anxieties about the counterculture, the decline of traditional sexual mores, the decrease in union membership, and the new tendency of whites to see themselves as home owners, taxpayers, and school parents rather than workers, were reshaping their political thinking. Even more crucial, the Democratic Party's support for affirmative action, school busing, and welfare made these Northern and Southern white voters conclude that the party no longer protected *their* interests but rather those of African-Americans. In order to attract these disaffected voters into the GOP fold, politicians like Goldwater, Nixon, and Reagan developed a Southern Strategy, framing a color-blind discourse of rights, freedom, individualism, and "small government" that appealed to the values of middle-class suburbanites. Republican "color-blind conservatism" predominantly appealed to class advantage, economic rights, "freedom of choice," and cultural concerns, but race always hovered in the rhetoric. This ostensibly meritocratic discourse secured racial privileges like the spatial segregation of suburbs, and justified a minimum of diversity in public schools.[12] *Nut Country*, challenging this traditional narrative, argues that the GOP's Southern Strategy was born not in the 1960s but in the 1950s Southwest, and was in fact explicitly racial in motivation and application. Dallas Republicans were blazing the trail for the GOP Southern Strategy by making racial appeals to white Democrats as early as 1956.

Nut Country reveals the peculiar social and political significance of Dallas by highlighting not only the city's contribution to the Southern Strategy but its powerful local conservative movement. While historians have written engaging analyses of the postwar conservative movements forged in the metropolitan areas of the Sunbelt, the crescent of states along the southern rim that accounted for much of the nation's demographic and economic growth in the last half of America's century, none has fully examined conservative Republicanism in Dallas or Houston.[13] This is surprising, given that none other than Barry Goldwater observed that "there was no better place in the nation to study 1964 from the GOP grassroots level than the state of Texas."[14] *Nut Country* places Dallas center-stage in the story of the conservative ascendancy. The city's geographic position made it the crossroads of the South, West, and Midwest, and its status as a Sunbelt boomtown ensured the arrival of voters from a variety of locations. Dallas was not only a Southern city with a long-standing tradition of white racial supremacist views but also home to many Northern and Midwestern transplants who, while uncomfortable with overt racism, were susceptible to sophisticated encoded appeals to unacknowledged bigotry. The city was thus a perfect test kitchen in which the Republican Party could try out different racial strategies to change its political fortunes. When party leaders in Dallas perfected their dish—through victories such as the landmark election of Republican John Tower to the US Senate in 1961—they could deliver it to the rest of the country. Conservative Dallas Republicans tested spicier versions, but its blander form—a comparatively subtle appeal to white racial superiority—would be served up by the likes of Barry Goldwater, Richard Nixon, and Ronald Reagan in the years to come.

The story shows how the central religious tenets of Dallas ultraconservative Republicans advanced their secular political ideology. The Republican Party's original Southern Strategy was partly grounded in a spiritual defense of segregation, which held that the Bible prohibited the integration of blacks and whites. Biblical literalism and premillennial dispensationalism fostered ultraconservative Republicans' preoccupation with eschatology and spiritual cabals, which they then projected onto the secular world of politics. Many employed apocalyptic rhetoric, purporting that America was always in its death throes. Their embrace of fundamentalism undergirded an absolutist understanding of secular matters, reinforcing their devout belief in the correctness of their opinions and perception of the world as black and white. Their conviction that Satan's war against Christianity was history's biggest and longest-standing cabal also likely fed into their preoccupation with conspiracies. For ultraconservative Republicans, history was a grand plot, and conspirators were ubiquitous, omniscient, and omnipotent; random events, when closely scrutinized, were found to fit preconceived patterns that confirmed their conspiratorial worldview.[15]

This tale features characters who were charismatic, prepossessing, uncompromising, and fiercely ambitious, among them General Edwin Walker, who was reprimanded by the Kennedy administration for distributing John Birch Society literature to his troops. After resigning from the US Army, Walker became an ultraconservative icon, establishing his headquarters in Dallas, but ultimately proved unable to handle the pressures of celebrity status. Walker's latent homosexuality in a place and time that did not openly permit such a lifestyle likely contributed to his downfall. We will meet W. A. Criswell, the powerful pastor of the First Baptist Church of Dallas. In the early 1960s, Criswell defended segregation and doubted that John F. Kennedy, the 1960 Democratic nominee for president, could ever remain free from "church domination." The cast also includes Edward "Ted" Musgrove Dealey, the publisher of the *Dallas Morning News*. Under Dealey's tenure, quipped the retail magnate Stanley Marcus, the *News* was "opposed to social progress, the United Nations, the Democratic party, federal aid, welfare, and virtually anything except the Dallas Zoo." As a guest at the White House in 1961, Dealey insulted the president in front of other Texas reporters, calling Kennedy and his administration "weak sisters," and claimed that the president was "riding Caroline's tricycle."[16]

Kennedy's frustration over Dealey supplies this book's title, a sharp riposte uttered on the last day of the president's life. In a Fort Worth, Texas, hotel room on the morning of November 22, 1963, the president's mood had soured as he read the day's edition of the *Dallas Morning News*. "Welcome Mr. Kennedy to Dallas," read a full-page advertisement placed by three members of the John Birch Society, which went on to claim that the city's success was due to "conservative economic and business practices," not "federal handouts," and to accuse the president of Communist sympathies. "How can people say such things," Kennedy asked his wife, who was donning a new pink Chanel dress. "We're heading into nut country today," he muttered. "You know who's responsible for that ad? Dealey."[17]

But *Nut Country* is not only about outspoken publishers with a penchant for reactionary politics, brilliant if eccentric oilmen, and obstinate preachers with an affinity for the Lost Cause; it is also a story of men and women like J. Erik Jonnson and Margot Perot—the new power brokers of Dallas, the Sunbelt's new buckle. They were the housewife activists and politicking corporate magnates who mobilized and built the scaffolding of the Dallas GOP. The new power brokers migrated from all parts of the country, but especially the Midwest and Northeast. They came seeking new economic and political opportunities in the free-market environs of Dallas. George Herbert Walker Bush and his family were hardly the only "Lone Star Yankee" immigrants. Jonnson hailed from Brooklyn, New York, moved to Dallas, ascended to the presidency of Texas Instruments in 1953, became active in Republican politics, and was elected mayor of Dallas in 1964. A lifelong Republican originally from Pennsylvania, Margot Perot was the wife of H. Ross Perot, who founded Electronic Data Systems, and a mother to five children. By the 1960s, Margot was not only president of the Valley View Republican Women's Club but teaching others how to organize precincts and serving as the recording secretary of the Dallas County Council of Republican Women.[18]

These power brokers were a cohort of upwardly mobile, bright, and modern men and women preoccupied with establishing institutional frameworks, raising money for the party, raising children, recruiting quality candidates, and above all, winning elections. They realized that building a successful party organization required eschewing intransigence and absolutism and staking out moderate positions. They drew their economic worldview from the principle that the abundant private interests that sought to influence the free-market system represented a lesser threat to the individual than a hegemonic state.

Bruce Alger, Dallas's Republican congressman from 1955 through 1965, serves as the window through which much of this story is told. Alger personifies how Dallas's moderate conservative and ultraconservative Republicans fought for hegemony, forcing public officials to adjust to each new turn in the contest. Born in Dallas in 1918 and raised in the St. Louis suburb of Webster Falls, Missouri, Bruce Alger attended Princeton University on an academic scholarship and flew B-29 long-range bombers during World War II. After the war he returned to Dallas, where by the mid-1950s he had become a successful real estate developer. He was elected in 1954 as the first Republican congressman from Dallas since Reconstruction. Alger was a dashing figure with jet-black hair and tight-fitting dark suits. Many of his contemporaries thought he resembled Gary Cooper, and today he could easily stand in for *Mad Men*'s Donald Draper. Alger ultimately established a reputation as one of the country's most reactionary congressmen, though he bounced between the ultraconservative and moderate conservative camps. Historians have largely shrugged off Alger and his attacks on the size of government, his denunciations of Social Security, his condemnations of public housing, and his censures of a federal milk program.[19] In truth, Alger was far more complicated, interesting, and important a figure to the future of the Republican Party than historians have realized.

Most importantly, Alger's 1956 reelection campaign served as a seminal precedent for the racialization and future Southern Strategy of the Republican Party. It marked the first time that a Southern Republican had abandoned his initial measured stance on desegregation and embraced segregationist positions to maintain and build his electoral coalition. With the ranks of the far right swelling, a moderate stance on integration became politically untenable for Alger. Alger made the baldly political decision to signal to white voters that he was antagonistic toward the interests of civil rights and blacks. His precedent made it unequivocally clear that Dallas Republicans opposed civil rights as well as "handouts" and "special treatment" for African-Americans. Alger's decision established a powerful precedent that was followed thereafter in a consistent and steady pattern by such Dallas Republicans as Senator John Tower and Dallas County Republican chairmen Maurice Carlson and Peter O'Donnell, as well as 1964 Republican presidential nominee Barry Goldwater.

Nut Country explores the larger development of the modern Republican Party during a profoundly important rebuilding phase, from 1952 to 1964. For the national GOP, these turbulent years of political reconstitution were instrumental in exorcising a great impediment to its future success: its legacy as the party of Radical Reconstruction, of Abraham Lincoln, and of black male suffrage and office-holding. In the mid-1950s, the GOP began the incremental process of breaking from, albeit never completely, its long-standing identification as the party of Lincoln. With Dallas as its progenitor, this newborn GOP evolved into a party that opposed expansion of federal civil rights legislation, and that paved the way for its ascension in the once solidly Democratic South.

While Dallas's centrality to this story has been overlooked, it is important not to take the implications of this too far. As Geoffrey Kabaservice and Joseph Crespino point out, it is an overstatement to say that the national parties completely swapped positions.[20] Well into the 1960s throughout the South, segregationist Democrats like Georgia governor Lester Maddox and Alabama governor Lurleen Wallace won elections. In a nuanced and exhaustive recent study of race and the Republican Party, historian Timothy Thurber found that in the 1970s "Republicans, especially those in the Senate, proved crucial to fending off attempts by conservatives (usually southerners) in both parties to roll back reforms" crucial to African-Americans.[21] Indeed, although never inspiring the excitement and activism of racially conservative Republicans, moderate and liberal Republicans of the 1960s and 1970s—Everett Dirksen, Nelson Rockefeller, and William Scranton—stood at the forefront of the major civil rights accomplishments of the period.

Moreover, Republicans—with some Dallas Republicans leading the way—altered their political strategies on race in the wake of Goldwater's loss. The resounding losses of both Senator Goldwater and Congressman Alger in 1964 convinced many Dallas and national Republicans that the old stratagems (appealing to fears of Communism and the loss of property, asserting white supremacy) were no longer effective with enough of the electorate. Some abandoned thinly veiled appeals to racist sentiments, adopting a color-blind language of justice for all in order to widen their electoral reach. While such discourses of tax relief and libertarian economics were sometimes rhetorical strategies couching racial conservatism, many times they were genuine and embodied practical appeals to the newly affluent in the booming Sunbelt. Some Republicans, including Dallas Republicans like Frank Crowley, Peter O'Donnell, and W. A. Criswell, experienced genuine changes of heart on the matter of race throughout the course of the long civil rights era, not only moderating their approach but earnestly reappraising the place of blacks in American society.

And yet, despite the reality of color-blind rhetoric—whether born from genuine conviction or from political calculation—Dallas's contribution to the racialization of the Republican Party during the seminal period from 1952 to 1964 continues to loom large into the present. The more nuanced, color-blind discourse after 1964 became possible and appeared relatively benign precisely because of the more provocatively racial stratagems that Dallas originated and Goldwater delivered. Blacks were among the first to recognize how much the Republican Party had changed by 1964, and many have neither forgiven nor forgotten it. Barry Goldwater received the same percentage of the black vote in 1964 as Mitt Romney did in 2012: 6 percent.[22] Bob Dylan, the period's most influential folk singer, could have been speaking to the enduring legacy of the Dallas GOP on race: "the line it is drawn / the curse it is cast."

1 Big D

The Ins and Outs

In 1950, no Republican from Texas had served in the US Senate since 1877. No Republican from Dallas County had served in the US House of Representatives since Reconstruction. No Republican had served in a Texas statewide office since Governor Edmund J. Davis in 1874.[1] Republicans always lost in Dallas.

Volunteering for the Dallas Republican Party in the 1940s was a taxing experience with few rewards. Party work itself was hard, tedious, and exhausting. A few campaign workers did the work of many and kept long hours. The incessant ringing of the telephone at party headquarters made too much coffee necessary and cigarette breaks all too infrequent for the rare receptionist. Volunteers had to tolerate the constant stain of mimeograph fluid underneath their fingernails. Sleep-deprived, crabby candidates needed to be coddled. Campaign workers had to keep a watchful eye out for the forgetful ones who left behind yard signs or those who bossed around the college volunteers. Of course, volunteers experienced such travails only when the party fielded a candidate, which in the 1940s was uncommon.

The Texas GOP fared no better. Between 1923 and 1950, state Republican chairman Rentfro Banton Creager oversaw a party that possessed little power beyond doling out patronage. Creager enjoyed his small circle of admirers and relished the meager spoils that trickled in from Washington, but he showed little inclination to invigorate the party by seeking out candidates. The candidates it did field received scant financial or logistical support.[2] Grizzled campaign veterans knew enough to temper their enthusiasm for any candidate lest they grow despondent when the Democrats trounced him in November.

The party of Abraham Lincoln had little appeal to Texans. When the guns of the Civil War fell silent, Republican-led Reconstruction sought to rebuild a South decimated by four years of conflict. Republicans determined the size and scope of federal policies designed not only to build new political institutions in the South, but also to help newly emancipated African-Americans adjust to their new lives as free men and women. African-Americans supported a Republican Party that endorsed their civil rights with amendments to the Constitution. Republicans were identified with misrule, military occupation, and government by "carpetbaggers": as a result, the party was unpopular with Southern whites. Humiliated by Yankee occupation, Southern whites voted out Republicans, disenfranchised African-Americans, and voted solidly Democratic throughout the late nineteenth and first half of the twentieth century. Texans supported Democrats in every presidential election until 1928, when voters preferred the Protestant and "dry" Herbert Hoover to the Catholic and "wet" Al Smith.[3]

Dallas itself was, in the 1940s, a socially conservative but Democratic-voting town, an uncomfortable political juxtaposition which would soon change. The widening gap between the views of conservative Texas Democrats and a national Democratic Party increasingly sympathetic to the social and economic rights of blacks and the working class provided opportunities for Republican growth in the state. Factional discord between more liberal national Democrats, championing a more activist state, and conservative Texas Democrats, supporting minimal social services, segregation, and restrictions on labor unions, produced a cohort of voters who were there for the taking. In each of the presidential elections of 1944, 1948, and 1952, many conservative Texas Democrats bolted from their party and voted for the Republican nominee, but the 1952 election was the first instance in which Republicans reaped clear benefits. That year, conservative Democrats, especially Texas oilmen, wanted the federal government to recognize Texas's claim to the oil-rich tidelands ten and a half miles off its coast. The national Democratic Party, including President Harry Truman, favored federal ownership of the tidelands. Democratic governor Allan Shivers, who wielded control over the Texas Democratic Party apparatus and its national convention delegates, would not endorse Democratic presidential nominee Adlai Stevenson unless he supported the state's ownership of the tidelands.

Republican presidential nominee Dwight Eisenhower, a native of Denison, Texas, had already committed to returning the tidelands to Texas. When Stevenson refused to support state ownership, Shivers, who himself was up for reelection, threw his support behind Eisenhower. Eisenhower defeated Stevenson in Texas, receiving 53 percent of the vote. By putting a rift in the once Solid South, Eisenhower's victory marked, in the words of historian Kenneth Bridges, a "realistic and palatable alternative" and "the turning point in the evolution" of a two-party South.[4] And it was conservative Democrats in Dallas who made a key difference. Eisenhower ran remarkably better in Dallas County than in the state as a whole, drawing 118,218 votes to Stevenson's 69,394.[5]

Why Does Dallas Exist?

An important factor in early-1950s Dallas that contributed to the enthusiasm for Eisenhower, and for Republicanism in general, was the city's origin myth.[6] Hollis McComb, a Texas journalist, crafted a quintessential précis of the origin myth, according to which Dallas "never should have become a city. . . . Dallas was set astride no natural routes of trade. . . . There was no port nearby. Beneath the city were none of the raw materials—oil, gas, and sulfur—that made other Texas cities rich. . . . The climate in summer is practically unendurable. Yet there Dallas stands—its skyscrapers soaring abruptly up from the blackland like Maxfield Parrish castles. . . . Dallas doesn't owe a thing to accident, nature, or inevitability." Dallas, he concluded, was "the Athens of the Southwest" "because the men of Dallas damn well planned it that way."[7] Celebrating the unlimited potential of any individual possessing what McComb called "sheer determination," the myth expressed and fostered a powerful economic faith in the virtues of the ordered chaos of unfettered frontier capitalism, discouraging the receipt of federal funds and rejecting any need for social services.[8] Moreover, it drove Dallas's predilection for conspicuous consumption, conferring a kind of sainthood on those whose spending provided outward proof of their virtue.[9]

Yet the myth bore only a loose resemblance to the truth. With an abundant water supply and rich soil, Dallas was, as Michael Phillips has observed, "the logical place for an important commercial settlement."[10] Founded in 1841 by John Neely Bryan, who pioneered a number of settlements in Arkansas, Dallas remained a marginal agricultural trading post until its selection as a county seat in 1850. Dallas's agriculture-based economy in the nineteenth century, along with its strong Protestant evangelical heritage, instilled in the region a powerful Southern traditionalist conservatism that stressed the importance of self-reliance, strict moralism, social hierarchy, and segregation. Deeply ensconced well before Dallas became a financial, oil, and aerospace epicenter, these predispositions, shared by many Dallasites, included a belief in the Bible's inerrancy, a revulsion for the corner saloon, and a fear of new immigration. The advent of the railroads in the 1870s turned a sleepy agricultural hamlet into a bustling hub for manufacturing, ensured more intensive cultural and economic exchanges with St. Louis and the Northeast, and increased the city's population from three thousand in 1873 to forty thousand in 1890. In the 1910s and 1920s, the horse-drawn streetcar accelerated the city's expansion. The aggressive promotion of Dallas by local businessmen, an influx of migrants, and the annexation of Oak Cliff in 1904 combined to swell Dallas's population to almost three hundred thousand by 1940.

Changing socioeconomic circumstances only made the myth more purchasable, while contributing to Republican growth on their own. The city's position near East Texas and its capacity for innovation in banking allowed it to capitalize on the oil booms of the 1920s and 1930s. With the discovery of the East Texas oil field, which by 1931 was supplying a quarter of the country's oil needs, Dallas became the oil capital of Texas.[11] The oil industry underwent a transformation as Dallas bankers concluded that oil underneath the ground was a bankable asset and supplied oilmen with generous credit to fund discovery wells and pioneer geological advances in oil production.[12]

World War II and the Cold War increased manufacturing in Dallas and accelerated the population surge. Aircraft, missiles, and electronics were the mainstays of Dallas manufacturing. Total manufacturing employment in Dallas grew from 26,700 in 1940 to 75,750 in 1953, three times faster than the national average, outpacing all of the country's top forty manufacturing hubs save Los Angeles.[13] The 49,000 manufacturing jobs added during that period resulted in a dramatic population increase of 273,250 people.[14]

Many of the new arrivals were either members of the military or employees in new defense-related industries doing contract work for the federal government. Prior to the war, the cities of the Northeast and the Midwest had been the primary sites of military installations and recipients of contracts for weaponry. A federal decision mandating the relocation of airplane manufacturers from the coasts to less central and safer locations between the Allegheny and Rocky Mountains proved a boon to Dallas and other Sunbelt cities.[15] Airplane manufacturing became a priority of the federal government after President Roosevelt ordered the building of fifty thousand planes in 1940. Fearful that other Southern cities would land the lucrative federal plums, Dallas boosters aggressively promoted their city, lobbied for military bases, and encouraged the relocation of Eastern defense-related companies. While manufacturers could determine the specific location, Dallas boosters helped them decide, emphasizing Dallas's crystal-clear horizon and tradition of anti-unionism.[16] Manufacturers were likely aware that Dallas police and business leaders had brutally resisted the CIO's attempts to unionize dressmakers in 1935 and Ford employees in 1937.[17] In August 1940, the Navy chose Dallas for its Reserve Aviation Squadron Base. The city leased nearby Hensley Field to the Navy and expanded the runways. An administrative command for the armed forces, the US Eighth Service Command, along with its three-million-dollar annual payroll, also arrived in the 1940s. By 1942, the Dallas Chamber of Commerce was claiming that its city was the "War Capital of the Southwest," an interesting boast for a city whose political culture would soon be cast in a strongly anti-Washington pose.[18]

Although Dallas's food companies, construction firms, and clothing manufacturers were among the first recipients of defense contracts, tapping more than ninety million dollars between January 1940 and February 1941, as Robert Fairbanks has pointed out, "no single business entity more profoundly affected the city than aircraft manufacturing."[19] Not a single individual was making airplanes in Dallas in 1940, but by 1953 one-quarter of all employees in manufacturing—19,300—were producing airplanes, almost all of them under a defense contract and without a union.[20]

North American Aviation constructed a plant west of the city and built twenty thousand planes during the war, providing seven thousand jobs by 1942 and forty-three thousand by 1943. Southern Aircraft Company in nearby Garland and Lockhead's Aircraft Modifier Plant at Love Field brought thousands of military families to the region.[21] And the growth continued after the war. Aviation workers who had boosted their skills during World War II found plenty of employment in Dallas during the Cold War. The ties that bound Washington and Dallas in wartime forged the military-industrial complex of the 1950s and bolstered the region's commitment to a more aggressively anti-Communist foreign policy. The federal government encouraged even more relocations to the nascent Sunbelt in the postwar period, inundating Dallas and other Texas communities with munificent defense-related contracts. In 1948, Uncle Sam bankrolled the relocation from Connecticut of aviation giant Chance Vought, which had made the Corsair for the Navy in World War II. "Billed as the largest industrial move in the nation's history," the company was, by 1953, providing twelve thousand jobs.[22] The city's dry climate, equidistant location between the east and west coasts, and proximity to oil, gas, and bustling Love Field—as well as its historical reputation as an amiable partner of business—all made Dallas a natural home for relocating Midwestern and Eastern companies. Funded in part by the federal government and founded by Robert McCullough, who had previously worked for North American Aviation, Texas Engineering & Manufacturing Company (Temco) employed 5,250 in the manufacture of airplanes, airplane parts, missiles, and washing machines.[23] Small wonder that historian Harvey J. Graff called Dallas in this time a "city at the crossroads" and Michael Phillips termed it "the hinge" of the South and West.[24]

The city's white-collar economy had begun to thrive by the 1950s. It brought with it engineers and scientists in the oil and aerospace industries and businessmen and accountants in the banks and insurance companies. By 1960, 25 percent of employees in Dallas were professionals or managers. An additional 30 percent either clerked in the city's financial institutions or worked as salesmen in its many department stores.[25] Enjoying high incomes, many of the ascending upper-middle-class Dallasites in the oil industry, oil-related insurance and banking industries, and the flourishing aerospace industry moved into higher tax brackets, began paying 90 percent, the top marginal tax rate of the income tax, and started looking to the Republican Party for tax relief.[26] While some oilmen like Clint Murchison were "presidential Republicans" who backed Eisenhower but supported Democrats Lyndon Johnson and Sam Rayburn for their unequivocal support of the 27.5 percent oil depletion allowance, other Dallas oilmen, including Jake Hamon, H. L. Hunt, and Harry Bass turned more consistently to the Republican Party, which embraced even more generous tax breaks for the affluent.[27]

The nexus between the financial sector and the oil industry also fostered the growth of the city's electronics and aerospace industry, which provided another factor in the strong base of support for Republicans in the 1950s. Geologist and Dallasite E. L. DeGolyer spearheaded the use of the refraction seismograph and reflection seismograph to survey underground geological structures.[28] In 1936, he founded DeGolyer and MacNaughton, which prepared estimates of oil reserves for the major and independent oil companies.[29] Earlier, in 1929, he had established Geophysical Service Inc., which, after receiving a cash infusion from the First National Bank of Dallas in 1951, became Texas Instruments (TI).[30]

Midwestern Migrants

Many of the white-collar workers who filled the ranks of the oil, banking, and aerospace companies powering the city's economic engine came from the Midwest. In the 1940s and 1950s, the Dallas region drew a heavy flow of migrants from Ohio, Indiana, Missouri, and Kansas. For sure, there were also more modest streams of migration from the South, the border South states of Arkansas, Tennessee, and Oklahoma, the piney woods and rolling red hills of East Texas, and the Northeast.[31] While Southern-based, often fundamentalist newcomers infused Dallas with hard-right conservatism, Midwestern transplants like H. N. Mallon brought a more pragmatic conservatism to the city.

Many of the migrating Midwesterners had experienced firsthand the catastrophic natural disasters and tumbling commodity prices of the Depression years.[32] Many had served honorably when called upon by their country and were tested by war and combat. That these itinerant young men and women charted their course, collected their belongings, bade goodbye to their loved ones, and made the long journey south revealed their belief in a better tomorrow.[33] Their destination itself helped spur such confidence. While many Southern communities languished amid declining commodity prices, severe unemployment, and population exodus, the inland city of Dallas, with its bustling economy, itself driven by federal largesse, offered the intrepid traveler an opportunity to create great personal wealth.[34]

Many Dallas Republicans of the 1950s and 1960s arrived thus, often venturing from GOP strongholds in the Midwest, such as Ohio, Indiana, and Missouri. Arguably the core of the GOP Right in the 1940s, Ohio produced such conservative Republican stalwarts as Senator John Bricker and Robert Taft, and was an important departure zone for the more mainstream moderate conservative Republicans of Dallas. The progressive municipal reformer Brand Whitlock once observed, "One became in Urbana and in Ohio for many years, a Republican just as the Eskimo dons fur clothes." Although divided between Marcus Hanna's northern Ohio machine and George "Boss" Cox's southern Ohio faction, Republican hegemony in the state commenced in 1896, achieved its apogee with the election of Ohio newspaper publisher Warren G. Harding to the presidency in 1920, and remained unchallenged until the Great Depression. In the 1940s, Ohio's businessmen and Corn Belt farmers formed a conservative coalition and reestablished the state as a conservative Republican stronghold.[35]

Indiana was another such point of embarkation for the Dallas Republican Right. The birthplace of the John Birch Society, Indiana sent far-right Republican William Jenner to the US Senate in 1946 and was the home of University of Notre Dame Law School president Clarence Manion, also a conservative Republican. By the turn of the twentieth century, a more progressive breed of Republicans had become the dominant power in the state, and they maintained hegemony until the early 1930s. At the end of the 1930s, the centralization of state government under Democratic governor Paul McNutt and expanding powers of the federal government under the New Deal precipitated a Republican backlash that continued unabated into the 1950s.[36]

While the Democratic Party of Missouri produced such figures as Harry Truman, the notorious "Boss Tom" Pendergast, and James Reed, one of the "irreconcilables" who fought President Woodrow Wilson's League of Nations, the Show-Me State also had a long-standing Republican tradition of championing low taxes and fiscal frugality in national and state-wide affairs. In addition to the backlash against the growth of federal power under the national Democrats, widespread corruption in Missouri's Democratic Party, support from two of the state's major newspapers, the *Star* of Kansas City and the *Globe-Democrat* of St. Louis, and the emergence of new leaders like Monsanto Chemical's Edgar Monsanto Queeny and the St. Louis lawyer Barak Mattingly all contributed to Republican strength into the 1940s.[37] Many Kansans seeking lives devoted to temperance, family, community, and self-perfection became loyal to a Republican Party that championed government efficiency, defended moral rectitude, and voiced some reservations about Wall Street. Kansans' tendency to embrace Methodism, Catholicism, and other moderately conservative denominations accounted, at least in part, for the foundering of radical movements and the success of Republicanism. Since the passage of the Kansas-Nebraska Bill of 1854, the state has voted Republican in thirty out of thirty-eight presidential elections.[38]

The influx of Midwestern Republicans eventually drew sharp distinctions between Dallas and the politics of the otherwise solidly Democratic South. Along with their partisan loyalties, the predispositions of the people themselves helped transform the region's character. Unlike their Southern brethren, who yearned for the time before the Yankee invasion and still celebrated the principles of the Lost Cause, and even some Northern Brahmin contemporaries, who still lamented the ascendency of the Irish in America, Midwesterners were less nostalgic and shed few tears over changing circumstances.[39] For them, that family farms were subdivided and became the small shops on Main Street was simply a sign of progress. And prosperity went hand-in-hand with progress. Unlike the Southern-based, fundamentalist-leaning ultraconservatives—premillennialists who saw things getting worse—the Midwestern Republican arrivals were predominantly Protestants of a postmillennial temperament, with grand expectations for the future and good reason for optimism.

Journeying from small towns and farms in the Midwest, North, and South, many of the newcomers settled and raised their families in the comfortable, commodious tract homes of North Dallas. The most distinguished and affluent citizens of Dallas County lived in the Park

Cities, which included Highland Park and University Park. During the 1940s and 1950s, more white migrants arrived from the Midwest and the Northeast. White Dallas natives also found work as professionals and managers, fleeing the deteriorating downtown sections of South Dallas and West Dallas for the affluent neighborhoods of North Dallas and bulging suburban communities like Grand Prairie, Garland, and others north of the city limits.[40] By the 1950s, the 169,695 families living in the county enjoyed higher incomes than other American families. The median family income was $3,433, and 26 percent of families earned $5,000 or more.[41] These citizens found the policies of the Republican Party consonant with their desire to preserve private property, lower taxes, and reduce regulation.

While these heartland-born sojourners may have abandoned their native region and its declining manufacturing base for better employment, bigger homes, and the luxuries of postwar consumer culture, they maintained their commitment to rugged individualism and their suspicion of regulated markets. Like their ancestors, who farmed the Great Plains in the Gilded Age and wanted free trade to spread their crops far and wide, many of these migrating Midwesterners championed unfettered free enterprise and unbridled enthusiasm in the face of strife.[42] Torn from loved ones "back home," launched into an unfamiliar region, they were also impressionable, influenced by the prevailing ideology and customs of their new milieu. The ubiquity of conservative thinking in Dallas thus reinforced their own ideological heritage and made them even more prone to follow what they heard at church on Sunday, caught on their radios, or read in the *Dallas Morning News*.[43]

Dealey's Daily

With a circulation of 250,000, the *Dallas Morning News* sold more copies than any other paper in Texas by the early 1960s. Writing in 1974, Stanley Marcus of Neiman Marcus recollected that the *News* "spread a venom that helped poison a large segment of the community."[44] Yet until World War II, the *News* had taken a moderate, even progressive, stance. It played a major role in driving the Ku Klux Klan from power in Dallas in the late 1920s. In the 1930s, the *News* supported recognition of Russia, advocated for some New Deal programs, praised Franklin Roosevelt and Alf Landon for their opposition to teachers' loyalty oaths, supported the *Daily Worker*'s right to freedom of the press, and denounced the efforts of Hearst's newspapers to suppress academic freedoms. In 1936, an editorial observed that "Red-hunters" were "gullible victims of racketeers who live luxuriously from the profits of Red Scares."

In the 1940s, and especially after E. M. "Ted" Dealey became publisher and assumed control of the newspaper from his father, George B. Dealey, the *News* swung editorially to the right.[45] Ted Dealey was a rabid anti-Communist who loathed welfare, federal aid, and the United Nations. Whereas his father could be progressive, once outlawing any references to "Jew girls" by his writers, Ted could be strident, coarse, and mossback, peppering his language with salty racial epithets. The *News* under Ted Dealey provided right-wing organizations with a prominent and sympathetic medium to express their viewpoints. The newspaper called the American Civil Liberties Union the "Swivel" Liberties Union. The Supreme Court was the "judicial Kremlin" and "a threat to state sovereignty second only to Communism itself." The New Deal was the "Queer Deal," and members of Franklin Roosevelt's Brain Trust "were subversives, perverts and miscellaneous security risks."[46] The New Deal, editorialist and self-styled "Columntator" Lynn Landrum wrote, was "a series of improvisations strung pretty much upon a single string. The single string is that the underdog is bound to be the best dog. . . . All the rest is spur-of-the-moment strategy, shot-in-the-arm therapy, rabbit-out-of-the-hat showmanship." "Taxes," the Columntator added, "are the poorest form of molasses to attract industrial flies" and "as effective at keeping out enterprise as would an electrified fence."[47]

Along with endorsing union-busting measures like the Texas "right to work" law, the *News* promoted the careers of such right-wing stalwarts as Senator Joseph McCarthy and Representative Martin Dies, a Texan who chaired the House Un-American Activities Committee from 1937 to 1944 and conflated Communism, civil rights, and labor activism.[48] The *News* even supported McCarthy after his precipitous downfall, observing that his censure was "a happy day for Communists." As one contemporary observed, "The conservatism of the *News* over the past fifteen or twenty years has taken on the tone of the radical right. . . . All United States presidents since Franklin D. Roosevelt's day have been subject to its wrath—even Eisenhower, who was much too liberal in some of his policies for the *News*."[49]

New Right, Old Time Religion

Along with popular newspapers, preachers in their pulpits played a role in fostering the city's conservative ethos. The religious beliefs that Dallasites embraced, especially dispensationalism and Word of Faith, constituted a crucial reason for the rise of the Republican right in Dallas. During the years of the city's astronomical growth, the United States experienced what Billy Graham called the "greatest religious revival in American history." In 1953, the first vehicle in the newly sworn-in president Dwight D. Eisenhower's inaugural parade was called "God's Float." By 1961, 112 million Americans—60 percent, the highest percentage ever—were active church members. Sunday schools in the United States enrolled forty-two million. In 1960, Americans spent a billion dollars on the construction of new churches.[50]

Dallasites were even more devoutly religious than most of their American contemporaries. Dallas was the "religious capital" of Texas, wrote John Bainbridge.[51] At midcentury, Dallas County boasted the largest churches in the United States for each of three denominations, with 12,000 members at First Baptist Church, 8,750 members at Highland Park Methodist Church, and 5,200 at Highland Park Presbyterian Church.[52] Faith had been important in Dallas since the city's founding. Yet the growth in denominational membership and the construction of churches in Dallas County suggests that Dallasites' willingness to tie themselves to denominations became even stronger during the years after World War II. Migrating Midwesterners as well as some deracinated Northern fundamentalists cherished the liberty of importing their own traditions, structuring society through the formation their own churches, or settling comfortably into existing religious institutions.[53] By 1960, of the 945,000 people living in Dallas County, 500,000 were members of one of the nine hundred Protestant churches. Missionary programs and evangelism accelerated the growth of Holiness and Pentecostal denominations, which included the Church of Christ, and of the Assemblies of God. Expanding in Dallas County more quickly than the mainline churches, by 1960 the Assemblies of God had 10,000 members and ninety-two churches and the Holiness and Pentecostal denominations had 25,000 members and eighty-two churches.[54]

The Dallas vicinity also produced Assemblies of God minister Kenneth Hagin, the "father of the modern Word of Faith movement." Word of Faith revolutionized postwar America's charismatic movement by tying together God, fundamentalism, and capitalism.[55] Born in McKinney, Texas, in 1917, Hagin suffered from a congenital heart defect that left him bedridden as a youth. During his incapacitation, he claimed that he "went to hell" three times in 1933. After returning for the third time, he committed his life to Jesus Christ, who revealed to him the passage in Mark that became the cornerstone of his ministry: "What things soever ye desire, when ye pray, believe that ye receive them, and ye shall have them." Hagin's theology taught that God instilled knowledge in believers not through the senses but directly. God wanted his followers to be prosperous, declared Hagin, who summarized his theology as "say it, do it, receive it, tell it." In other words, God spoke the world into existence, and ordinary men and women had the same powers of creation. Anyone who unequivocally believed in the inerrancy of the Bible and then verbally expressed the word of God could create material wealth. Believers could also cure disease by enunciating scripture and believing in physical health.[56]

With its promise of prosperity, the Word of Faith movement was tailor-made for the Dallas ethos, which celebrated free-market principles and often conspicuous consumption.[57] Word of Faith, according to its followers, even strengthened capitalism in Dallas because, according to its tenets, God had sanctioned moneymaking and encouraged the pursuit of wealth.[58] In October 1951, a Dallas realtor named F. Ivy Boggs spoke to three thousand of the Texas Baptist Brotherhood: "I submit that the soundest economic plan ever devised is given in the Bible's parable of talents. It is clearly taught in the parable of talents that it is a sin not to make money."[59]

Despite the remarkable growth of Pentecostal and Holiness groups, they still lagged behind the mainline denominations in numbers. Numbering approximately fifty-three thousand in 1949, Methodists grew to seventy-nine thousand and boasted eighty-eight churches in the county by 1959.[60] Other mainline denominations had far smaller memberships.

The liturgical Lutherans and Episcopalians had seventeen thousand and eight thousand members, respectively, by 1960. The Christian Church, or Disciples of Christ, increased its membership in Dallas County from approximately thirteen thousand in 1950 to twenty thousand in forty-three churches by 1960.[61] Doubling the size of their denomination since 1950, Southern Presbyterians reached a membership of twenty thousand and filled twenty-three churches by 1960. By 1950, Dallas was also a foothold for Catholicism, which had arrived in 1869 when Father Joseph Martiniere established a humble parish called Sacred Heart. In 1902, Dallas became the seat of a Roman Catholic diocese.[62] The Dallas Catholic community surged in the first half of the twentieth century, numbering 125,000 by 1954.

Southern Baptists were, however, the largest and most influential denomination in Dallas County, growing in membership by 58 percent between 1949 and 1959, when it boasted 156,000 members and church property worth forty-five million dollars.[63] Baptist church construction was particularly remarkable in the years after World War II. There were 121 Baptist churches in the county in 1948, and 220 by 1959.[64] Dallas was the headquarters of the Baptist General Convention of Texas (BGCT), which had 3,850 churches and 1,568,000 members. With a circulation of 355,332, the *Baptist Standard*, the organ of the BGCT, was based in Dallas. Southwestern Baptist Theological Center, the largest ministerial training center in the world, was located in nearby Fort Worth.[65]

Dallas Baptists believed the Bible to be infallible, practiced a stern individual morality, and, in general, refrained from the social gospel, instead believing that societal change was the product of individual conversion. Baptist institutions and ministers nurtured and fostered anti-Communism, social conservatism, economic conservatism, and racial conservatism. In the 1950s, the largest of the churches in Dallas, and the largest in the entire Southern Baptist Convention, was the First Baptist Church, whose most famous congregant was Billy Graham. H. L. Hunt, also a congregant of First Baptist, testified to his coreligionists that his baptism was the "greatest trade that I ever made because I traded the Here for the Hereafter."[66] Located adjacent to the skyscrapers of downtown Dallas, by 1960 First Baptist Church had an operating budget of over one million dollars and a staff of fifty employees. In addition to its church, First Baptist owned a seven-story recreational building that contained a basketball court, skating rink, and four bowling lanes.[67] In 1950, it had a membership of 9,128 and an endowment of $562,100; by 1960, its membership had reached 12,108 and its endowment, $1,488,568.[68] From 1897 to 1944, Pastor George W. Truett captivated audiences every Sunday at First Baptist. After his death, Dallas radio stations continued to rebroadcast his engaging sermons, into the 1960s and beyond.[69]

Truett's successor, the square-jawed W. A. Criswell, was his antithesis. Where Truett was reserved and cerebral, Criswell was a bundle of nervous energy, moving incessantly around the pulpit, stomping his feet. He gesticulated forcefully, arms flailing. His fists pounded the lectern. His deep voice bellowed across the church. Initially worried that his spirited manner of preaching would restrict him to a rural congregation, Criswell's teacher of elocution assured him, "I'm not saying to you that everybody will like you, but they will listen."[70] From the age of six, Criswell had wanted to be a preacher. Despite the reservations of his parents, who worried that he would be entering a life of destitution and urged him to become a doctor of medicine, he pursued that goal, graduating from Baylor University in Waco, Texas, in 1927 and the Southern Baptist Theological Seminary in Louisville, Kentucky, in 1937.[71] Truett's death in 1944 opened a vacancy for Criswell, who became pastor of First Baptist Church of Dallas after Carr P. Collins, a local insurance executive, recommended him.[72]

Criswell vociferously attacked what he saw as the interrelated evils of Communism, socialism, and liberalism. After visiting four continents in 1950, he grew more convinced of the threat of Communism both to the nation and to the individual. He emphasized the need for a stronger national defense and universal military training for US citizens. Yet even with a strong military, Criswell emphasized, America was still vulnerable to Communism unless it embraced a strong Christian faith.[73] "In the way of atheistic Communism," he observed, "lies Christian America. As long as there is a strong America, the Communists will not triumph."[74]

Criswell also lamented what he saw as a sharp decline in morality. The country, he said, was devolving into an "amorphous society that has no morality, that gives itself to drunkenness and drugs, to debauchery and lack of personal responsibility, that is filthy and dirty and whose language is unspeakable and unacceptable."[75] Never one to avoid political themes in his sermons, Criswell taught that the Bible, which he held to be unerring, supported existing social and racial hierarchies.[76] He denounced the teaching of biological evolution, declaring that "man came from God rather than gorilla."[77]

Good Government

Along with essential social, economic, and cultural factors, political factors spurred rapid Republican Party growth in early 1950s Dallas. A long heritage of commitment to nonpartisan institutions in Dallas had checked the growth of the Democratic Party. Founded after most other major American cities, Dallas had avoided the bossism that came to dominate cities in the urban North. In 1907, it became one of the first cities in the United States to abandon its aldermanic system and adopt a commission form of government, in which an elected, nonpartisan commission held power. Then, in 1930, Dallas leaders, believing that the cornerstone characteristics of a successful city were growth and order, opted for the city manager–council form of government, in which a trained expert was hired to administer the municipality. The dearth of machine politics in Dallas enabled policymakers to implement reforms that aimed to restrict the power of political parties: as a result, city politics remained nonpartisan and there existed no powerful Democratic machine with its concomitant bloc-delivered votes, patronage, and spoils system.[78]

Voting laws in Dallas in the 1950s also contributed to Republican strength. In the 1880s and 1890s, policymakers in the American South had worked to restrict the voting rights of blacks, employing onerous residency requirements, cumulative poll taxes, and secret ballot laws to keep blacks, as well as some whites, from going to the polls.[79] Many of the devices that deterred voting were still in place in the 1950s. The poll tax in Dallas was particularly burdensome since it had to be paid each year on January 31, nine months before the general election. Working-class Dallasites, who voted primarily for Democrats, were impacted more significantly by these provisions than the middle- and upper-class professionals who increasingly voted Republican.

A conservative strain of populism long present in the region's political culture also contributed to the emerging Republicanism. To be sure, the business-friendly conservative populist impulse that developed in Dallas by the 1940s and 1950s was vastly different from the anticorporate protests of the late nineteenth century. Yet both shared an aversion to the influence of the Northeast. Whereas nineteenth-century populism loathed the Eastern banks that forced many farms into foreclosure, Dallas's conservative populist impulse of the twentieth century directed its ire against Washington, DC, and held that the federal government was either incompetent or traitorous in the fight against Communism.[80]

In hindsight, these factors that predisposed Dallas to become a Republican stronghold give an air of inevitability to the ascent of the Right in the early 1950s there. The city's fledgling Republican Party drew on the innate conservatism of a town experiencing explosive economic and demographic changes, breeding a perfervid climate of anti-Communism, in which a growing number of residents imbibed the reactionary columns of the *Dallas Morning News* while connecting with the robust local religious traditions grounded in Baptist fundamentalism and burgeoning Catholicism. Yet, while these contributing factors may have precipitated the ascendancy of Republicanism, they did not sustain it. Republicans in Dallas needed to establish the institutions and organizations, raise the monetary resources, attract the grassroots foot soldiers, and provide the viable candidates to forge a sustainable party. These factors that constitute a movement came from two distinct subgroups: moderate conservatives and ultraconservatives.

2 Party Women and Organization Men

Hit the Road, Jack

On the night of Tuesday, February 27, 1962, temperatures approached freezing in Dallas. Anyone willing to brave the cold weather had many choices for evening entertainment. *Breakfast at Tiffany's* was playing at more than one downtown theater. The Carousel Club, a local hotspot owned by Jack Ruby, showcased "Torrid Toni" Turner, billed as "Dallas's first and only reptile charmer." Yet on that frigid night, ten thousand people filed into the Dallas Memorial Auditorium to hear the address "What Price Freedom?" by New Dealer–turned–conservative Republican Ronald Wilson Reagan, host and star of *General Electric Theater*. Dallas mayor Earle Cabell, scores of civic leaders, and hundreds of students from Dallas high schools and universities flocked to the event. Thirty-five students from Howard Payne University traveled more than 340 miles to hear the Hollywood star. Local businesses, including the Republic National Bank, Red Ball Motor Freight, and H. N. Mallon's Dresser Industries, sponsored the event and arranged to telecast the forty-seven-year-old actor's address.[1]

Reagan issued a powerful riposte to President Kennedy's recent assertion in Los Angeles that the "real danger" from Communism "comes from without, not from within." Reagan exhorted Kennedy to take the offensive against the Communists both at home and abroad. To the delight of his audience, Reagan urged Kennedy to roll back Communism. "We're at war," Reagan roared, "so why the heck don't we act like it!"[2]

Reagan's speech drew praise from the *Dallas Morning News*: the speech was "stirring" and "held that audience in rapt attention for more than an hour." "Mr. Reagan," the paper gushed, "exploded a score of liberal myths, built a foolproof case against centralized government and outlined one of the best platforms for conservatism ever heard in Dallas, a conservative stronghold." Porter "Pete" Gifford, the chairman of Freedom Forum, the local conservative group that put the evening together, called the speech "one of the finest addresses I have heard on the subject of freedom."[3]

The speech drew high praise from the moderate conservative Republican community because Reagan was one of them. Like Reagan, an Illinois native, many of Dallas's moderate conservative Republicans hailed from the Midwest. They loathed liberalism, big government, and what Reagan called the "self-perpetuating" federal bureaucracy of the Kennedy administration. Like Reagan, who identified himself as a Presbyterian, many of these Republicans were not coming out of fundamentalist, Baptist traditions. Theirs was the more centrist conservatism of the region's mainline denominations: Methodism, Presbyterianism, Episcopalianism, and Catholicism.[4] As Midwesterners, they had embraced small government and frugal governance, and they found their own worldviews reflected in Reagan's speech extolling the virtues of free-market economics. And just like Reagan, moderate conservatives of Dallas in the 1950s and early 1960s were preoccupied with fighting Communism, inside and outside the United States.

The background, worldview, and motivations of the moderate conservative Republicans of Dallas had much in common with those of Ronald Reagan. Although there has never been a consensus over Reagan's exact ideological leanings, in the context of Dallas in the 1950s, his reputation was that of a moderate Republican. To some today, the ideological makeup of many of the moderate Republicans of that time may appear downright immoderate. But their positions were unquestionably more measured than those of ultraconservative Republicans. The ultraconservatives remained on the periphery of party politics while moderate conservative Republicans occupied themselves with the nuts and bolts, building the scaffolding of the GOP and concentrating on the duties of the party machinery—finding good candidates, raising money, and getting out the vote.

Distinguishing Pinks from Reds

Moderates saw little difference between liberals and socialists, but unlike ultraconservatives, they did draw distinctions between liberals and

Communists. Still, like ultraconservatives, they viewed the pluralism and moral relativism of American liberalism as an insufficient rampart to protect the country from Communism. On economic questions, moderates staked out less extreme positions than ultraconservatives. For instance, both factions wanted to lower taxes, but only the ultraconservatives wanted to eliminate the income tax. On education, ultraconservatives expressed skepticism about intellectuals and the academy, whereas moderate Republicans took their inspiration from conservative intellectual traditions and placed a high value on education. Many of the city's moderate conservatives had attended the best schools in the country and benefited materially from their degrees in fields like business administration or engineering. Quite naturally they did not share the hard right's suspicion of intellectuals.

Moderate conservative and ultraconservative Republicans shared an understanding of the Cold War as a political and military struggle, but it was for both primarily a religious conflict. Many of the moderate conservatives who hailed from the Midwest had brought with them their staunch anti-Communism, bolstering Texas's special affinity for Joseph McCarthy, whose frequent trips to the state contributed to his reputation as "Texas's third US Senator."[5] In 1956, Hungarians revolted against the Soviet Union and won their freedom, however briefly. Frederick Wilhelmson, a University of Dallas professor and moderate conservative contributor to the National Review, explained that the power of God accounted for the uprising. Wilhelmson pointed out that experts had insisted that "revolution behind the Iron Curtain not only could not succeed but that it could not even get underway. What they forgot was that the Faith is not of this world."[6]

Dallas Freedom Forum also presented Communism as a diabolical menace seeking to eradicate truth and eliminate Christianity. Freedom Forum nurtured conservative convictions, rallied the grassroots, and helped assemble the institutional framework for moderate conservative Republicanism. Begun by Fred Schwarz—an anti-Communist Australian émigrée, physician, and founder of the Christian Anti-Communism Crusade—Freedom Forum was soon sponsored by Dallas civic leaders, especially Texas Power and Light's W. W. Lynch, and was launched as a four-day seminar in September 1960.[7] The keynote speaker declared that "this country has been protected by a spiritual force" and America was given the atomic bomb "for our deliverance." Pacifists, he warned, were the "pawns of a Godless religion," Communism.[8] Doctor Clifton Ganus, a Church of Christ minister and Harding College history professor, warned his audience that "creeping socialism" would become "out and out socialism" unless Americans increased their devotion to God.[9] A member of the Freedom Forum advisory board, Genie Farrow, argued, "We must choose faith in God or our children and generations of the future will not have the freedom of life, liberty, and the pursuit of happiness." "We are losing ground as a Christian nation," she concluded, "because we aren't as dedicated as individuals to the word of God."[10] Freedom Forum's message of Christian anti-Communism appealed to the distinguished business and professional elite of Dallas. Hundreds of professionals attended. Scores of local businesses sent their employees on company time.[11]

Moderate conservatives revered figures like Schwarz and J. Edgar Hoover. In December 1960, when Dallas became the first district in the state of Texas to require that its high school students study the differences between American freedom and Soviet Communism, the only books approved by the board as course material for the unit on Communism were written by Schwarz and Hoover.[12] Conservative moderates also embraced as heroes erstwhile comrades who quit the Communist Party to wage war on it. Such informers, having lived inside the belly of the monster, understood better than anybody its beguiling power. Consequently, they served the invaluable purposes of naming names and explicating the Communist mindset.[13] In 1961, moderates turned out in droves when Frank Meyer, a former Communist turned conservative Republican intellectual, appeared at the University of Dallas and charged that liberals suffered from a "mass delusion."[14]

Still, moderates were willing to acknowledge distinctions, albeit sometimes small ones, between liberals and Communists. To be sure, they still saw liberalism as an insufficient ideological bulwark to challenge Communism and ensure the survival of the West. What's more, the aggrandizement of the welfare state and the concession of Eastern Europe to the Soviet Union demonstrated for many conservatives that liberals and Communists often found too little room for disagreement.

Western civilization, many moderate conservatives concluded, would remain in its death throes so long as liberals settled for peaceful co-existence, ignored the fact that the enemy was merciless, and denied that the battle was spiritual. In their view, American liberals, who possessed a detestable affinity for moral relativism, failed to understand the power of the Communist conspiracy.

Yet moderates did not claim that liberals actively colluded with Communists.[15] While moderates believed wholeheartedly in the international Communist conspiracy, they never settled completely on the existence of an American conspiracy, in which high-level public officials in the State Department or the White House consciously conspired with Moscow. Despite regarding American liberalism with almost as much antipathy as Communism, the moderates tended to equate it with European-style socialism.

Liberals further earned the condemnation of moderate conservatives in Dallas because they strove for greater entitlement programs and stronger protections for the rights of African-Americans and organized labor. Illustrating that they leaned to the right of nationwide Republicans, Dallas moderate conservatives resisted modern Republicanism, Eisenhower's selective endorsement of progressive education, labor, and social welfare reforms.[16] Dallas moderates conflated the struggles for civil and labor rights with socialism and in doing so made their case against the aggrandizement of state power. "Texas," the *Dallas Morning News* warned, "is a primary target for the Liberals. They've tried to put a poll tax into the hands of every qualified Negro voter. They have been diligent in labor's ranks."[17] The paper denounced the "CIO-ADA-NAACP ideas of government" and sought to stop "labor, the minorities," and "the gimmecrats" from leading the country "into European-style socialism."[18] "Quit playing with your putters and get involved in politics," one prominent moderate Dallas Republican and businessman urged. "If you don't," he warned, "a combination of liberal labor leaders and left-wingers will have America completely socialist before you know it."[19]

By the late 1950s, moderate conservatives in Dallas had abandoned older isolationist stances and advocated strategies to free nations from Communism, characterizing foreign policy under presidents Eisenhower and Kennedy as disastrous. When Russia quashed the Hungarian uprising, conservatives condemned the failure of the Eisenhower administration to live up to its doctrine, "roll back" the Soviet advance, and "liberate captive peoples."[20] Proximity to the ultraconservatives only made the moderates more reactionary; the gap between the Eisenhower administration and moderate Dallas conservatives widened further when the president invited Nikita Khrushchev ("the great murderer," according to one Dallas conservative) to the United States.[21] During one address after John F. Kennedy ascended to the presidency, Frank Meyer pounded the lectern, to the delight of an enraptured Dallas audience, hurled invective at the Kennedy administration for the Bay of Pigs fiasco, and called for "immediate counter-attack all down the line." If Castro could not be overthrown by Cuban troops, "then it's up to U.S. troops to do the job," he roared. "If we don't fight in Cuba, then where? On Long Island?"[22] Conservative moderates held as folly the notion that the United Nations could ever effectively supplant independent nation-states. They not only brooked but encouraged imperialism, bragging of Western advances in education and medicine, and argued for its necessity. After all, Western hegemony had protected the newly formed African countries from becoming Soviet satellite states.[23]

Rand(om) Acts of Selfishness and the Road to Hayek

Backing a free market, celebrating limited government, and rejecting the encroaching assertion of federal power over states' rights, Bruce Alger embodied the moderate conservative Republican worldview. Moderate conservatives concurred with Alger's frequent condemnations of socialism, denouncing the "socialistic" Democratic Party. A Dallas County Republican Party newsletter asked those "who are not yet working," "what's the matter with your fighting heart?" "Don't you realize," it continued, that we are "in the middle of a battle for the survival of our economic system? . . . A Democratic Congress—even though tempered by a few conservatives—will be the direct road back to Socialism."[24] The activism of the Roosevelt, Truman, and Eisenhower administrations threatened the economic freedoms that moderate conservatives like Alger held dear.

Under all three administrations, the federal government had grown steadily. Roosevelt's New Deal regulated the banking system and financial markets, arbitrated conflicts between employers and labor, distributed European-style old-age pensions and unemployment insurance, and assailed wide-scale unemployment and poverty by "priming the pump" with federal dollars. President Eisenhower continued to expand the scope of government in the 1950s. During his "hidden-hand" presidency, as Fred Greenstein observed, Eisenhower "tempered his private conservatism" and acquiesced to liberal programs to build a strong Republican majority. When Eisenhower left office, the popular New Deal and Fair Deal programs remained snugly ensconced as vital features of American life. In fact, social welfare programs had expanded during the Eisenhower years: Eisenhower created the Department of Health, Education, and Welfare, acceded to a higher minimum wage, established more magnanimous Social Security benefits, set up a meager health care scheme for indigent seniors, and pioneered the National Defense Education Act.

Frustration over the persistence and growth of the welfare state and, more important, inspiration from libertarian intellectuals who challenged such policies shaped the economic worldview of Dallas moderate conservatives.[25] One intellectual who had a particularly profound influence on Dallas conservatives was the radical libertarian and Russian émigrée Ayn Rand. Rand believed that selfishness was a virtue. An individual's liberty was absolutely sacrosanct and should never be restricted by religion, which she regarded as superstition. She once teased the conservative editor William F. Buckley Jr. that he was too intelligent to believe in God. Rand's novels were vehicles for an ideology she called objectivism, which taught that individuals had a moral obligation to follow their desires. Rand believed that the state should only protect the rule of law and provide for national security. She wholeheartedly rejected the welfare state and celebrated unbounded free enterprise.[26]

As a philosophy major at Princeton University, Bruce Alger followed Rand's work closely. He read all of her books and corresponded with her in the early 1960s. Spellbound by Rand's literary skills, Alger appreciated her emphasis on the individual but disagreed with her on the role of religion in society.[27] A champion of natural law, Alger believed that divinely inspired and universal principles of morality were knowable to all and binding for every individual.[28] In advocating an extreme form of libertarianism not grounded in religion, Rand was sanctioning moral relativism and was therefore dangerous, according to Alger. Atheism was repugnant to Alger on moral-political grounds, since he understood the Cold War as a spiritual battle between the Christian West and godless Communism. Implementation of Rand's ideas would actually restrict liberty, he argued, since an "individual's importance and freedom results from his accountability to God, his reason for being."[29]

While there were undoubtedly Rand acolytes in Dallas, Friedrich Hayek's views on the market were even more popular among moderate conservative Republicans. Most moderate conservatives held that the best justification for economic individualism was not that capitalism required selfishness, but that corporations, the free market, and private property were less likely to act coercively toward the individual than was the state. As one put it, "The right of free enterprise is a basic right which our forefathers held came from God, not government."[30] Dallas libertarians lamented the loss of individual freedom in modern society, and they found a strong case for this view in the works of Hayek and other libertarian intellectuals who revived classical liberalism in the postwar West. Celebrating small government, free markets, and private property, Hayek argued that the seeds of Nazism were sown by the very socialistic policies that Britain and the United States were now following. Hayek believed that any form of collectivism—whether Communism, socialism, or even liberalism—would lead a country further down what he called "the Road to Serfdom" and culminate in totalitarianism.[31] The writings of Hayek's intellectual mentor and fellow Austrian, Ludwig von Mises, also attracted the moderate conservatives. Mises argued in his 1944 book *Bureaucracy* that the bureaucratic system of management—the antithesis of the profit system—was constraining creavity and contaminating both the public and private sectors in the United States.[32] More uncompromising in his defense of the market than Hayek, Mises argued that only "under perfect capitalism, hitherto never and nowhere completely tried or achieved" could peace be sustained in the West.[33] Mises championed a state that had a tiny role to play, and his vision of an unhindered profit system for private enterprise appealed deeply to Dallas businessmen.[34]

In *The Road to Serfdom*, Hayek, who was more famous than Mises, opined that even limited dalliances with state planning paved the way toward totalitarianism. A professor at the London School of Economics, Hayek lamented the growing embrace of centralized planning that characterized Western economies during World War II. Planning was inherently misguided, he said, because the complexity of the ever-changing marketplace made it impossible for anyone to understand what was occurring at a given moment. Moreover, planning compromised individual freedom, because it was impossible in a democratic system for planners to agree on goals. Consequently, all decision-making responsibilities would fall to a small minority of the most unscrupulous, ruthless, and self-interested individuals. This minority would prohibit equal treatment under the law and construct a coercive society based on an entirely different value system. Therefore, Hayek argued, planning was a slippery slope toward dictatorship. The only path safeguarding individual freedom involved unleashing the "spontaneous forces of society" by embracing the principles of classical liberalism: the free market, private property, and competition.[35]

Dallas's moderate conservative Republicans drank deeply at this well of renascent classical liberalism.[36] In 1962, newly elected Texas senator John Tower, who succeeded Lyndon Johnson, praised Hayek's *Capitalism and the Historians* as an "excellent read."[37] When Porter "Pete" Gifford took the helm of Dallas Freedom Forum, a symposium previously known for its anti-Communism, not only did he infuse it with Hayekian ideas, he invited Hayek and Leonard Read, the president of the Foundation for Economic Education, to a secluded ranch in Mineral Wells, Texas, where they held a special seminar with members of the Freedom Forum advisory committee.[38]

Dallas moderates defined freedom as a condition that prevails when there is an "absence of coercion,"[39] and the state, with its power to control the "legitimate use of force," was thus potentially the greatest threat to liberty. Consequently, many Dallas conservatives supported a limited state and decried government control. "Republicans," party activist Jo Kanowsky observed, "stand for the freedom of the individual to work, live, and do business responsibly as he sees fit without central government control."[40] Denouncing the power of the state in spiritual terms, Bruce Alger said there were "68 words in the ten commandments," but "26,000 words in the O.P.A. [Office of Price Administration] order concerning the price of cabbage."[41] He argued that federal money for urban renewal led to a loss of freedom, as did "federal control of wages" and "forced integration" in public housing.[42] Rejecting federal aid for schools, L. J. Wathen of the Past President's Association of the Dallas Federation of Women's Clubs claimed that Washington wanted to "control our schools."[43] The "acceptance of federal funds," the Dallas Morning News observed, "is gradually pushing this country toward a new order in which the Federal Government is taking over."[44]

Dallas moderates saw economic freedom as a paramount issue. "The loss of economic freedom," Alger declared, "would mean the loss of all freedom." Like Ludwig von Mises, who declared that "private property is inextricably linked with civilization," moderates equated private property with economic freedom. This worldview explained why so many moderate conservative Republicans like Dick Smith opposed urban renewal.[45] As Smith put it, urban renewal "abrogate[d] the Free and unfettered enjoyment of Property" because it enlarged the city's right of eminent domain and thus increased the opportunity for the individual to suffer financial loss.[46] "Because libertarians saw property rights as absolute," historian Lisa McGirr astutely observed, "the welfare state's redistribution of property through taxation was perceived as a form of socialism."[47] Consequently, moderate Republicans fulminated frequently against high taxes. Rita Bass, for instance, assailed reliance on "exorbitant taxes . . . to finance reckless government spending."[48] Frank Slay wanted lower taxes for those in high brackets because they needed to "have some incentive to continue to work and produce."[49] And A. D. Peabody, a small business owner, asked, "Isn't it about time" that Congress "quit passing the buck and get busy and cut expenses and taxes generally?"[50]

Again, many moderate conservative Republicans in Dallas hailed from the Midwest, which had long celebrated the virtues of moral and capital development. Their embrace of small government and frugal governance was consonant with the values expressed in the works of such postwar libertarian intellectuals as Hayek and Rand. Their own values, grounded in the centrist conservatism of Methodism, Presbyterianism, and Episcopalianism, complemented what they read. It seemed familiar, harkened back to their pasts, and instilled them with a confidence that they were on the right track. Because they seemed to be following familiar paths, their political methods never veered to the radical, despite what *they* thought was revolutionary behavior.[51]

The moderate conservative Republicans practiced a political pragmatism, focusing on the day-to-day activities that won elections and established the institutional networks essential to a viable party. As natives of a region still experiencing rapid industrialization during their formative years, these Midwestern transplants were filled not only with boundless optimism over the greater economic opportunities that lay ahead, but also with the confidence to seek out new friendships, forge new networks, establish new institutions, and construct the scaffolding of the Dallas Republican Party.[52] Examples are plentiful. Ellen McCready was a Cleveland native who canvassed her neighborhood as a block worker, rendered drawings as art director of the Dallas County Republican newspaper *Battle Line*, and served as vice president of the Dallas County Council of Republican Women. Pat Tuttle, originally from Indiana, helped build the institutional skeleton of the Dallas Republican Party in her capacity as the president of the Town North Republican Women's Club. Mary Krueger, an Indiana native, moved to Dallas with her family at the age of eight. As an adult, she balanced working behind the scenes as the campaign activities chairman of the Pleasant-East Republican Woman's Club with throwing her own hat into the ring as a candidate.[53]

We All Made Money Fast

Libertarian economics also made sense to moderate conservatives because many were growing very wealthy. Engineers and scientists from the oil and aerospace industries, along with businessmen and accountants from the banks and insurance companies, predominated in the party and often became Republicans because they wanted to promote lower income and business taxes.[54] As one oilman observed, "We all made money fast. We were interested in nothing else. Then this Communist business burst upon us. We were going to lose what we had gained."[55]

The upwardly mobile oilmen who profited handsomely in the booming economy and filled the ranks of Dallas Republicanism include some of the city's most prominent citizens. In 1960, the petroleum engineer and Republican activist Clifford Goldsmith moved his wife, Taffy, and two children into a brand new home on Forest Ridge. By 1964 the family was living in a more spacious abode on Lanshire, holding neighborhood meetings and cocktail parties for the Texas Young Republicans and the Dallas County Republican Party.[56] George McDaniel, a Dallas native, MIT graduate, and independent oilman, served as Republican precinct chairman.[57] Stanford-educated Nancy Jane Clark, who worked at the Dallas-based DeGolyer and MacNaughton oil firm, served as a precinct worker starting in the early 1950s and was poll tax chairman of the Park Cities Republican Women's Club. John "Jack" Crichton moved to Dallas with a master's degree from MIT, became vice president of DeGolyer and Mac-Naughton after serving as a field artillery officer in World War II, and was chosen as the Republican nominee for governor in 1964. Crichton had been one of the first Americans to recognize the enormous volume of Middle Eastern oil. Surrounded by thick cigarette smoke, innumerable coffee cups, slide rules, and maps of the Middle East in a New York hotel suite in the 1940s, he and his colleagues had calculated (with some accuracy, it turns out) that Kuwait's Burgan field contained ten billion barrels of oil. Crichton made a respectable showing in the gubernatorial race but lost in that year's Democratic sweep.[58]

The fundraising acumen of oilmen Harry and Dick Bass helped to sustain the Dallas GOP into the 1960s. Business conservatives elsewhere in the 1950s were donating funds to conservative organizations like the National Association of Manufacturers and the Foundation for Economic Education but avoiding involvement in electoral politics. In Dallas, however, the Bass brothers were raising money from business associates for the Republican Right.[59] Working diligently from their downtown offices in the Mercantile Building, the Basses not only safeguarded the family's oil fortune but established a coherent network of Republican Dallas businessmen eager to defend capitalism, champion the rights of management, and attack labor unions.[60]

While Harry Bass was the reserved and stern workhorse whose shock of grey hair perhaps testified that raising money was an arduous task, his brother, Dick, charmed donors with his gregarious appeal. After taking a geology degree from Yale in 1950, Dick continued his education at the University of Texas, where he studied petroleum engineering. In 1953, he married Rita Crocker and started working for his father's firm, H. W. Bass & Sons, an independent oil and gas company with interests ranging from South Texas to Canada.[61] Harry served in the Navy for two years in the Pacific Theater during World War II, attended the University of Texas and Southern Methodist University, and learned the oil business while working for his father's other company, Can-Tex. In 1957—at the age of thirty—Harry became president of H. W. Bass & Sons. Harry Jr.'s first foray into Dallas Republican politics came in 1952 when he campaigned for Dwight Eisenhower.[62] He attributed his Republican participation to his father, who shared a "deep-seated respect for conservative politics." The Basses were magnanimous benefactors to the Republican Party. One activist attributed the rise of the county party to the "very generous people like Harry and Dick Bass," who "gave above and beyond what anybody should be expected."[63] Even more important than their individual donations, however, were Harry's keen and aggressive fundraising abilities, which his peers recognized early in his career.[64] "The money must come first," he told his "fellow conservatives," imploring his fellow businessmen to write solicitation letters to their own colleagues.[65] Rising quickly in the party hierarchy, Harry was a member of the Dallas County Republican Finance Committee by the mid-1950s and chairman of the Dallas County Republican Party by 1957.[66]

Technology enhanced the Basses' fundraising. In the late 1950s, when few political operatives employed computers, chairman Bass pioneered the use of the new technology to compile statistics on precinct voters and contributors and wrote some of the earliest campaign software to display voting trends and donation patterns.[67] He also seems to have pioneered automatic deductions for political donations, writing in the early 1960s, "$10, $5, or $2 a month deducted regularly and automatically from your bank account will save you time and will supply our organization with the continuing broad base of support that we must have." Foreshadowing practices of the national Republican Party of the twenty-first century under the helm of Karl Rove, Harry Bass strengthened the party infrastructure not only by creating a database with donor information but by soliciting donations from business associates with thoughtful correspondence that appealed to conservatives.[68]

Dallas's electronics and aerospace industry provided another base of support for Republicans. J. Erik Jonnson, the president of Texas Instruments (TI) from 1951 to 1958, was a prominent Republican. TI's executive vice president, Fred Agnich, was a Catholic from Minnesota who also embodied pragmatic moderate conservative Republicanism and supported, in his own words, "the American system of free enterprise" and the "importance of placing some limitations upon the powers of strong central government." At the same time, he stipulated that he was "not subservient to the ultra reactionary dogmas of the past."[69] A talented organizer and administrator, Agnich amassed money for candidates in the 1950s, chaired Republican presidential nominee Richard Nixon's fundraising drive in 1960, and presided over the Goldwater Dinner Committee when the Arizona senator came to town in 1961.[70] By the 1970s, Agnich represented Dallas in the lower house of the Texas legislature. When Karl Rove stopped by the Austin statehouse looking for work, it was Agnich who secured the young man his first job in Texas politics.[71]

Doctors, lawyers, and bankers also found prominent roles in the Dallas Republican Party. Eldon Siebel, a thoracic surgeon, was a delegate to the 1962 Republican state convention. Before serving as chairman of the Dallas County Republican Party in the 1970s, George McKenzie graduated from Southern Methodist University Law School, established his own law firm, and represented the widow of Lee Harvey Oswald before the Warren Commission.[72] L. E. Guillot, president of Southwest Savings and Loan Association, styled himself as the self-deprecating practical jokester of the Dallas Republicans, jocularly revealing that he was the worst precinct chairman in the history of Dallas County, since his recruits had a bad habit of nailing campaign signs upside down. Despite Guillot's avowed incompetence, George Herbert Walker Bush, an oilman from Midland, selected Guillot to manage Dallas County in his campaign for the United States Senate in 1964.[73]

Big business was not alone in supporting the party of laissez-faire economics: Dallas's small business owners were active in the party as well. Indiana native Jo Kanowsky recollected that her Republican parents, who owned a wholesale grocery business, taught her the value of frugality, hard work, and persistence. She followed their lead in advocating for conservative causes in public life and owning and managing her own business, KAL Distributing, a Dallas-based plastics distributor for the aerospace industry. Kanowsky settled in Dallas in 1945, became a Republican precinct chair in 1952, directed the "Thank you, Mr. President" fundraising drive in 1956, and rose to state Republican committeewoman in 1960.[74] Another small businessman epitomized the active Dallas Republican whose hard work and initiative significantly improved his social standing. Dillard Radke was born and raised on a family farm in St. Joseph, Missouri. Having escaped a penurious childhood, he went to business school and worked for twenty-five years in the motor freight industry before establishing his own business, Dillard Radke Enterprises, which specialized in selling office supplies and repairing typewriters. He first pulled the lever for Herbert Hoover in 1928 and cast votes for Republicans thereafter. In the 1960s he coordinated Republican activities in the Oak Cliff section of Dallas.[75]

The political socialization of many Dallas Republicans began as youngsters and predicted their later activism. While Joan Gaidos's political activism "really got started" in Dallas, she credited that interest to her family's partisanship and Chicago background. "When you grow up in Chicago, it's kind of hard not to be interested in politics," she remembered. "I belonged to a northern Illinois family that God would have struck any of us dead if we had voted Democrat. So it wasn't as if I were converted."[76] Many Republicans shared stories similar to that of Anne Goode, who got involved in the Dallas conservative movement in 1956 by doing mundane precinct work and by the early 1960s had worked her way up to becoming president of the Hillside Republican Women's Club. Goode hailed from a family of staunch Republicans in western Pennsylvania. Growing up in Pittsburgh, Goode remembered, "I began my Republican career by collecting more Hoover lapel pins than any other child in the neighborhood." The college-educated mother of one recollected proudly that her own mother had run as the Republican candidate for tax collector in a district that was heavily Democrat.[77]

Others joined the conservative movement in Dallas because a friend encouraged involvement or a spouse blazed the trail. As historian Michelle Nickerson found, friends and married couples "pushed and pulled each other rightward," sometimes obscuring "who led whom."[78] In the case of Katie McDaniel, who was a delegate to the Republican National Conventions in 1956 and 1960, the answer was clear. Despite attending Democratic rallies with her family as a youth in Lubbock, Texas, McDaniel was drawn into the Republican Party through her husband, an independent oilman, whose friend was running for office in Pampa, Texas.[79]

Other Dallas moderate conservatives became involved in the Republican Party as a result of exposure to what they perceived as radical left-wing politics. Babs Johnson, a native of Wichita Falls and a fourth-generation Texan, credits her decision to become involved in conservative politics to her strong reaction against liberal professors at the University of Chicago. Advancing rapidly in Dallas politics, Johnson started out in 1954 as block chairman and, by 1964, served as the president of the Dallas County Council of Republican Women, which coordinated the duties of the Republican Women's Clubs.[80] Gwen Pharo, the secretary to Sam Rayburn, joined the Republicans "to shape it into a party that understood the Soviets." "A lot of the most prominent people aligned themselves with the Republicans simply because we thought the Democrats were just riddled with subversive people," she said. "Our whole government was being served by foreign elements," and Republican Party work "became the thing to do."[81] In Glenna McCord's case, living under the radical military dictatorship of Venezuela's Marcos Perez fostered her allegiance to the Dallas Republican Party. While her husband, Bob McCord, was oil prospecting in Venezuela for four years, the Dallas native and her family also took up residence there. The experience convinced her that Venezuelans were unable to speak out as individuals and determine their fate. By taking freedom "for granted," McCord observed, ordinary Americans "really fail" their government. Concluding that participation in conservative politics was absolutely necessary to safeguard such freedoms in the United States, she became a vehement supporter of Bruce Alger in 1954 and vice chairman of the Republican Party in Dallas County by the early 1960s.[82]

Ideas Have Consequences

Unlike the ultraconservatives, who displayed a blatant anti-intellectualism, moderate conservative Republicans relied on the appeal of the written and spoken word to draw thousands into their movement. For Porter

"Pete" Gifford, a graduate of Cornell and the president of Gifford-Hill, the journey to the Republican Right began in 1950 when he read John T. Flynn's *The Road Ahead*.[83] "It startled me to realize," Gifford recalled, "how close we were to socialism. As a result, I sent copies of the book to two or three hundred people."[84] Similarly, the Public Affairs Luncheon Club donated copies of Russell Kirk's *The Intelligent Woman's Guide to Conservatism* to the Dallas Public Library and Southern Methodist University's library and student center.[85] Convinced that the mainstream media was dominated by liberalism and collectivism, conservative moderates turned to sympathetic bookstores and a growing array of conservative publications for their news and information.[86] Many erstwhile Democrats became staunch Republicans after concluding that leftists were concealing the truth and conservative authors were the only reliable sources.

By the 1960s, conservatives in Dallas County had gained two additional weekly newspapers owned by local Giles Miller. A onetime Democrat who turned Republican in 1962 to run for Texas's only at-large congressional seat, Miller purchased *Park Cities News*, a small local paper, and changed its name to the *North Dallas–Park Cities News*. Miller then hired some of the country's most distinguished conservative editorialists, including Fulton Lewis, Morris Ryskind, and Barry Goldwater, to write features. Miller's own column censured the supposed liberalism at Southern Methodist University, vilifying the school's Perkins School of Theology as harboring dangerous ideas. He also compiled editorials by conservatives in the *Digests*, which evolved into a weekly newspaper called the *Richardson–Park Cities Digest*, with features by Paul Harvey and Dean Manion. "A conservative newspaper for the conservative heart of Texas," read its masthead.[87]

The American Bookstore, located in the conservative Republican bastion of University Park, sold patriotic phonograph records, pamphlets, and books by conservative authors. With an inventory running the gamut from laissez-faire economics to anti-Communism to traditionalist conservatism, Henry and Val Whorley's storefront in Snyder Plaza afforded Dallas conservatives the chance to purchase bumper stickers with such slogans as "Don't Worry—They're Still 90 Miles Away," "Goldwater for President," and "Kennedy for King." Henry Whorley was a mineral prospector who turned to bookselling after realizing that other bookstores did not carry conservative books. Patrons could purchase for three cents Reverend Carl McIntyre's speech "Why Christians Should Fight Communism"; pick up Congressman James Utt's attack on UNESCO, "Communism's Trap for Our Youth"; or obtain a copy of Texas native Fred C. Koch's "A Businessman Looks at Communism." Material from the Dallas County Republican Party was a mainstay at the American Bookstore: Whorley's stock included the party newspaper, *Battle Line*, and a broadsheet from county headquarters detailing fifty-five ways "the New Frontier Has Helped the Reds." One pamphlet decried the federal government's attack on the American family, accusing the Department of Health, Education, and Welfare of encouraging schoolchildren to declare, "My father is a tyrant," "I think about sex a great deal of the time," and "I'm losing my faith in religion." Such literature, one Dallasite said, "converted many women, mothers of women, into militant conservatives."[88]

The Housewife: Backbone of the GOP in Big D

As the examples of Katie McDaniel, Babs Johnson, and Glenna McCord illustrate, the ones who put the institutional framework in place and gave rise to the Dallas Republican Party were to a large extent moderate conservative women. Previously, politics had been "left to the men," with women expected to be "invisible," observed Gwen Pharo. Republican women, she said, "made politics socially acceptable."[89] Peter O'Donnell, the Dallas County Republican chairman, explained that women were "the backbone of our effort," the "stand-up and be counted people." "Women provided the majority of the workers," he remembered.[90] Dallas Republican activist Mary Lou Wiggins recalled, "We looked on this as a mission—conservatism. We felt like we are doing this for our children. . . . We felt like we were pioneers."[91]

The institutional framework of the Dallas Republican Party grew by fits and starts. But the establishment of the Texas Republican Club's Women's Division in early 1947 was the first concerted effort in the state to incorporate women into the party apparatus. The Women's Division contained a strong Dallas contingent. Of the nine female directors, seven came from Dallas. Speaking in January 1947 at the Adolphus Hotel, Texas Republican Club chairman J. F. Lucey declared, "Leading men and women in every walk of life in Texas have constantly voiced the opinion that this state needs a two-party system."[92] To accomplish that end, he said, the organization would establish Republican clubs in every precinct across Texas. Dallas, he added, would be the organization's center, and women would reinvigorate the Texas GOP. Despite Lucey's optimism, the Texas Republican Club was a disappointment. Suffering from a lack of funds and finding its female arm expendable, the organization terminated the Women's Division in October.[93]

But despite the Texas Republican Club's early demise, a change in party leadership gave Dallas women new reason for hope. In October 1950, R. B. Creager, the longtime head of the Texas Republican Party, died; a powerful impediment to party building was thus removed. Yet even more important than Creager's departure was the arrival of new female leadership. In 1952, Thelma Black of Dallas, who had been active in the Women's Division, became the National Republican Committeewoman from Texas.[94] Black actively spearheaded an initiative to organize women's Republican clubs throughout the state, and during her tenure they exploded in popularity.[95] Dallas County Republican women led the way, striving to establish clubs in every precinct by 1956.[96] On Wednesday, October 28, 1953, twenty-three Dallas women established the Preston West Republican Women's Club, the first of its kind in Dallas.[97] Led by activist Allie Mae Currie, other Dallas Republicans formed the Inwood Republican Women's Club in November 1954. The clubs were most common in more affluent areas of the county, such as the Park Cities. Yet clubs in the working-class Oak Cliff section of Dallas were soon organized as well.[98] With the formation of the Preston Crest Republican Women's Club in May 1955, the number of clubs in Dallas County reached twenty.[99] As coordination between these clubs grew increasingly difficult, their presidents established the Republican Women's Council.[100] With Dallas blazing the trail, Republican club formation statewide spread like brushfire. By 1955, Texas had attained the requisite number of clubs to establish its own delegation to the National Federation of Women's Republican Clubs of America (NFWRCA). While only nine Texas Republican clubs had joined NFWRCA prior to 1950, sixty-four clubs became members between 1950 and 1955.[101]

In 1954 Republican women's clubs in Dallas County combined modern media techniques and more traditional shoe-leather campaigning to elect Bruce Alger to Congress. The Dallas County Women's Republican Club recruited new members for the election with an old-fashioned membership drive. In May 1954, the membership committee of the club sat at a dining room table, drank bottomless cups of coffee, and stuffed envelopes. They formed an efficient assembly line: one addressed envelopes, another signed letters, a third folded and sealed, and a fourth worked the phones.

The Republican clubs applied new technologies, including slides and home movies, to rally the troops to the gospel of the GOP.[102] Clubs employed telephone committees to get out the vote on Election Day. Walter Fleming, chairman of the Dallas County Republican Executive Committee, urged precinct workers to "make only six telephone calls that produce six definite votes by your friends." "Please *telephone—telephone—telephone*," he pleaded, "from NOW until the polls close at 7:00 p.m. on Tuesday, November 2nd. The *telephone* is now the key to Victory."[103] Many of the women lost their soles in politics, canvassing door-to-door in search of votes. Mrs. J. F. W. Hannay, an indefatigable doorbell-ringer, observed, "My fore-finger was down to the knuckle, but it is an honorable wound and worth it!"[104]

Supporting moderate conservatives was not the only priority of the Republican women's clubs. Perhaps even more important, the clubs were schools in ideology. The Republican women spread moderate conservative thought to the public by organizing speaking engagements for national Republicans like Barry Goldwater and local Republican leaders like Frank Crowley, a Dallas County commissioner. Early in the 1950s, the Republican women organized forums and panels on topics that became synonymous with conservatism. They ensured there was a strong right-wing base by locating the halls, distributing the tickets, contacting the media, and publicizing the events.[105]

Republican women raised children and tended home full-time, but they also journeyed beyond their domiciles and entered a world that was traditionally masculine.[106] Those two spheres often intertwined, and children tagged along.[107] As Gwen Pharo said, "We were all young marrieds with small children. When I used to sell poll taxes [a ballot-denying measure that was abolished with the passage of the Twenty-fourth Amendment in 1964] in my precinct which was down in old Highland Park, I would drag one of them by the hand and push the other one in a stroller and go door-to-door."[108] Taffy Goldsmith recalled, "I went to rallies around the state on trains and buses. . . . We went wherever we could to get anything started. . . . It was easy for me to go into any hostile group as a pregnant woman with a red white and blue outfit."[109]

Their singular advantages provided these women the means to pursue their interest in conservative causes. Affluence allowed Dallas Republican women to have important connections and commodious houses. Often married to powerful executives or themselves professionals who had access to figures with clout, many Dallas Republican women traveled in elite circles, rubbing shoulders with wheelers and dealers at country clubs, church socials, and Sunday barbecues. With their numerous contacts, these Dallas housewives could reach farther and more quickly than working-class women to locate recruits and forge sustainable networks. These women also benefited from the space at their disposal. Many of them had little trouble inviting fifty or so people into their homes to prepare a mass mailing, listen to a guest speaker, or even hold a precinct convention.

"Frankly, they had the time," Peter O'Donnell recollected. "There weren't as many women in the workforce as there are today."[110] Republican women often scheduled meetings during the day, when their husbands were at work, or during the evening, when their children were sleeping. The consumer culture of the 1950s, with its new appliances and other time-saving innovations (e.g., processed foods), also contributed to their ability to perform their domestic duties and still have time for political activism. Plus they had the help of "domestics." When asked how she managed all her duties, Mary Ann Collins remarked, "I'd like to get a plug in for my maid, my right hand, Lacene Hollins. I couldn't do it without her."[111] Because these women were able to pursue their political interests while their husbands worked full-time in lucrative positions that provided mobility and the accoutrements of a middle-class lifestyle, their activism, rather than fostering any left-of-center politics, actually reinforced their commitment to traditional gender roles.[112]

While disposable time and socioeconomic means allowed these Republican Dallas housewives to become political activists, their motivations for doing so had to do with what political involvement could offer them personally.[113] Often highly educated elsewhere before following their husbands to Dallas, they discovered that engagement with conservative ideas satisfied their desire for continued intellectual growth. Political work "gives you an opportunity to use your brain," remarked Glenna McCord, who had attended Trinity University in San Antonio.[114] Discussing Russell Kirk's 1953 book *The Conservative Mind*, attending a Fred Schwarz speech and filling a notebook with copious notes, writing an article for *Battle Line*, or slogging through F. A. Hayek's *Constitution of Liberty* during an infant's nap—such activities provided these women with mental stimulation and quenched their yearning for intellectual fulfillment.[115] In sum, at a time when women had fewer opportunities to pursue fulfilling careers, Republican activism was a socially acceptable and satisfying intellectual outlet.

For these moderate conservative Republicans, the intelligent and upwardly mobile men and women who put in place the party's organization in Dallas, building the institutional frameworks needed to secure political power trumped commitment to ideological constancy. Compromise was acceptable because the stakes were huge. At the heart of the Cold War lay not only a military struggle but also a religious confrontation between Christianity and atheism. Despite indicating a willingness for cooperation, moderate Republicans abhorred liberalism for failing to comprehend the indefatigability of the Communist nemesis and sharing too much with Communism. In its very essence, liberalism, with its predilection for moral relativism, was far too anemic an ideology to safeguard the West.

In economic matters, moderate conservatives often found justification for capitalism not in the Randian maxim that "greed was good" because it fulfilled a human desire, but in the conclusions of postwar libertarian intellectuals that corporations, free enterprise, and private property were less likely than the state to tyrannize the individual. Laissez-faire economics appealed to a growing number of newly affluent people in the booming Sunbelt. The prospect of tax relief motivated many affluent Dallasites to embrace the Republican Party. At the same time, other factors also accounted for the party's appeal for this emerging demographic: classical political socialization, intellectual curiosity, negative perceptions of radicalism, and an aversion to the civil rights struggle (largely couched in states' rights rhetoric) all motivated moderate conservatives to join the ranks of the Dallas GOP. At the same time, ultraconservative Republicans developed their own set of appeals to their own set of constituencies.

3 Heralds of Apocalypse

Black Gold Battles the Red Menace

By 1954, the United States was "all set for surrender . . . into International Bondage," according to Ida Darden. Two years earlier, she had said that the presidential campaign of 1952 signaled an important moment for the country because it might mark the last time a candidate embraced Americanism. America was always on the verge of collapse, according to Darden. Although such eschatological prognostications proved spurious time and time again, she continued to predict the end. "It looks like it won't be long now," she announced in 1960, only to renew the prediction in 1961: "this looks like it might be it." Indeed, she characterized far-right polemicist Revilo Oliver's 1960 forecast that Soviet occupation was only four years away as excessively optimistic.[1]

H. L. Hunt was another ultraconservative Republican who employed apocalyptic rhetoric. Peaceful coexistence, Soviet premier Nikita Khrushchev's belief that war between the United States and the USSR was not inevitable, meant the "end of freedom," according to Hunt.[2] Just after John F. Kennedy assumed the presidency in 1961, Hunt wrote that the "United States is in such grave danger . . . the American people may mistakenly set up in desperation a fascist dictatorship."[3]

Hunt's Facts Forum was the flagship of a vast radio, television, and print media empire. At the zenith of its influence in the mid-1950s, the organization claimed five million viewers and listeners in the United States. It won the hearts and minds of thousands of Americans with its free-circulating collection of twenty thousand books and its organ, *Facts Forum News*, which reached sixty thousand subscribers.[4] Within three years of its birth, Facts Forum boasted 125,000 members nationwide, including John Wayne, Norman Vincent Peale, and Sears, Roebuck chairman Robert E. Wood.[5] The policy prescriptions most enthusiastically endorsed by Facts Forum included abolishing the income tax, curbing suffrage and other rights of disadvantaged groups, championing the rights of the states over federal encroachment, and conflating Communism, socialism, and liberalism.

Facts Forum's most successful grassroots operation was in Dallas, the organization's national headquarters. Organization began at the local level with the formation of Facts Forum chapters, neighborhood discussion groups of around sixty individuals. Within a week of its founding in June 1951, seven chapters, including 225 members, had been organized in Dallas County. By July, the number of units in Dallas County had grown to twenty-one. By October, members had established its fiftieth chapter.[6]

The origins of this ultraconservative media empire can be traced to the oil beneath the red clay of East Texas.[7] In 1930, the unscrupulous septuagenarian Columbus M. "Dad" Joiner discovered in East Texas what would turn out to be the largest pool of oil ever found in the United States. The column of crude that roared out of his well, Daisy-Bradford No. 3, should have been a blessing, but it was a source of worry for Joiner, who had the bad habit of buying up leases and selling them to multiple investors. Suffering from bad health, Joiner didn't want to wait for the courts to sort out his overlapping land titles. He was an eager seller. H. L. Hunt was a willing buyer, purchasing Joiner's leases for $75,000 in cash and, so long as the land yielded crude, $1,260,000 in oil revenue. This oil field would produce four billion barrels of oil and make Hunt the nation's largest independent oil operator and the world's richest man. It would also provide the funding for Facts Forum, his powerful clearinghouse for ultraconservative Republican ideology.[8]

Along with H. L. Hunt and Ida Darden, television reporter Dan Smoot and historian J. Evetts Haley embodied the worldview of the ultraconservative Republican. While all four began their political lives as Democrats, they increasingly voted Republican by the early 1960s, thus illustrating the seismic political shift of the era.[9] Each found a different medium for distributing his or her ultraconservative messages. Whereas Hunt had multiple vehicles, the ruggedly handsome, silver-tongued Smoot focused on print and television. From the late 1950s to 1971, he published a weekly newsletter, the Dan Smoot Report, and in 1957, ten years before William F. Buckley connected intellectual conservatives and political conservatives with his popular public affairs television program *Firing Line*, launched his own widely viewed television show, also called the *Dan Smoot Report*, from a studio in Dallas.[10] Ida Darden, a native of nearby Fort Worth, was best known for her ultraconservative organ the *Southern Conservative*, which was published from 1950 to 1961. J. Evetts Haley, called the "region's Thomas Paine" by one Texas newspaper, was a cowman and prolific historian who wrote twelve books on history and biography. While active on the speaking circuit and an occasional political candidate, Haley was most famous for his condemnatory appraisal of President Johnson in *A Texan Looks at Lyndon*, which reportedly sold seven million copies.[11] Like other ultraconservative Republicans, Haley often expressed himself in apocalyptic terms. An ardent backer of Barry Goldwater, Haley concluded that the 1964 Civil Rights Act would "end the American Republic."[12]

Doomsday Machine

Such ominous predictions of the death of the Republic, Soviet occupation, or "the end of religious freedom in America"—the consequence, according to W. A. Criswell, of electing a Catholic president—illustrated just how deeply religion molded the worldview of the ultraconservatives.[13] Their predictions of secular finality were facilitated by and carried over from their belief in both the inerrancy of the Bible and premillennial dispensationalism, which proposed that the Bible foretold the end of the world.[14] Smoot, for one, was a member of the nondenominational Scofield Memorial Church (originally the First Congregational Church of Dallas), whose original pastor was premillennial dispensationalism's most important popularizer, Cyrus Ingerson Scofield.[15] Hunt's apocalyptic view of secular matters also derived from his premillenial dispensationalism. In addition to being a member of Criswell's First Baptist Church, Hunt hired dispensationalist Church of Christ ministers, including Wayne Poucher as moderator and James Dobbs as commentator, for his political forum, *Life Line*. Dr. George Benson, president of the Church of Christ College in Arkansas, served as Hunt's close advisor, while Dr. Barrett Batsell Baxter, a member of the Bible Department at a Church of Christ school in Nashville, was on the *Life Line* board of directors.[16]

All the characteristics of their secular doomsday—the grandiloquent and provocative announcements of finality, the anticipation of imminent and inevitable ruin, the specific date for the end, and the antipathy toward the United Nations and the Soviet Union—were carried over from their belief in a divinely inspired day of reckoning. Prophetic belief in the end times has been a powerful phenomenon throughout American history, from the conclusion of William Miller, the Baptist preacher and founder of Adventism, that October 22, 1844, would be the world's last day, to scenarios predicting that Adolf Hitler, Benito Mussolini, or Franklin Delano Roosevelt—or eventually JFK—was the Antichrist.

Dallas was an important location for this sort of biblical prophecy. In addition to Cyrus Ingerson Scofield, the city was home throughout the 1950s and 1960s to other prognosticators, such as Dallas Theological Seminary president John Walvoord and faculty members J. Dwight Pentecost and Merrill Unger, who produced sophisticated and widely read expositions describing the last days and the importance of the Soviet Union in prophecy.[17] For example, with Khrushchev and Kennedy sparring over Berlin in 1961, Pentecost foretold that Ezekiel's prophesy of war was coming to fruition.[18] Unger also predicted that the last days were near: "billions will perish in the cataclysm."[19] Billy Graham declared that "secular history is doomed. . . . The world is hurtling toward a war greater than anything known before."[20] As the historian Paul Boyer explained, "nations" were of primary importance to prophecy writers, for in their view, nations needed to exist independently in order for the Antichrist to rule over them. They favored the arrival of the Antichrist, which would signal the imminent return of Jesus Christ. Therefore, they vehemently opposed global alliances and supranational organizations like the United Nations and, indeed, identified them with the Antichrist.[21] Among all nations, the most important was the northern nation ruled by Gog, which prophecy scholars identified as the Soviet Union; the end times, they said, would commence with its invasion of Israel. As early as 1916, Scofield observed that Russia's identity as the nation of Gog was "well-nigh universally held."[22] Walvoord and Pentecost also claimed that the Soviet Union would bring forth the Antichrist.[23] Accounting for ultraconservative antipathy for the United Nations, the Antichrist would then destroy Russia and, according to Pentecost, "rule over all the earth. There will be one world government, one world religion, one world dictator."[24]

Not a Choice, an Echo

Unshakably confident in their conclusions, Dallas ultraconservative Republicans rejected any opinion that diverged from their worldview. H. L. Hunt, Dan Smoot, and Ida Darden personified this predilection for binary thinking.[25] In exhorting Congress to impeach the *entire* United States Supreme Court for its decision in *Brown v. Board of Education of Topeka*—its "vicious and corrupt" plan to mongrelize America—Darden went even further than the John Birch Society's Robert Welch, who concentrated on chief justice Earl Warren.[26] Having concluded that history was a spiritual battle between atheism and Christianity, Hunt called for vanquishing not only the Communist Soviet Union but also liberalism—in order to stave off America's own collapse.[27] The ultraconservative Public Affairs Luncheon Club denounced Southern Methodist University for inviting John Gates, the erstwhile editor of the *Daily Worker*, to speak, despite his public disavowal of Communism. While the purpose of Gates's visit was, according to SMU president Willis M. Tate, to "intelligently scrutinize" the subject of Communism, the club remonstrated fiercely, urging the governing board of SMU's Student Center to rescind the offer to Gates, whom the club called a "self-acknowledged atheist and unregenerate follower of the Communist line."[28]

The same absolutism characterized their position on taxes. Darden's brother, Vance Muse, dedicated the 1940s to repealing the Sixteenth Amendment, which allowed for the income tax. Darden took up his cause, arguing that the "federal tax racket is the worst form of organized vice in human history," and proposed the return of the whipping post for legislators who backed a Texas sales tax.[29] Smoot shared their view of taxes. At a time when the most affluent Americans paid 90 percent of the income that fell in the highest bracket out of their total compensation to the federal government, Smoot believed that the Reed-Dirksen amendment fixing the top rate at 25 percent did not go far enough and instead favored California congressman James Utt's proposal to repeal the Sixteenth Amendment.[30] According to Smoot, spending income tax dollars on anything save national defense violated the Constitution.

An unwillingness to compromise also characterized Dallas ultra-conservatives' attitudes toward foreign policy and labor unions. Smoot advocated impeaching John F. Kennedy for his foreign policy errors, abolishing all disarmament treaties, ending foreign aid, and removing the United States from the United Nations.[31] Moreover, he condemned the UN as the "machinery for world government."[32] Considering his pre-millennialist bent, he was undoubtedly preoccupied with the fear that the United Nations was Satan's design. According to Darden, the United States could defeat Communism by pulling out of the United Nations, withdrawing recognition of Russia, and sending a company of Marines to "take care of the Cuban beatnik."[33] Ultraconservative Dallasite John Penter encouraged President Kennedy to "break off diplomatic relations with the U.S.S.R."[34] No friend of labor, the ultraconservative Public Affairs Luncheon Club took the position that labor organizations should be treated as corporations. Unions, club president Sue Fitch declared, ought to "be brought under the provisions in the Sherman Anti-Trust statutes."[35]

With God on Our Side

The ultraconservatives' fundamentalist backgrounds led them to embrace a literal interpretation of the Bible.[36] Dan Smoot's absolutist world-view derived, at least in part, from his belief in biblical inerrancy. He had grown up in a family of fundamentalists. As a youth, his Aunt Blanche had taken him on evangelical preaching tours, where the "principle [sic] themes were hellfire and damnation" and "warnings of the wrath to come."[37] Smoot remembered his grandmother's "lucid narration of Bible stories," and her view that "the Bible told her that the horrible consequences of World War I and of the devastating flu epidemic were manifestations of God's wrath against a sinful world, echoing His wrath of old against Sodom and Gomorrah."[38] Smoot's premillennial dispensationalism also informed his Manichean worldview. One of the principal beliefs of premillennial dispensationalism was the division of the world between those with Christ and those with the Antichrist. That Smoot carried these beliefs over into secular matters is clear.[39] Smoot himself said, "I regard the Bible as The Authority." "The Bible," he said, "contains absolute, revealed Truth."[40] Ultraconservatives' belief in a literal reading of the Bible, which held that Satan conspired to eradicate Christianity, only reinforced the ultraconservatives' commitment to eviscerating atheistic Communism and Satan's brother in arms, the Soviet Union.

In contrast to the Midwestern influences on moderate conservatives, Southern roots informed the ultraconservative variety of Republicanism. Hunt's paternal grandfather was a captain in the Confederate army and a farmer who moved his family from northern Georgia to find richer soil in the Ozarks of Arkansas. His Georgia-born father, Haroldson Lafayette Hunt Sr., had served as a trooper for the Confederacy. H. L. Jr.'s own love of the soil and farming ran as deep as his detestation for the New Deal and Fair Deal. "The healthiest thinking in this country is being done by people who live on medium-sized farms," he said. The oilman revered George Washington, a Virginian, and lived in Dallas in a replica of Mount Vernon, albeit five times larger. Hunt claimed that he descended from one of the original founders of Jamestown, as well as James Oglethorpe, who had established the colony of Georgia for debtors. He honed his talent as a stellar poker player in the bunkhouses and among the river-boat gamblers of the Mississippi River. Unaware of Hunt's status as the world's richest man or even his true identity, his second wife, Frania Tye Lee, knew him only as "Major Franklin Hunt." When she asked whether he had served in the military, Hunt replied that he had not, but "every-body in the South is called major or colonel."[41]

The Invisible Government

The biblical literalism of the ultraconservatives went hand in hand with conspiracism since, in their minds, the greatest conspiracy of all was Satan's ongoing battle against Christianity. For ultraconservatives like Dan Smoot, the Cold War between the atheistic Soviet Union and a Christian America was merely a secular episode in this spiritual battle. As he wrote in *The Hope of the World*, "The great struggle of our time, is a war to the death between the Christian forces of freedom and the atheistic forces of slavery."[42] From here, it was a small jump to envision an invisi-ble "real" government. In *The Invisible Government*, Smoot concluded that the Council on Foreign Relations, along with some secondary govern-ment agencies, constituted the actual government of the United States and was seeking to turn America into a Communist state, setting the stage for a one-world system.[43] Dallas native, grassroots ultraconservative Republican, and John Birch Society member J. McCarthy was in complete agreement. Upon discovering that the Rockefeller Foundation provided funding for the Council on Foreign Relations, McCarthy argued that rescinding the foundation's tax-exempt status would "eliminate the Council on Foreign Relations and its subsidiaries."[44]

Dallas ultraconservatives like Smoot and McCarthy charged that conspiracy, rather than the separate actions of individuals across time, drove history.[45] Titillated by the discovery of a truth that others could not see, these enlightened ultraconservatives often became determined to inform the benighted of the vastness of the conspiracy.[46] Ida Darden concluded that not only did a few principal figures of the New Deal and officials of the State Department furtively favor Communism, but that the election of Franklin Delano Roosevelt had inaugurated a sustained conspiracy that reached into every corner of American life—its churches, media, government institutions—and had as its object the downfall of a sovereign United States and the ascent of a Communist world government.[47] On other occasions, she concluded that the conspiracy began under the Democratic administration of Woodrow Wilson.[48] Yet, according to Darden, the Republican administrations of Harding, Coolidge, and Hoover had been immune to the conspiracy.[49] Throughout the pages of the *Southern Conservative*, she seethed against Roosevelt and urged the swift repeal of all social legislation passed since 1933.[50] Roosevelt was to blame for Pearl Harbor, she claimed, and Alger Hiss had controlled all the events at Yalta while Roosevelt relaxed.[51] Darden concluded that the "Unseen Master" infiltrated the churches as well. Her evidence was that ministers had forsaken a literal interpretation of the Bible for the social gospel, which held that God's kingdom was of this earth, that worldly matters were improving, and that an activist government should alleviate the suffering produced by the free market.[52]

While initially pleased by the election of Republican president Dwight D. Eisenhower, many ultraconservatives soon came to the conclusion that the erstwhile general's caution was actually appeasement and perfidy.[53] Eisenhower's inaction after the uprising in Hungary, refusal to defend Senator Joe McCarthy, and appointment of Earl Warren, under whom the Supreme Court issued the landmark *Brown v. Board* ruling, led them to conclude that Ike was taking his cues from the Kremlin.[54] With her conspiracy loom working, Darden wove in even more threads: Eisenhower was actually the Russians' preferred candidate in the 1956 election. After all, she reasoned, Eisenhower had already been indoctrinated by the Soviets while serving as president of Columbia University, and thus had four years more experience as a Communist infiltrator than his challenger.[55] According to Dallas ultraconservative Republican Earnest B. Foote, Eisenhower worked to "promote Red activities while head of Columbia University," accepting from "Communist Poland $30,000 to finance Communistic propaganda" and appointing as professor "a notorious exponent of Marxism." "This record," Foote said, "can not be ignored by any American patriot."[56]

Conspiracy theories had been prominent throughout American history and served many important functions for ultraconservatives. Knowing "the truth" provided a sense of empowerment to believers who lacked personal or political influence.[57] Conspiracy theories worked to fill in the unexplained lacunae in peoples' belief and knowledge systems. Fastidious fact-collecting accompanied the conspiratorial thinking of Dallas ultraconservatives. For those inclined to conspiracism, precise dissection of historical phenomena, however arbitrary, uncloaked secret pasts and nefarious plots. As Heather Hendershot put it, ultraconservatives "were information packrats. No detail was too minor to find a place in a filing cabinet."[58] They gathered facts incessantly, amassing quotes and statistics to buttress the narrative they already believed in. H. L. Hunt referred to anybody who disagreed with his positions as "the Mistaken." Only the rigorous collection and deployment of "facts" could debunk and illuminate their error. Having observed, for instance, that "9 out of 10 Americans think we should not leave the U.N.," Hunt responded with a barrage of "facts." "The public," he complained, "apparently failed to recognize" that "Khrushchev . . . can control the U.N. at will," "the head of the U.N. Military Staff is always a Communist," and "the existence of the U.N. supplants the sovereignty of the U.S."[59] Ultraconservatives stockpiled "evidence" of treason through a process of examining decisions made by American policymakers and presupposing that errors in judgment were conscious, intentional, and sinister. They combined this preoccupation with heaping up facts with a predilection for leaping to dubious conclusions. For instance, *The Politician*, by John Birch Society founder Robert Welch, backed up its claim that President Eisenhower was a Communist with more than a hundred pages of footnotes.[60]

Conspiracy theories brought together individuals from different backgrounds, classes, and regions since subscribers often had the same fears, spoke the same language of conspiracy, held the same affinity for amassing evidence to bolster their case, and shared the same intense thrill of knowing what others did not.[61] Finally, as historian Kathryn Olmstead has argued, a belief in conspiracy theories became more prevalent in twentieth-century America, particularly in the post–World War II era, because *actual* government conspiracies were on the rise: "as the government grew, it gained the power to conspire against its citizens, and it soon began exercising that power."[62] After all, during the Cold War, government officials *had* spied for the Soviet Union, had worked with mobsters to kill a foreign head of state, had provided weapons to terrorists in exchange for hostages, and had, without informed consent, conducted LSD experiments on Americans in bars.[63]

An Iron Curtain over America

For all this fine parsing, ultraconservatives still came to simplistic and strident conclusions. Their predilection for conflating Communism, liberalism, civil rights, and atheism betrayed an antidemocratic and cynical worldview of the American people as obtuse and ignorant. Dan Smoot frequently attacked democracy on his television program. H. L. Hunt wrote *Alpaca*, a fictional tale of a country that granted additional votes to citizens who paid higher taxes. Those who paid the highest taxes received seven votes, and anyone who agreed to forgo government benefits received two.[64] In June 1951, Hunt's Facts Forum established its own reading program, recommending Clarence Manion's *The Key to Peace*, which assailed democracy and "unrestrained majority rule" as tyrannical.[65]

Along with eschatological themes, a frenzied style characterized the speeches of many ultraconservatives, who wrote them with the purpose of stirring controversy and bringing down the house. Hailing from the Panhandle, Texas historian J. Evetts Haley may have wandered sometimes in his loyalty to the Republican Party, but his violent rhetoric never ceased. In 1936, Haley endorsed Republican Alf Landon and charged that "just as the owner of the sheep leads them, [President Roosevelt] leads the people, and when the fattening period is over—and January 4, 1937 is the day set for slaughter—the American people, his sheep, will be slaughtered."[66] In the 1950s, Haley defended segregation, promising to meet the federal enforcers of *Brown v. Board* "at the state line with our Texas Rangers."[67] While usually running as a Republican, as he did in an unsuccessful bid for Congress in 1948, Haley ran for Texas governor as a Democrat in 1956, roaring in one particular stemwinder that "interposition"—the declared right of a state to impose itself against the federal government—"is just as Constitutional as ham and eggs."[68] In November 1961, Haley appeared in Dallas to support the National Indignation Convention, which was established by Dallas native Frank McGehee to protest the sale of surplus fighter planes to Yugoslavia and which inspired other Dallas ultraconservatives to boycott any products from Communist countries.[69] Upon being introduced by Tom Anderson, a John Birch Society member, Haley bellowed, "Tom Anderson must be turning moderate. He only wants to impeach Earl Warren. I'd hang him."[70]

Dallas ultraconservatives often displayed a prejudice against African-Americans. Many of them expressed a fear that their own race was losing cheap African-American labor, including male servants and female "help." For ultraconservatives, the existence of the National Association for the Advancement of Colored People was just another symptom of the Communist conspiracy that engulfed every facet of America. As historian Jeff Woods showed, "the more national criticism of the region's racial institutions grew, the more southern segregationists looked to Communism to protect the traditional social order."[71] Ida Darden was an incorrigible racist whose newspaper, the *Southern Conservative*, fought integration by fabricating stories of black boys sending salacious notes to white females and "making indecent exposure of their persons in the classroom." Darden proposed two responses to forced integration: reviving the Ku Klux Klan and throwing black children out of classroom windows.[72] Celebrating the virtues of the open shop, Darden's brother, Vance Muse, observed that it "help[ed] the nigger. Good niggers, not these Communist niggers." "I like the nigger in his place," he added.[73]

For Dan Smoot, integration was "an American tragedy" concocted by the "notorious" NAACP. Underscoring that *Brown v. Board of Education* was the primary reason many ultraconservatives wanted to impeach Earl Warren, Smoot wrote that *Brown* "set the precedent for the Warren Court's lawless behavior."[74] Downplaying the extent of the racial problem in the white South, "prior to the late 1920s and early 1930s," Smoot observed, "American whites and negroes were solving their 'racial problems' with miraculous speed."[75] Northerners in the NAACP and the Communist Party, he concluded, exacerbated an unfortunate but rather inconsequential legacy of the Civil War and Reconstruction.

To be sure, Smoot would deny any personal racism, but his warnings against "the real and final intimacy of inter-marriage" between "colored and white people" demonstrate that belief in white superiority remained at the forefront of his thinking. "The ultimate objective" of the NAACP, he opined, "can never be reached until black and white races are submerged in each other—until they intermarry and procreate a racially blended population of light brown people."[76] Underscoring his belief that the dreadful conditions of African-American bondage in the New World had been exaggerated, Smoot stated that for these "barbarians," slavery was "an actual improvement upon the life which they had made for themselves in Africa."[77] According to Smoot, "cotton picking was an annual late-summer festival which [blacks] thoroughly enjoyed."[78] His descriptions of black "children romping and shouting from house-to-house" and "grown-ups sitting on front porches laughing" illustrated his belief that black people were childlike and simple. "Negroes," he remembered, "seemed to put a smile, if not a broad grin on everything."[79]

Although it was gradually disappearing as a primary mode of attack by the early 1950s, some Dallas ultraconservatives still employed anti-Semitism. After having met fellow Republican Mrs. Earnest B. Foote and listened to her views, S. T. Darling, a Dallas woman, expressed alarm at Foote's assertion that Dallas papers supported Eisenhower because the "papers were owned by Jews" and Eisenhower himself was a "Swedish Jew."[80] According to John Owen Beaty, an English professor at Southern Methodist University and the author of the *Iron Curtain over America*, Communism derived from the Jews, who descended from a lost Southern Russian tribe called the Khazars.[81] Beaty's assertion prompted a critical article in the autumn 1953 journal of *Southwest Review*. Beaty responded with the pamphlet "How to Capture a University," which alleged that Jews, particularly Stanley Marcus of Neiman Marcus, controlled Southern Methodist University. Beaty received the full support of Ida Darden, and Stanley Marcus noted pointedly that the *Dallas Morning News* "didn't use its editorial power against" Beaty.[82]

Ultraconservatives embraced the long-standing nineteenth-century notion that the Constitution, rather than providing rights, was in fact designed to restrict them. In this view, the Constitution was intended to protect property rights, safeguard the power of the states relative to the federal government, and curtail democracy in order to preserve privilege and the status quo. Deriving directly from John C. Calhoun and other slave-owning politicians of the antebellum Old South, the concept of the Constitution as a restrictive document was embraced by segregationists in the New South.[83] Dan Smoot was undoubtedly overstating things when he called himself a constitutional conservative since he only accepted as valid the first ten amendments. Like many ultraconservatives, he subscribed to the belief that the Fourteenth and Fifteenth amendments were "inorganic accretions," as William F. Buckley put it, tacked onto the Constitution by the "victors-at-war by force" to punish the South and make African-Americans the equals of white men.[84] Having never been ratified appropriately, Smoot believed the Fourteenth Amendment, which safeguarded for all citizens due process and equal protection under the law, to be null and void.[85]

Mental Heath, Dental Heath

Ultraconservatives detested particular institutional and cultural manifestations of Dallas's increasing urbanity, including the new emphasis on mental health, dental health, and modern art.[86] One Dallas ultraconservative condemned the inclusion of an article about the father of psychoanalysis, Sigmund Freud, in *American Opinion*, the John Birch Society organ. "Please clean up the liberal tone of Jack Moffitt's column," she complained. "I was very displeased, to say the least, to find such *trash* as the article on Freud in the American Opinion. How can you expect members to recommend A.O. to prospective members and have to apologize for its contents. There is no excuse for such editing."[87] In one of her more interesting articles, Darden wrote that a scientist from California was performing experimental trials on spiders with a conformity serum concocted from patients under psychiatric care. His goal was to introduce uniformity across the entire general population and make Communism more viable in the United States. Water fluoridation was also, Darden suggested, about capturing minds and bringing about Soviet occupation and eventual world government. She doubted that fluoride prevented cavities and argued that dentists would never support something that undercut their material interests.[88] In 1959, the ultraconservative Dallas Public Affairs Luncheon Club, which consisted of five hundred Dallas women, also protested the fluoridation of the Dallas water supply. "While there are competent medical men still available to prescribe drugs for their patients," club president Sue Fitch declared, "public servants have no place prescrib[ing] medication for the people of Dallas."[89]

The Public Affairs Luncheon Club had earlier declared, in a 1955 resolution, that the Dallas Museum of Fine Arts "promotes and acquires the works of artists who have known Communistic affiliations."[90] While fretting about restrictions to artistic expression, Jerry Bywaters, the museum's director, observed that the primary issue was club members' aversion to contemporary art. "The so-called art has no meaning" and "leave[s] our youth with a baffling question," said Florence Rodgers, past president of the Luncheon Club. "When you simply put streaks and vagaries on a piece of canvas, you have nothing."[91] In the end, the museum's board of trustees decided that avoiding controversy was their priority and drafted new guidelines for exhibiting artwork. The merits of the work itself would no longer exclusively determine the museum's decisions; political affiliation, especially Communist affiliation, would also be considered.[92]

According to ultraconservatives, educational institutions and faculty (who were allegedly engaged in the Communist conspiracy) threatened to corrupt the minds of students. Because the conspiracy entered every sphere, schools and museums were a key battleground. One ultraconservative, who had "a daughter in college," bemoaned the influence of "some instructors in regard to governmental control of economics." "Students and young job holders," he lamented, "seem to have no particular goal, and if they are neglected, we may lose them to wishy-washy thinking and thus to socialism."[93] "Many an intellectual in America to-day," complained Dallasite Elizabeth Staples, a former editor of H. L. Hunt's *Facts Forum News*, is "blithely supercilious about the government which affords him . . . rich privileges and pleasures. . . . Is any American exempt from the stern dictum . . . that eternal vigilance is the price of freedom? Why should anyone . . . take life, liberty, and the pursuit of happiness for granted? . . . We cannot possibly retain possession of them if we are somnolent; we will lose them by default. There are times when . . . a free citizen, must resist threats of serfdom; must be a rebel against tyranny."[94] Ida Darden charged that teachers had been subverted by the United Nations Educational, Scientific, and Cultural Organization (UNESCO) and the National Education Association.[95] Ultraconservatives engaged in aggressive and often tenacious campaigns to eradicate Communist literature and persons said to have Communist affiliations. In the early 1950s, after hearing the protests of the Minute Women, an anti-Communist women's group that successfully elected some members to the Houston school board, the city censored high school textbooks that contained favorable references to the United Nations.[96] Darden was a strong advocate for the Minute Women, who attacked the patriotism of the city's teachers. She also endorsed the investigation of a University of Texas economics professor who called the free market decadent.[97] Such actions contributed to the ultraconservatives' anti-intellectual ethos.

There were some who kept close tabs on "subversive" professors.[98] One ultraconservative wrote Robert Welch, informing him that Claude Allen, an English professor at the University of Texas at Austin, had told a class of freshmen that "it was the prudishness on the part of girls that was causing all the racial strife." "Girls must forget their inhibitions," the professor had reportedly said. The informant also made these charges: "Some of the male students . . . report his advocacy of living with negroes and they have seen him with negro women."[99] For H. L. Hunt, subversive intellectuals had shattered the American people's faith in laissez-faire economics. "International correspondents largely with Harvard, Columbia, and New York University backgrounds . . . freely refuse to accept any pro-freedom commentary."[100] Above any other issue, historian J. Evetts Haley embraced local control of education, adding that Texas schools needed to do more with less money for students.[101] After launching an unsuccessful attack in 1960 on Southern Methodist University, which he called a haven for left-wingers, Haley turned his attention to the Texas textbook market, which annually grossed from six to ten million dollars. Urging that high school students "should be taught only the American side," Haley argued, "the stressing of both sides of a controversy only confuses the young and encourages them to make snap decisions based on insufficient evidence." The State Textbook Committee acquiesced to censors like Haley, removing or expurgating schoolbooks that included favorable references to integration, the United Nations, and activist musician Pete Seeger.[102] At a meeting in Dallas in 1962, Haley put it to Dallas school superintendent W. T. White that textbook censorship had not gone far enough, although he felt that the current method of selecting textbooks worked in Dallas because its teachers were more conservative than elsewhere. Terry Eastland, a twelve-year-old junior high student, shared Haley's concern that current textbooks were undermining Texans' faith in free enterprise and Christianity. As Eastland put it, "We'll never get peace until the second coming of Christ. They talk about world peace in there and I'm not in favor of that."[103]

Many ultraconservative Republicans hailed from the South, shared a belief in a literal interpretation of the Bible, and subscribed to premillennial dispensationalism. Their religious beliefs bolstered their animus toward the atheistic Soviet Union, which they claimed sought to divest Americans of their religious faith. That they shared a strong belief that history was a binary struggle between atheism and Christianity accounted for, or at least did not interfere with, their rejection of pluralism and their peremptory judgment that their worldview was the correct one. Their belief that Satan's war against Christianity was history's biggest and most long-standing conspiracy fostered a more general preoccupation with conspiracism. History was seen as a grand plot, with conspirators everywhere, all-powerful and all-knowing. Dissecting random events and fitting them into patterns consistent with their preconceptions helped ultraconservatives make sense of a complicated world and derive power from its complexity, forging ties with those who saw things similarly and construing those with other views as enemies, a nefarious Other.

Ultraconservatives often expressed antidemocratic sentiments and shared a violent prejudice against African-Americans. As we will see in chapter 4, these racist sentiments in some respects complemented their religious backgrounds. The ultraconservatives were religious zealots, yet their apocalyptic discourse extended to the secular world, where they found conspiracies behind the fluoridation of drinking water. These central features of the ultraconservative worldview were not always static.

Ultraconservatives and moderates nonetheless influenced each other, helping to define and reinforce their respective core beliefs but also to modify them. Through personal interactions and rhetorical exchanges, an ideological swapping often occurred, as a result of which many characteristics of ultraconservative Republican thought became woven into the fabric of positions taken by many once-moderate conservatives.

4 Whistling Dixie

Cheegros

Speaking to a South Carolina Baptist evangelism conference on February 21, 1956, W. A. Criswell, the fiery pastor of Dallas's First Baptist Church, interjected himself into the national conversation on race with statements in favor of segregation. A capacity crowd filled the pews of the First Baptist Church of Columbia to listen to the charismatic preacher, whom Billy Graham called "my pastor."[1] Criswell issued a powerful invective against "this thing of integration." He argued that segregation was God's intention and that any deviation from that plan was contrary to the will of God. Integration, he said, was a "denial of all that we believe in." Ecumenical religious leaders who supported desegregation were "just as blasphemous and unbiblical as they can be." The "universal Fatherhood of God and brotherhood of man" was a "spurious doctrine." He then assailed the Supreme Court for the "idiocy" and "foolishness" of attempting to alter the folkways of the South. Civil rights advocates were likewise subjected to Criswell's lash. "Let them integrate," he declared. "Let them sit up there in their dirty shirts and make all their fine speeches. But they are a bunch of infidels, dying from the neck up." Criswell then excoriated the National Council of Churches and the National Association for the Advancement of Colored People. The "good-for-nothing fellows," he roared, "are trying to upset all of the things that we love as good old Southern people and as good old Southern Baptists." His address grew increasingly confrontational and angry. "Why the NAACP has got those East Texans on the run so much that they dare not pronounce the word chigger any longer. It has to be cheegro." Criswell called anybody who professed to be desegregated "soft in the head" and reminded his audience that denominations "mutually agree to worship apart."[2] The following day, Criswell presented his biblical defense of segregation for the second time, to the South Carolina legislature and Governor Strom Thurmond. The speech again included the "cheegro" reference. Legislators rose from their seats and cheered enthusiastically, then passed a resolution encouraging the United States Justice Department to place the NAACP on its subversive list.

The Burden of Jim Crow

Throughout its history, Dallas embraced Jim Crow and other racially based practices. Those opposing these practices often met with violence. In the nineteenth century, the white primary, poll taxes, and other instruments of Jim Crow restricted the rights of black people. In the early twentieth century, public lynchings, the egregious neglect of social services, and campaigns against untrammeled growth all exacerbated racial animosities. In 1910, a lynch mob entered a Dallas courtroom where Allen Brooks, an African-American, was on trial for allegedly accosting a white female. The mob fitted a loop around Brooks's neck and threw the opposite end of the rope out the window. A crowd swarming in the dusty Dallas streets below grabbed the rope and pulled Brooks to his death.[3] In the 1920s, Dallas leaders bolstered residential segregation even further through the passage of seven draconian ordinances.[4]

A revitalized Ku Klux Klan found Dallas to be a congenial environment in the 1920s. Founded by William Simmons in 1915, and popular throughout the Midwest, especially in Indiana, the new Klan maintained the pageantry, secret passwords, and antipathy toward black people of the Reconstruction-era Klan but saved its deepest ire for Catholics, Jews, and the new immigrants. Consisting of thirteen thousand members by 1924, the Dallas chapter, Klan No. 66, was the largest in the nation. Hiram Wesley Evans, a dentist and Disciple of Christ who was the Dallas chapter's Cyclops, or presiding officer, gained notoriety in 1922 by becoming the Imperial Wizard for the national organization. Essential to the success of the Klan was the support of Dallas church leaders, including the pastors of Westminster Presbyterian Church, First Methodist Church, First Presbyterian Church, Forest Avenue Baptist Church, and the Cole Avenue Baptist Church. Terrorizing Dallas's black community, the Klan accused some black people of accosting white women and punished them by branding "KKK" into their foreheads with acid. Courts provided little relief for black people because the juries and police were often Klansmen themselves.[5]

Throughout the 1930s and 1940s, Dallas's African-Americans continued to suffer from harsh segregation policies. They frequently received random beatings by white people, were consistently denied adequate housing as well as educational and occupational training, received scant social services, and worked the most menial jobs as washmen, waiters, and shoe-shiners.[6] If African-Americans, 13.5 percent of the population of Dallas County in 1950, were able to obtain housing at all, they were restricted to the poorest sections of West Dallas and South Dallas.[7]

City leaders embraced a commitment to unregulated capitalism and minimal government unless instability threatened prosperity. Concerned that poor infrastructure and bad housing would hurt business and have a detrimental impact on what Robert Fairbanks called "the city as a whole," leaders in the 1930s accepted federal monies for improvements in roads, sewers, and parks, and for Texas's only Public Works Administration public housing project, a facility for whites only. Moreover, because poverty lines harmed commercial interests, boosters drew on such New Deal programs as the Federal Emergency Relief Administration, which provided four million dollars in desperately needed relief for the city's unemployed.[8]

Daniel Decries Desegregation

In 1955, the year following the landmark *Brown v. Board of Education* decision, in which the US Supreme Court ruled that "separate education facilities are inherently unequal," Carey Daniel invigorated the biblical defense of segregation with the publication of *God, the Original Segregationist*, which sold a million copies and even appeared in abridged form in the *Dallas Morning News*.[9] Daniel was not only the pastor of the First Baptist Church of West Dallas, he was also the first vice president of the Texas Citizens' Council, which in 1955 claimed twenty thousand members.[10] "Negroes," the council's president, Ross Carlton, observed, were "unwitting and dumb tools of the Communistic propagandists in the NAACP."[11] Daniel's racial conservatism derived from his premillennial dispensationalism. In the early twentieth century, the popular *Sco-*

field Reference Bible had espoused a strong racial conservatism. Cyrus I. Scofield claimed that black people descended from Ham, whom Noah cursed after the flood. According to Scofield, black people were meant to be "inferior and servile," and the Bible offered spiritual justification for segregation, Jim Crow, and other forms of subjugation.[12]

In *God, the Original Segregationist*, Carey Daniel wrote that after the biblical flood, God "made a sharp division in the land" for the descendants of Noah's sons, Shem, Ham, and Japheth. Shem's descendants were the Jews, Ham's were dark-skinned people, and Japheth's were white people. Ham's descendants were given the continent of Africa, and Shem's were granted Israel and all the lands to the Euphrates River. White people received everything else.[13] A subset of Ham's children, the Canaanites, were allowed to inhabit God's Promised Land but had to remain separate from all white people. Because they "dared to violate God's sacred law of segregation by moving into and claiming the land farther east," God ordered their destruction. The one who "first conceived of the idea" of desegregation was, in Carey Daniel's view, Ham's grandson Nimrod, whom Daniel called "the mouthpiece of the devil." In other words, according to Daniel, Satan was the original desegregationist.[14]

Rank-and-file congregants, historian Jane Dailey put it, used "the language of miscegenation" as a bulwark of segregation. One of their sources was Daniel's book, which exemplifies how some ministers raised the issue of miscegenation, amid sexually charged language, to maintain what it regarded as God's divine plan. At the heart of the question of desegregation, according to Daniel, was interracial sex and marriage. "I would be a fool to think [interracial marriage] impossible if desegregation is *thrust* upon us," he proclaimed. "Does anyone really doubt that intermarriage and mongrelization are inevitable if this happens? [Black men] have felt a *renewed urge* to cohabitate with white women."[15] Perhaps hoping to drum up white fear by making an implicit analogy between the fall of Sodom and Gomorrah and the impending desegregation of Dallas, Daniel turns again to stereotypes of black sexuality: "Anyone familiar with the biblical history of those cities during that period can readily understand why we here in the South are determined to maintain segregation." The book concludes with an exhortation to his "segregationist friends": "WRITE OR BETTER TELEGRAPH YOUR TOP

POLITICAL LEADERS AND CONGRESSMEN DEMANDING CONTINUED SEG-
REGATION IN OUR PUBLIC SCHOOLS."[16]

Daniel's "segregationist friends" wrote lots of letters. Whether they read *God, the Original Segregationist* or heard Daniel in church, Dallasites absorbed his teachings and repeatedly invoked God's will throughout 1955 to defend segregation. "God hates the sin of mongrelization," observed H. T. Finsch, a Dallas citizen. "At the Tower of Babel they were all of one mind and language, integrated, an ancient 'United Nations.' And God scattered and confounded them."[17] "I too think segregation is ordained by God and all nature proclaims it," stated Martha Pearson of Dallas. "The Bible plainly states that God did not want the races to mix."[18] Lee Cannon of nearby Sherman, Texas, observed, "I am a Negro, [and] it never was my desire to mix with any race other than the Negro race. . . . Had God intended for such, why did he make different races?"[19]

W. A. Criswell's unabashedly racist address in South Carolina drew praise from many in Dallas and further catalyzed others to assert a biblical defense of segregation. Like Daniel, Criswell used the *Scofield Reference Bible* as a point of reference and proclaimed as late as 1979 that black people suffered from "the curse of Ham."[20] While approval of his speech was by no means universal in Dallas, no vociferous opposition arose, and other Dallas clergymen joined in. Ralph Langley, the pastor of Dallas's Wilshire Baptist Church, supported Criswell's remarks, even suggesting that "separate but equal facilities for the Negro satisfie[d]" *Brown v. Board of Education*. Earl K. Oldham, another Dallas Baptist minister, held that "segregation is the will of God" and urged "every Bible believer" to "make a protest against integration." "Three cheers for Dr. Criswell," Daniel exulted just days after Criswell's speech. "All white citizens who want to stay white—and all who believe in the preservation of the white and Negro races as God made them to remain—should unite with the Texas Citizens' Council for segregation."

Many ordinary white Dallas men and women likewise stood behind Criswell or echoed his biblical defense of segregation. Some stated their views in letters to the *Dallas Morning News*. Thomas Fisher exclaimed, "At last, Dallas and the Southern Baptist convention have a Billy Sunday in Dr. W. A. Criswell," adding, "I believe that Dr. Criswell speaks for the majority of Southern Baptist church members." Martha Pearson opined, "The people who are so ready to sacrifice segregation are no Bible students. . . . I wish we had more men of Dr. Criswell's caliber." Robert Crow observed, "To advocate integration is to defy God," and he added, "If God abhors anything, it is mongrelization, which inevitably follows integration." According to Margaret Evans, "Criswell and all other ministers opposed to integration have always quoted scriptures to back their convictions. . . . What better guide can we use than the word of God?" S. A. Beard called Criswell's address "a firm stand for God and his people who He created and segregated," and concluded, "It is His will that they remain that way." Homer Matthews remarked, "Many thousands of people of the South are of the same opinion [as Criswell] and have been waiting for a Christian leader of any denomination to present our views." Dallasite Sue E. Easley declared, "It is good to know someone is standing up for us whites. The Supreme Court should be impeached." Thomas Cleary declared, "I am delighted to know that we have one high-class Christian, God-loving man in Texas who has the courage to look the world in the face and speak the truth as it is written in God's word."[21] Lynn Landrum, the self-named "Columntator" for the *Dallas Morning News*, praised Criswell's admonition that segregation is "going to get into your family." "Maybe the good doctor over-said himself," Landrum allowed, "but, praise the Lord, he didn't mumble. It ought to clear the air." "This is true, brethren," Landrum concluded, "and we might as well face it. If you want to raise White Face Herefords, you keep Milking Shorthorns out of the pasture."[22]

Sue Fitch and the Public Affairs Luncheon Club

While Carey Daniel and W. A. Criswell were promoting their case for segregation, the women of the Public Affairs Luncheon Club and its president, Sue Fitch, were galvanizing support for Jim Crow in Dallas. If hunting Communists was the club's pastime in the first half of the decade, denying equal opportunities to African-Americans was its principal vocation in the second half. Only a week after the *Brown v. Board of Education* ruling in May 1954, the club passed a resolution that the "amalgamation of white and Negro children in the public school system not be implemented or enforced by federal directive."[23] Because of Criswell's increasing popularity among segregationists, advocates of massive resistance became regular speakers before the club after his

South Carolina address. By the spring of 1956, it was becoming abundantly clear that the leaders of the Public Affairs Luncheon Club would be fierce interpositionists to the bitter end.[24]

A week after Criswell's address, the club's vice president, Mrs. Ross Carlton (wife of the first president of the Associated Citizens' Council of Texas), introduced a speech by Virginia broadcaster W. E. Debnam.[25] He fired up the crowd with his spirited defense of segregation: "I have a tremendous regard for the white race. I have a tremendous regard for the Negroes and I think we will all go to heaven but I don't believe we'll go to the pearly gates by sitting in each others laps."[26] After the speech, the luncheon club passed a resolution backing interposition. "The public school system of Texas is not a federal institution," read the resolution, "but was created by the State and the maintenance and control of the schools left to local communities." *Brown v. Board of Education*, the resolution concluded, was an "unprecedented decree" and "a violation of the Constitution of the United States."[27]

Carlton and, especially, Sue Fitch made the Public Affairs Luncheon Club a forum for the leading figures of interposition and white supremacy. Chicago-born Fitch was educated at Southern Methodist University and served as chairman of the club for the 1956–1957 season. A collector of antiques, Fitch spent much of her time showcasing homes as a broker in Dallas's booming real estate market. The rest of her time she committed to ensuring that segregation did not become a relic of the Southern past, attending meetings of the Daughters of the American Revolution and securing for the luncheon club speakers who were in favor of massive resistance. "I feel the No. 1 issue is usurpation of power by the Supreme Court," she declared in 1956. "I am sure we will support a bill to curb the power of the Supreme Court."[28] That fall, Fitch invited as a speaker Judge Tom Brady, the founding father of Mississippi's white Citizens' Councils and the author of the racist and anti-Semitic booklet *Black Monday*,[29] where comments such as this can be found: "The social, political, economic, and religious preferences of the Negro remain close to the caterpillar and the cockroach. . . . There is nothing fundamentally wrong with the caterpillar or the cockroach. It is merely a matter of taste. A cockroach or caterpillar remains proper food for a chimpanzee."[30] According to Brady, the Supreme Court's "socialistic" ruling left white citizens with the choice between "segregation and amalgamation." Safeguarding the purity of their race, he said, depended on whites' willingness to establish a new territorial state for blacks, abolish public schools, expose Communism in the churches, elect Supreme Court judges, and form resistance groups in the former states of the Confederacy.[31]

Fitch and many other former Midwesterners viewed segregation as a societal norm. Many adamantly dismissed the notion that Southern blacks even supported civil rights. Many refused to acknowledge the ubiquity of racial prejudice and the injustice of segregation.[32] In Dallas, the long-standing racial prejudice of the slave and Confederate state of Texas became wedded to the Midwest's own tradition of white suprematism.[33] A broader conservative worldview often accompanied, very often complemented, and sometimes even accounted for their defense of white supremacy. For instance, they often held that Communists provided the backbone of the civil rights movement. They were also persuaded that liberals championed civil rights as a means to secure other, more important objectives of the socialist program, including greater benefits for labor and a more equitable distribution of wealth. In their assaults on integration and the civil rights movement, many eventually displaced Jim Crow racism with an antistatist, Cold War anti-Communist discourse. This colorblind rhetoric proved advantageous not only because it allowed a defense against charges of racism but because it ultimately fastened the southern white cause to a broader conservative program.[34]

Massive Resistance at Mansfield High

Inspired by local ministers like Daniel and Criswell, backed by grassroots supporters, and bolstered by speakers scheduled by Fitch, segregationists in August 1956 resisted the desegregation of the high school in Mansfield, Texas, a community thirty miles southwest of Dallas. In Mansfield, for the first time in Texas history, a federal court had ordered the desegregation of the schools. Assisted by the mayor and the police chief, an angry mob of four hundred whites thwarted the enrollment of three black students on August 30 and 31. One voice from the crowd jeered at the sheriff, "You can protect them tomorrow and the next day, but you can't stay with them forever." Enraged whites carried signs with such inflammatory slogans as "A DEAD NIGGER IS THE BEST NIGGER" and "COON EARS $1.00 A DOZEN," telephoned blacks with bomb threats, and hung three effigies representing the students. One effigy hanging from the school flagpole bore the sign "STAY AWAY NIGGERS." "I didn't put it up there," insisted the principal, "and I'm not going to take it down."[35]

Throughout the crisis, opponents of integration invoked a spiritual basis for their position. "If God had wanted us to go to school together He wouldn't have made them black and us white," one teenager observed.[36] Integration, Addie Barlow argued, "violates God's law."[37] According to Earl Anderson, the pastor of Munger Place Baptist Church in Dallas, "It would be a miracle indeed if someone would come up with just one verse in the Holy Bible which even inferred that God did not ordain these natural races and that He did not intend for them to keep themselves pure within their own natural racial boundaries until the end of this natural world."[38] Walter Moore of Dallas asserted, "Violation of God's law regarding the races would bring about more crime, . . . intermarriage, a mongrel race, and ultimately a fallen nation."[39] Texas governor Allan Shivers, who defended segregation in Mansfield by sending the Texas Rangers to the school, embraced this religious defense of segregation, observing that "no court can wreck what God has made."[40]

The governor's action went unopposed: President Eisenhower faced reelection in 1956 and declined to intervene in Mansfield. (A year later, he would respond differently to a similar crisis, sending federal troops to enforce the integration of Central High School in Little Rock, Arkansas.) Congressman Bruce Alger also felt the effects of the Mansfield crisis on his campaign. Indeed, its repercussions extended beyond Dallas politics and altered the Republican Party's discourse on race relations throughout the South.

Alger v. Wade

Encouraged by community leaders, Bruce Alger had successfully run for Congress in 1954, aligning himself with President Eisenhower. "I am an Eisenhower Republican," he declared in that campaign. "You elected Ike. Now support him. If you are for Ike, you are for me."[41] One campaign advertisement pictured Alger shaking hands with the president. A bumper sticker reminded drivers to "Back Ike—Vote for Alger for Congress."[42]

While hitching his wagon to a popular sitting president certainly gave Alger an advantage, he was also an attractive candidate in his own right— young (thirty-six), dashing, eloquent, and hard-working. He worked Dallas's skyscrapers from the basements to the top floors in search of votes.[43] All potential voters, from office secretaries to company presidents, received his warm smile and business card. A coterie of Dallas debutantes flocked to his campaign, walking precincts and making phone calls.[44] Alger also proved adept in the use of television. He had experience with the new medium, having worked after college as a management trainee for RCA,[45] and he actively targeted the television audience. Tell your friends, a Dallas County Republican newsletter urged, to watch *Coffee Time with Bruce* at 9:30 a.m. each Monday and Friday.[46]

Alger also benefited from the miscalculations of his opponent, Wallace Savage, a conservative Democrat who opposed unions, supported right-to-work laws, and fought federal antilynching laws. Whereas Alger took a measured position on integration and ran on a simple promise to support the grandfatherly Eisenhower, Savage embraced reactionary positions on race and other issues. Throughout a grueling primary campaign against Leslie Hackler, a more liberal Democratic challenger, Savage had stood as a staunch proponent of segregation. "Much of Savage's campaign," the *St. Louis Post Dispatch* said, "was based on charges that the ADA [Americans for Democratic Action] and CIO-PAC controlled Hackler's campaign."[47] The divisive primary depleted funds intended for the general election.[48] Important liberal constituencies, who had historically voted Democratic, became alienated by Savage's extremism. In the general election, liberals either did not vote at all or voted for Alger, the seemingly uncontroversial and hard-charging newcomer who promised to "back Ike."[49]

Alger would eventually break with "modern Republicanism"— Eisenhower's selective endorsement of progressive education, labor, and social welfare reforms. Yet, until the summer of 1956, he remained a moderate on integration and the civil rights of African-Americans. To be sure, Alger was never a champion of civil rights, but he appeared to acquiesce to the inevitability of desegregation. With Savage attacking the NAACP and integration, Alger won Dallas's black precincts in 1954.[50] Following the announcement of *Brown v. Board of Education* in May 1954, he observed that his hands were now tied on the matter of integration: "The Supreme Court, the final word in interpreting our Constitution and law, has said that segregation in public schools must be abolished. There is no higher court to go."[51] "It would be foolhardy of any of us to think we can turn the clock back and deny rights to any of our citizens because of race," he remarked in 1955.[52] As late as August 22, 1956—eight days before the confrontation in Mansfield—Alger stated on the question of integration, "I believe in gradualism."[53]

Alger was the only Southern Republican congressman who refused to sign the "Declaration of Constitutional Principles," otherwise known as the Southern Manifesto, which was written in early 1956. Inspired by the editor of the *Richmond New Leader*, James J. Kilpatrick, who called *Brown v. Board of Education* a "rape of the Constitution" and argued that states had a "basic right" to interpose themselves "against federal encroachments," the Southern Manifesto declared *Brown v. Board of Education* an "unwarranted exercise" of "naked judicial power" and announced its support for resisting "forced integration" by "any lawful means."[54] The manifesto was signed by nineteen of the South's twenty-two senators and eighty-two of its representatives, but Bruce Alger assailed it as "a statement of open defiance . . . which in itself accomplishes nothing," "a denouncement of the Supreme Court of the United States which is a cornerstone of our American government." "We've made great headway in solving this national problem over recent years," he said. "Our spiritual leaders, not lawmakers can lead the way. Nothing will be solved, and only damaging distraction will result, if we resort to defiance."[55]

During the 1956 congressional campaign, race took center stage. Alger's opponent, Henry Wade, was a conservative Democrat and the popular district attorney of Dallas County. In early September 1956, just days after the mob action that prevented the enrollment of three black students at Mansfield High School, Wade challenged the claim of Alger and the Republican Party to be running on a "platform of peace": "We don't have peace in . . . Mansfield, Texas."[56] "Republicans are running on a platform of peace," Wade retorted. "They forget they were born of the most devastating war in our history—the Civil War." Citing a remark attributed to Alger, Wade engaged him in a memorable war of words: "[Alger] said anyone who thought the Supreme Court segregation ruling was unconstitutional was 'whistling Dixie.'" "Dixie," Wade said, "is a grand old tune—a tune both my grandfathers marched to in war. And you'll find Henry Wade 'whistling Dixie' whenever the Supreme Court or anyone else in Washington tries to take away states' rights or local self-government."[57] Wade's unabashedly racist campaign was rife with polarizing statements and incendiary charges, like his statement that the Republicans were distributing gifts and "all sorts of promises" to "Negroes," from tax cuts to cabinet positions, to gain their votes.[58] Wade also assailed Alger's endorsement of Vice President Richard Nixon, the recipient of an honorary membership in the NAACP, claiming Alger "was running on the coattails of a member of the NAACP."[59] As a result of this barrage of attacks, Alger found himself in an increasingly precarious position.

Alger was under considerable pressure from colleagues and constituents to jettison his moderate stance on race. John Tower, a professor of political science and Republican activist in nearby Wichita Falls, had argued the merits of segregationist rhetoric as early as 1952. "We have got to remove the shadow of Thaddeus Stevens and Charles Sumner from the Republican Party," he said. "We have got to convince Texas people that the Democratic Party no longer serves their interests."[60] Throughout Alger's tenure in office, Frank C. Slay, a self-proclaimed "fellow Republican and Realtor," exhorted Alger to "fight for States' Rights" and "do all you can to preserve segregation." "I know that you do not want a mongrelized race of people in this country," Slay wrote Alger. "Throughout the history of the world, the Negro race has had to be assimilated, segregated or eliminated, and surely segregation is the best of the three."[61] Dallasite Homer Massey observed that "favoring civil rights will spell defeat in November." Tellingly, Massey anticipated Richard Nixon's Southern Strategy twelve years in advance when he argued, "If the Republican Party will keep off of civil rights and stay off and support states' rights, they will be assured of the support not only of the South but other parts of the country as well."[62]

Conversion

In the face of Wade's unceasing attacks, pressure from within his party, and growing segregationist sentiments among his constituents (whether religiously based or influenced by arguments for interposition), Alger began to buckle, his support of "gradualism" morphing into a harder line against segregation. Responding to Wade's lyrical musings about Dixie during a debate, Alger assured his audience that "responsible Negro leaders" had told him that blacks never wanted integration in the first place but only "equality of education."[63]

After Mansfield, Alger concluded that even in an urban setting as sophisticated and cosmopolitan as Dallas, racial moderation was an untenable position for a Republican seeking reelection in Texas, a state dominated by conservative Democrats. It became clear to him that the citizens of Dallas wanted to keep traditional racial practices in place, and he modified his approach to race-related issues in order to succeed within his political climate. The success of his approach set a precedent for Republicans in the South. He avoided the incendiary remarks associated with zealots and extremists (e.g., the venomous attacks against "mongrelization" by governors George Wallace of Alabama and Theodore Bilbo of Mississippi). Appeals to the crasser arguments of the "massive resistance" set would not mesh well with the demographics and sophistication of many of the Dallas conservatives, so Alger adopted a more subtle approach, suggesting an understated resistance to change, racial equality, and a strong federal government.

Alger's conversion from racial moderate to artful champion of Jim Crow was dramatic. To counter Wade's attacks, he employed a dual strategy, both condemning appeals to race and employing segregationist rhetoric himself. For example, Alger berated Wade for "making a political football of segregation" to attract white voters: "[Wade] comes out for white supremacy seeking by arousing prejudice and hate to gain votes." Yet arousing prejudice appears to be precisely the aim of other statements by Alger, such as his call for the "radical NAACP" to be "curtailed and dissolved." On school segregation, Alger remarked, "I do not believe the Negroes want to go to white schools," adding, "Under no circumstances should any child be compelled to be taught by a teacher of the opposite race." While avoiding the overtly racist discourse of a George Wallace, Alger nevertheless made it clear to white voters that he was antagonistic toward civil rights and black people, thus reversing the historical basis of the Republican Party. Appealing to attitudes prevalent among many white voters, Alger suggested that integrating black children into white schools was akin to mingling "the diseased with healthy," "morons with normals," "criminals with virtuous," and "filthy with clean children." The "converted" Alger now had this to say about segregation: "Who can ever repeal the law of nature that birds of a feather flock together?"[64]

With this maneuver, Alger rewrote not only his own positions on segregation but those of his party. Responding to Wade's assertion that the Eisenhower administration was responsible for "what's going on in Mansfield," Alger countered that the Republican Party deserved credit for the "separate but equal" doctrine of *Plessy v. Ferguson*.[65] (He signed off on this doctrine himself when he condemned the *Brown* ruling's undoing of formulations spelled out in *Plessy*: "I am for separate but equal facilities and against forced integration. . . . Legislation is powerless to eradicate racial instincts, or to abolish distinctions based upon physical differences.") When the *Plessy* ruling came down in 1896, Alger boasted, "the Supreme Court was composed of six Republicans and only three Democrats." This landmark "Republican" opinion "stood unchallenged for 58 years, until in 1954, another court composed of seven Democrats and only two Republicans, decided the same question just the opposite." "I see no reason," Alger concluded, "to change my convictions merely because a Democratic Supreme Court rejected the correct doctrine announced by a Republican Supreme Court 60 years ago."[66]

Alger also concealed his appeals to racism behind rhetoric denouncing the encroaching power of the federal government. To be sure, he also opposed the expansion of the federal government for reasons other than race. Alger's frequent attacks on the expansion of Social Security benefits and such legislation as the Federal-Aid Highway Act of 1956 suggest he was a sincere advocate of small government even before he changed his mind on integration. Yet the controversy that arose in Dallas over urban redevelopment demonstrates how Alger cloaked his calculated appeal to bigotry beneath objections to eminent domain, loss of private property rights, and federal encroachment; while warning Dallas citizens that accepting urban renewal funds meant federal controls and much red tape, race was never far from his mind. "Federal regulation," he observed, "follows use of federal funds, which means accepting forced integration in public housing, and wage rates on urban renewal land clearance set by the Secretary of Labor, not by the local people and local economy."[67]

Alger's constituency appeared to appreciate his change of course. "God bless you," wrote Albert Dixon, "for the clean White Christian work you are doing."[68] In elections after 1956, Alger continued to stave off competition from conservative Democrats who favored Jim Crow by adopting even more blatantly prosegregationist positions. By the end of the decade, he was known as a pro–states' rights Republican who celebrated the Confederacy. "The birthday of Robert E. Lee," the *Dallas Morning News* observed in 1960, "would have gone unnoticed in Congress this week except for Dallas Congressman Bruce Alger, lone Republican member from Texas."[69] "It was fitting, though ironical, that a Republican—Bruce Alger of Dallas—was the only congressman to get on his feet and salute Gen. Robert E. Lee on his birthday. Fitting, because Lee fought for the rights of the states. By resisting big government in Washington, so is Alger. Where were the Democrats—so called party of the South? Courting the support of Eleanor Roosevelt and the NAACP?"[70]

During the late 1950s, one of the forces keeping up pressure on Bruce Alger to maintain his commitment to segregation, the Public Affairs Luncheon Club, was increasingly throwing its support behind the Republican Party. By the end of the decade club president Sue Fitch had gone from being a conservative Democrat who backed Dwight Eisenhower to a Republican activist. By 1962, she managed the downtown campaign headquarters for Bruce Alger and Republican gubernatorial candidate Jack Cox.

At the same time, the club was growing more outspoken in its segregationist views. Throughout Fitch's tenure, it clashed with the NAACP. In 1957, Fitch urged Texas attorney general Will Wilson to rescind the NAACP's right to operate in Texas. When US district judge William H. Atwell reluctantly ordered that Dallas integrate its schools in 1958, Fitch blasted the decree as submission "to a federal judicial oligarchy composed of nine men who are determined to force their sociological ideas upon an unwilling people."[71]

When the presidency of the Public Affairs Luncheon Club passed to Mrs. Ross Carlton in 1957, the club remained a promoter of segregationists. A Dallas native and graduate of the University of Texas, Carlton was an ardent Alger supporter by 1958, the year she appeared on the cover of the *Dallas Morning News*, ostentatiously polishing her family's collection of guns for deer hunting.[72] When not bagging deer, Carlton was netting such segregationist speakers as James J. Kilpatrick, who inaugurated the club's 1957–1958 lecture season with a scathing address against integration. The *Dallas Morning News* showered Kilpatrick with praise, calling his efforts a "rear-guard action against the radical armies." Integration, the *News* stated, was a "demand that should never have arisen," and Kilpatrick spoke "forcefully" for "the fundamental constitutionalist."[73] The avowed Texas interpositionist Sidney Latham also addressed the women's club at the Baker Hotel and declared that "nobody wanted integration except nine Negro students in Little Rock and nine Supreme Court justices in Washington."

In 1959, Carlton organized speeches by segregationist Arkansas congressman Dale Alford as well as Senator Herman Talmadge, author of *You and Segregation* and erstwhile Georgia governor, whom the *New York Times* called the "South's foremost spokesman of white supremacy."[74] That Bruce Alger had come to be deeply embedded in a world of white supremacists was confirmed when he introduced the incorrigible interpositionist John Bell Williams to the luncheon club in 1958. Williams had declared in 1956 on the floor of the US House of Representatives that "mentally, the Negro is inferior to the white" and that blacks' "arrest and even deterioration in mental development is no doubt very largely due to the fact that after puberty sexual matters take first place in the Negroes' life and thoughts."[75] For his part, Williams praised Alger as "one of the most courageous men I've ever known—a man of integrity, scrupulously honest and utterly fearless."[76]

In the years after his reversal on race, Alger established himself as a leader of the ultraconservatives on other issues as well. In 1958, federal funding of the school milk program passed in the House of Representatives by a vote of 348 to 1. Alger was the only congressman in Washington to vote against "socialized milk," as Lynn Landrum, the *Dallas Morning News* columnist, called it.[77] Ultraconservative Republican H. L. Hunt praised Alger as "one of the five or six great men among the vanishing good men in Washington."[78]

Interposition ultimately proved untenable in Dallas. In the end, more moderate civic leaders, fearing the economic consequences and social strife that had engulfed Little Rock and New Orleans, defeated the nullifiers. The haunting prospect of closed public schools and violence affecting bottom lines made moderation more attractive than massive resistance. In the 1960s, Dallas civic leaders concluded that embracing token desegregation was the best course for the city.[79]

Alger's strategic conversion on race represents a seminal moment in the evolution of the Republican Party in the once solidly Democratic South. Carey Daniel, W. A. Criswell, and other Dallas ministers had popularized the argument that the Bible sanctioned segregation. This position, never unanimously embraced among Southern ministers, would eventually be vanquished by more centrist religious leaders.[80] But its hold on Bruce Alger's constituency, embodied in the streets in the summer of 1956 during the attempted desegregation of Mansfield High School, affected the political calculations of the Dallas congressman, who in 1956 adopted the earliest incarnation of the Republican Southern Strategy. Alger responded to the new climate and managed to retain his congressional seat in part by changing his positions to suit an increasingly reactionary constituency. While Bible-based enthusiasm for segregation was probably the biggest source of pressure, so too were furor over Eisenhower's use of federal troops in Little Rock, Arkansas, and the persistent anti-integration rhetoric of the Public Affairs Luncheon Club and its speakers. Foreshadowing the tactics of John Tower, Barry Goldwater, Richard Nixon, and other Republicans, Bruce Alger employed an understated advocacy of white superiority that eschewed the angry rhetoric of George Wallace but still appealed to the racial prejudices of the urbane middle- and upper-class whites living in Dallas and its suburbs.[81]

5 A Man on Horseback

Judas Johnson

Surrounded by some three hundred supporters, Texas congressman Bruce Alger vigorously pumped up and down a placard declaring "LBJ SOLD OUT TO YANKEE SOCIALISTS." Other signs read "LBJ, TRAITOR," "JUDAS JOHNSON," and "LET'S GROUND LADY BIRD." It was November 4, 1960—four days before the presidential election—and Alger and the crowd, primarily Dallas Republican women, stood outside the Adolphus Hotel in downtown Dallas and inside its lobby waiting for the arrival of Lyndon B. Johnson—US senator from Texas and running mate of the Democratic presidential nominee, John F. Kennedy—and his wife, Lady Bird. Alger and the women certainly had no love for Kennedy, whose recently adopted party platform included the most liberal civil rights plank in the country's history. Moreover, as Dallasite Stanley Marcus (of Neiman Marcus) quipped, "worse than being a papist," Kennedy "was suspected of being against the oil depletion allowance, which allowed oilmen to reduce their taxable income by 27.5% of their gross profit."[1] Like many Southerners, Alger and the women—many wearing white blouses, red coif hats, navy blue sailor collars, and red satin scarves from a campaign event earlier that day—were angry that Johnson had agreed to join the Democratic ticket.[2] They vowed to defeat, as one Austin paper editorialized, "the Yankee from Boston and the turncoat from Austin."[3]

Partisan bias prevents a complete and objective reconstruction of what actually occurred. The Johnsons reported being jostled by Alger and the Republicans and showered with curses, shouts, and spit.[4] Alger and others denied these or any other forms of disrespect. Republican Peter O'Donnell observed no jostling or spitting from his vantage on the street, and Rita Bass, who was inside the lobby, claimed the "episode was so overblown. . . . There was no spitting at Lady Bird or that kind of thing." Republican activist Joy Bell emphasized that the crowd inside the lobby could not have jostled the Johnsons because "everyone was so far away from him." "We were back behind the big brass rails . . . and the center had a ton of room." Bell's account of Lady Bird Johnson's demeanor during the episode differs strikingly from that in most histories. Whereas the traditional narrative portrays her as shrinking behind her husband, interviews with Republicans who were present indicate a poised, resolute, and competitive woman. According to Bell, Lady Bird verbally challenged her on two separate occasions. First, Johnson said that Bell was on "the wrong side." Then, she offered a wager that the Kennedy-Johnson ticket would win, to which Bell replied, "I don't bet."[5]

Whatever actually happened at the Adolphus Hotel that night, the encounter proved a boon for the Democratic ticket and a disaster for both the Dallas Republican Party and the Nixon-Lodge ticket. Millions of Americans read in their papers stories of unrest and saw on their television screens pictures of the senator and his wife surrounded by a crowd of scowling faces.[6] Lyndon Johnson handled the situation masterfully and to his political advantage, presenting himself as a martyr and using the occasion to reinvent himself: shedding the image of a drawling, regional politician beholden to the depletion allowance and states' rights, he became a national figure acceptable to a wider constituency. Upon seeing the protesters and the television cameras, Johnson purposely slowed down, taking thirty minutes to walk from the entrance of the hotel to the elevator. He told the Dallas police to stand aside and rejected requests from the commander of the Texas National Guard to remove the protestors from the Johnsons' path. As Bill Moyers, a Johnson aide, observed, "He knew it got votes for him. . . . The moment it happened, he knew."[7]

The event was a fiasco for the city of Dallas and the local Republican Party. Despite Alger's assertion that the demonstration was "good-natured and courteous," the front-page photo of the congressman holding his anti-Johnson sign and the stern visages of people in the crowd exacerbated and solidified the city's image as inhospitable and Alger's party as absolutist and reactionary.[8] Criticism of Alger and the Republican Party grew locally as well.[9] The usually friendly *Dallas Morning News* admitted that "damage was done." Many of Alger's supporters "deemed the incident unwise," observed the *News*. Shortly thereafter, one Dallasite observed, "Bruce Alger is still haggling with the lamplighter at Main and Akard. Claiming a monopoly on Americanism is one thing, but representing a bustling metropolitan area like Dallas in the jet age is a different and serious matter." Alger privately confessed to friends that holding the sign was ill advised and his actions had hurt the party.[10] The Kennedy-Johnson ticket won in Texas by 46,233 votes, capturing the presidency for John F. Kennedy. In the final analysis, the Adolphus incident presented a crisis for Dallas Republicans. The city began to be seen as a center of burgeoning extremism and its Republican Party as the force behind it. Outspoken Bruce Alger, the only US congressman to reject federal milk money for schoolchildren, suddenly realized the need to moderate the public perception of his zealotry and reactionary worldview.

The Candy Man Can

Just as the furor over the Adolphus affair was finally abating, a spate of newspaper articles appeared examining the actions of the John Birch Society as emblematic of a seemingly violent extremism. The John Birch Society was the brainchild of Robert Welch. Born in North Carolina at the turn of the century, Welch had been home-schooled by his fundamentalist Baptist mother. While he had strayed from some aspects of his childhood faith, Welch remained dogmatic in addressing secular matters throughout his entire life. A prodigy, he matriculated at the University of North Carolina at the age of twelve, graduating in 1916. Successful in business as a candy manufacturer, he was responsible for creating such childhood favorites as Sugar Daddies and Junior Mints. A highly skilled organizer, in the mid-1950s Welch amassed a small army of friends, colleagues, and employees to distribute his two widely read political tracts, *May God Forgive Us* and *John Birch* (an account of a Baptist missionary's life and murder by Chinese Communists). By the late 1950s, Welch had a reputation as a thoughtful figure among conservative intellectuals. Contemporaries hailed his organizational acumen and knack for sharp writing. At the time, few considered him a peddler of extremism. Attesting to Welch's reputation as a man of ideas, William F. Buckley declared that he had produced "two of the finest pamphlets this country has read in a decade."[11]

In December 1958, the candy man secretly assembled a cadre of conservative businessmen in an Indianapolis home and introduced his solution to the disease of Communism, which he said was rotting the body politic. The John Birch Society was born and set out to convince others of the "gigantic conspiracy to enslave mankind," a plot "controlled by determined, cunning, and utterly ruthless gangsters, willing to use any means to achieve its end."[12] The group painted with broad strokes when determining what constituted Communism. The prototypical ultraconservative, Welch warned against instruments of the Communist cabal that held America in its death grip; these included Social Security checks, civil rights laws, mental health laws, and even fluoride in the water supply.

Welch tolerated no dissension within the ranks; while his organization had a governing council, its apparent purpose was to elect a leader should Welch be assassinated. In the spring of 1961, a series of national magazine and newspaper articles, punctuated by a feature in *Time* magazine, explored the John Birch Society and concluded that it could evolve into something dangerous. The group, *Time* opined, was "one goose-step away from the formation of goon squads."[13] Public sentiment affirming its placement in the extremist camp was shaped in part by rumors that Welch had penned and distributed a manuscript labeling Dwight D. Eisenhower as a covert agent of the Communist conspiracy. Indeed, Welch had drafted a document titled "The Politician," which few had actually read, alleging that Eisenhower was appointing Communists to high-level positions in the US government: "Eisenhower and his Communist bosses and their pro-Communist appointees are gradually taking over our whole government, right under the noses of the American people," he wrote.[14] According to Welch, the executive branch under Eisenhower was "an active agency for the promotion of Communist aims," and the Supreme Court was "almost completely under Communist influence."[15] Welch called CIA director Allen W. Dulles "the most protected and untouchable supporter of Communism, next to Eisenhower himself." And President Truman's secretary of state, George C. Marshall, was "a conscious, deliberate agent of the Soviet conspiracy."[16]

Controversy over the organization stemmed in part from Welch's propensity to make apocalyptic statements. In the group's *Blue Book*, which, unlike "The Politician," was widely distributed, Welch predicted that his countrymen had "only a few more years before the country in which you live will become four separate provinces in a world-wide Communist domination ruled by police-state methods from the Kremlin."[17] Welch also attracted controversy for employing what otherwise like-minded people might consider "Communist methods" to defeat the conspiracy, instructing members to infiltrate the ranks of the PTA and establish front groups. Welch unabashedly admitted that he was in charge of the John Birch Society and would tolerate no insubordination. Convinced that most patriotic organizations were inefficient, he set out to establish a monolithic organization "under completely authoritative control at all levels."[18] Welch envisioned an organization in which women could be members and lead chapter meetings, but leadership roles were to be reserved for "the ablest men" of the corporate and professional worlds. Gender, wealth, and occupational status were all factors in the Birch Society's hierarchical structure.[19]

Birchism Was Their Business

Dallas was a national epicenter for the John Birch Society in early 1961. While not a member herself, Rita Bass noted that she "had a lot of friends who are members of the John Birch Society."[20] In April, Jim Lehrer, a rising young reporter for the *Dallas Morning News*, observed that approximately seven hundred members of the group lived in Dallas, making it "one of the most flourishing, enthusiastic John Birch movements in the country." Tom Wunderlick, an unpaid voluntary coordinator in the North Dallas–Park Cities section of town, estimated that Dallas had thirty-five Birch chapters. The city even had one of its own working in the Birch Society's Belmont, Massachusetts, headquarters. Tom Hill, a correspondence coordinator, was a former Dallas businessman. Hill maintained close contact with Buck McMann of Odessa, who served as the society's regional coordinator for Texas. Every two months, McMann made the 350-mile trek from Odessa to meet with Smith, Wunderlick, and Joseph P. Grinnan, another voluntary coordinator from North Dallas.[21]

One of Rita Bass's friends in the John Birch Society was Mary Ann Collins, whose story illustrates how the group emerged as a major force in Dallas and presented the Texas Republican Party with a significant dilemma. Collins was both a member of the Birch Society and a loyal Republican activist. A Catholic, she had grown up in a family that backed liberal to moderate national Republicans. The 1940 presidential campaign was her "real beginning," when Collins worked to elect Wendell Wilkie, the Republican nominee and a member of the party's liberal wing. Collins made homemade campaign signs, she recalled, "writing 'Win with Wilkie' and dropping them in her neighbors' doorways."[22] In the fall of 1952, she was teaching kindergarten during the day and volunteering her nights at the downtown Dallas headquarters to elect Dwight Eisenhower, a Republican whose ideological leanings were to the left of most Dallas moderate Republicans.[23]

The complex route Collins took to the ultraconservative Republican camp began with her joining the John Birch Society in the late 1950s. Robert Morris, president of the University of Dallas, attested to both the society's growing impact on Collins and her growing ultraconservatism. Collins and other "friends of the University" were "active in the JBS," he observed. "The idea of someone [Robert Welch] speaking directly . . . had an appeal for them and . . . they became vocal. . . . Mary Ann Collins was very vocal." Raising eight children in a household with a patriarch prone to alcoholism, Collins found in the John Birch Society a needed release. In 1960, while serving as a loyal acolyte of the GOP, she was also writing Welch and inquiring whether the society approved of three individuals as bona-fide anti-Communists.[24] The affable Collins found fulfillment in the social involvement the society provided and became fully immersed in its worldview. As a member, she came to view the Constitution not as an enabling document but a restrictive one. Championing "individualism" and "independence," she assailed "federal control of everything," attacked the Supreme Court, and called for a return to the antilabor, probusiness, and segregationist courts of the 1920s. She argued that "freedom of the individual" applied only to property owners.[25] Morris, alarmed by her outspokenness and increasingly reactionary demeanor, feared that she might attract negative publicity to the fledgling university and requested that Collins temper her rhetoric.[26]

Another force also drove Collins toward the ultraconservative wing of her party: the 1960 Democratic Party platform. Even though the Democratic nominee for the presidency was a coreligionist, his party's platform seemed an affront to Collins's worldview and the embodiment of everything she and the Birch Society opposed. It came out strongly in support of civil rights and, in her view, "federal aid to, and consequently federal control of, everything." "How," she wondered, "can any conservative, States' rights Texan swallow this?"[27]

After Dallas County Republican chairman Walter Fleming provided her with a copy of Barry Goldwater's *Conscience of a Conservative*, Collins became an avid supporter of the Arizona senator, whose beliefs reflected many of the central tenets of the John Birch Society. At the 1960 Republican National Convention in Chicago, the twenty-eight year-old Collins wholeheartedly defended her candidate, who ultimately lost the party's nomination to Richard Nixon. Goldwater placard in hand, Collins tried to join an impromptu demonstration in support of Goldwater's nomination, but, according to Collins, "the Sergeant at Arms wasn't going to let me back out on the floor." "That was in the days of high heels," she recalled. "I kicked that guy and I was back on the floor. That was the only way."[28]

Collins was a member of one of Dallas County's most affluent Birch Society chapters. Predominantly middle class, the Dallas chapters reflected the demographics described in nationwide sociological studies of the John Birch Society's membership.[29] Approximately 80 percent of the society's members lived in North Dallas or the Park Cities of University Park and Highland Park, more affluent sections of Dallas County. But members in Oak Cliff, a less affluent section of Dallas, refused to be outdone by any cross-town rival. "We're just beginning over here," Donald W. Smith, a voluntary coordinator in Oak Cliff said, "but we're gaining fast and I hope someday to catch them."[30]

Twenty-four people attended the Tuesday, April 11, 1961, meeting of Chapter 458 in Oak Cliff, including fifteen prospective members and nine regular members: an engineer, an electric company employee, a retail store employee, and six housewives. Birch Society meetings usually took place once a month, began with the pledge of allegiance, and included discussion, individual presentations, film viewings, and progress reports on the society's primary objectives. Meetings were usually limited to thirty individuals. Chapters whose meetings were regularly attended by more than thirty members were directed to split and form a new chapter.[31] The agenda for meetings rarely deviated from the outline included in the monthly bulletin. On the evening in question, the chapter first addressed the state of its campaign to impeach Supreme Court chief justice Earl Warren. The chapter leader inveighed against Warren, who was "a symbol of our contempt for the court and the pro-Communist decisions it has handed down." Meetings provided opportunities for members to trade conservative books and brief one another on the progress of letter-writing campaigns. At the previous month's meeting, the chapter leader had urged rank-and-file members to write letters to public officials encouraging them to work toward Warren's impeachment. At the end of the April 11 meeting, the chapter leader asked a fellow member, "Claude, you wrote Alger and Johnson, I believe, and received answers . . . would you read them?" Claude agreed to read the letter from Alger, in which the congressman balked at the request. "Sponsoring a futile gesture," Alger wrote, "would hurt the conservative cause."[32]

Alger's Switch in Time

Alger's response marked his drift away from ultraconservatism. If the Birch Society had nudged some Dallas Republicans, like Mary Ann Collins, rightward, it had driven Bruce Alger back into the orbit of the more respectable moderate Republicans. The Adolphus incident and resulting media storm had associated Alger with ultraconservatism at a time when America was becoming preoccupied with the reactionaries of the John Birch Society, and the organization now presented him with a dilemma. On one hand, it had many loyal supporters, and Alger risked alienating his most ardent backers if he distanced himself from the society. On the other hand, the viability of the Dallas Republican Party was in question; withdrawal from the controversial organization allowed Alger to escape from the embarrassment caused by the Adolphus incident.[33]

Interest in the John Birch Society among his constituents compelled Alger to comment on it.[34] Margaret Charlton, who directed Alger's downtown headquarters in 1960, asked for his thoughts about the society, noting that "many of your friends—many of my friends—are members."[35] Characterizing herself as "concerned about Communism" but also cognizant that a "misguided group is worse than none at all," she was among those who urged Alger to take a stand.

In March 1961—three months after the Adolphus incident—Alger appeared on *Today*, the morning television show airing on NBC, and adopted a harder line toward the John Birch Society. Barry Goldwater had lauded the society's members and eschewed commenting on Robert Welch or the goals of the society, but Alger went on the attack: "The society is led by one person and I do not like organizations that are controlled by one person." He lambasted not only its hierarchical structure, but also its central goal of impeaching Earl Warren, an effort Alger characterized as "a waste of time."[36]

By the middle of April 1961, Alger was distancing himself even further from the Birch Society and its leader. Criticizing its methods, he wrote, "We can not defeat Communism by adopting Communist tactics or giving up the rights of individuals to think for themselves." He vowed to defend the right "to think for ourselves and to determine our own destinies" in the face of "Communists, Federal Bureaucrats, and the founder of the John Birch Society."[37] But he also mitigated his attack, stating that his criticism was directed at the methods of the society and "in no way disparages the patriotism nor the motives of those connected with the organization."[38]

Many of Alger's erstwhile supporters blasted his derogatory appraisal of Welch. David Murphy, a constituent, opined, "If the prominent conservatives of this country disown and condemn the John Birch Society, they will be doing the anti-Communist movement great harm."[39] A Republican supporter, Katie Farrar, wrote to Alger, "[Your] 'I approve of their aims but not their methods' remark reminds me of the critics of the late Senator Joseph McCarthy." "Though you must not realize it, . . . [your comment] follows the Communist line to a tee."[40] Another Republican and Birch Society member, Richard Whittle (who had inaccurately claimed that "Welch did not call Eisenhower a Communist"), was apoplectic.[41] Taking the position that Alger had "turned on his staunchest allies,"[42] "Goldwater's 'forgotten people,'" Whittle said of the society's members, "They are intelligent, idealistic members of the middle-class who have no pressure groups to fight for them."[43] Robert J. George repudiated Alger's claim that the society was rigidly hierarchical. "I am for impeaching Earl Warren and

I have not been ordered by Mr. Welch to write this," he proclaimed. He had this advice for Alger: "Open your eyes before opening your mouth."[44]

Alger made other moves aimed at repositioning himself as a more moderate Republican. He distanced himself from the Dallas-based National Indignation Convention (NIC), which opposed sending foreign aid to Communist countries like Poland and Yugoslavia. When NIC's Frank McGehee, a Dallas native, petitioned Alger to address the group's convention, the congressman declined, explaining that since NIC endorsed candidates, his presence might prove awkward. Alger instead spoke to the convention by telephone, and drew the ire of McGehee by refraining from fully endorsing the NIC's mission.[45] Alger's criticism of both the National Indignation Convention and the John Birch Society drew clear lines of demarcation between his positions and those of the ultraconservatives.

Pro-Blue

If Robert Welch was the best-known figure in the John Birch Society, General Edwin Walker was its most controversial. Like Welch, the Dallas-based Walker challenged, molded, and solidified the identity of Dallas conservatives. Two episodes in particular—Walker's resignation from the Army in 1961 and his psychiatric incarceration in 1962—made him a lightning rod for the Dallas conservative movement. To appreciate the significance of these incidents, we must look at them in the context of the Kennedy administration's concern with activism on the Right.

The first Walker controversy erupted on the heels of the president's foreign policy debacle at the Bay of Pigs, where, contrary to the predictions of military advisors, a ragged band of twelve hundred anti-Castro guerillas failed to foment a general uprising and free the island nation of Cuba. The fiasco did little to quash right-wing criticism of a president who had won election by a wafer-thin margin.[46] During his first months in office, President Kennedy also had to deal with the consequences of a 1956 Army report that concluded some American soldiers captured by North Korea had been easily "brainwashed" because they lacked a sufficient understanding of Communism and the values of their own country.[47] The report resulted in a 1958 National Security Council directive requiring military officers to educate their troops about the nature of the

Communist enemy.[48] Kennedy spent many evenings reading Pentagon reports describing right-wing seminars full of retired and active military personnel occurring "in almost every area of the country." Military bases were often the venues for these seminars, headlined by speakers who viewed the international Communist threat as ancillary to the internal enemy and lambasted the president's domestic agenda, in Senator J. William Fulbright's words, "as steps towards Communism."[49] Along with his aides, including Robert Kennedy, Arthur Schlesinger Jr., and Myer Feldman, the president worried that political activism on the Right and the military's deepening involvement in political affairs were making it more difficult to ease tensions with the Soviet Union.[50] To counter these developments, his administration went to battle with some of the nation's most archconservative military brass, and General Edwin Walker became one of its primary targets.[51]

In the early spring of 1961, Walker had come to symbolize growing military involvement in political activities, and Kennedy sought to make an example of him. Having assumed command of the ten thousand soldiers of the 24th Division in Augsburg, Germany, in 1959, Walker zealously carried out the 1958 National Security Council order by establishing a "Pro-Blue" program: his troops were advised to vote exclusively for conservative candidates and prescribed a reading program that included Robert Welch's *Life of John Birch* and literature from the militant Christian anti-Communists Edgar Bundy, Billy James Hargis, and George Benson.[52] In a story that the *New York Times* picked up, *Overseas Weekly* (a rather salacious magazine for troops overseas that often appeared alongside *Stars and Stripes*) accused Walker of attempting to recruit soldiers for the John Birch Society and of characterizing former president Harry Truman, former secretary of state Dean Acheson, and former first lady Eleanor Roosevelt as "definitely pink."[53] On April 17, Walker was relieved of command pending an investigation requested by President Kennedy.[54]

With Kennedy's approval, the Army on June 12 "admonished" Walker for "injudicious actions" and casting aspersions on the character of public figures.[55] The White House also ended Walker's Pro-Blue program.[56] Walker thus suddenly became a martyr at a time when Dallas conservatives were looking for a "man on horseback." (As a guest at the

White House, Ted Dealey, the publisher of the *Dallas Morning News*, had publicly embarrassed the president by announcing to him in a room full of editors, "We need a man on horseback to lead this nation, and many people in Texas and the Southwest think that you are riding Caroline's tricycle."[57]) After Walker received his admonishment, protests poured into the White House comparing Kennedy's "muzzling" of Walker and Truman's firing of UN supreme commander Douglas MacArthur, who had urged an invasion of mainland China in 1951.[58] For a brief moment, many thought Walker was another MacArthur, a warrior around whom the Right could rally.

For many on the Right, the "muzzling" of Walker demonstrated either the federal government's weak commitment to fighting Communism or its perfidy.[59] The episode reinforced the Right's view that responses to foreign and domestic Communism, under Kennedy's and prior administrations, were either bankrupt or traitorous. Kennedy's sin was especially egregious: passivity could explain the loss of China and the stalemate in Korea, but the persecution of a dedicated patriot who was rallying his division against Communism was inexcusable.[60] Dashingly handsome in his Army uniform, with medals emblazoned across his broad chest, Walker certainly resembled MacArthur. Many on the Right traded stories of Walker's heroics: leading commandos on nighttime raids against the Germans in Italy during World War II, taking part in some of the bloodiest fighting, including the battle of Heartbreak Ridge, in Korea. He had volunteered for a paratrooper exam despite having never jumped out of an airplane, asking just before exiting the aircraft, "How do you put this thing on?" Meeting the test officer on the ground, he stoically declared, "Check."[61]

Walker Un-Muzzled

After Walker resigned from the Army in the fall of 1961, he felt free to speak his mind as a civilian. But his public appearances, starting with his rambling resignation statement, made it increasingly clear to some commentators that he possessed none of MacArthur's eloquence or flair for the dramatic and that he would be an embarrassment to their movement. Walker had said he was resigning from the Army to "find other means of serving my country in the time of her great need in order to pursue the dedication of a lifetime. To do this, I must be free from the power of little men who, in the name of my country, punish loyal service to it."[62] Hearing that, the perspicacious William F. Buckley kindly cautioned that "Walker is not necessarily the best formulator." The phrase "little men," for example, was "not-altogether-happy." To be sure, Buckley did not abandon Walker altogether. The general was still "hero stuff or nothing" and conservatives should not be "dropping flowers on his grave." But Buckley tried to dampen the enthusiasm of those who believed Walker was the Moses who would lead conservatives out of exile.[63]

After his resignation, Walker moved to Dallas and began to expound his views. While his anti-Communist credentials were well known, few knew his stances on other issues. Establishing his headquarters on Turtle Creek Boulevard, Walker traded in his military fatigues for a black suit and white Stetson. His fulminations about states' rights fleshed out his racially charged vision. Ironically, Walker had commanded the federal troops sent by President Eisenhower to Little Rock, Arkansas, in 1957. Publicly taciturn at the time, Walker divulged in late 1961 that he protested through "appropriate military channels" the president's decision to enforce the implementation of *Brown v. Board of Education*. In Jackson, Mississippi, on December 29, 1961, Walker praised the Mississippi Plan of 1875, which had employed violence and threats of violence against blacks to restrict their right to vote. "The plan not only brought freedom," Walker said, "it inspired the Southern triumph of 1877. It was the model of freedom from Oppression and Reconstruction—from the tyranny within our own white race."[64]

Walker's transformation also entailed trading a soldier's rhetoric for the increasingly apocalyptic exhortations of an evangelical preacher. He identified himself as a "Christian Soldier" and declared, "I have found . . . a host of dedicated, patriotic and militant Christians."[65] "I stand firm in the Gospel of Christ," he asserted. "If He be with us—who can be against us except Satan and the Atheistic Communist Conspiracy allied with him?" On December 12, 1961, at a "Welcome Home" rally in the Dallas Municipal Auditorium, he observed, "The friends of Daniel refused to bow down at the sound of the King's music. . . . They endured and they lived through the fiery furnace in loyalty to their faith." "I would say to you," he intoned, "stand up beside Daniel and be counted."[66]

H. L. Hunt proudly displays his book, *Alpaca*, a fictional tale about a country that gives additional votes to citizens who pay higher taxes. Those who pay the highest taxes receive seven votes. Any person agreeing to refuse government benefits receives two additional votes. © Bettmann/CORBIS.

In August 1956, segregationists resisted the integration of the high school in Mansfield, Texas, a community thirty miles from Dallas. Four hundred whites tried to stop the enrollment of three black students. One effigy hanging from the school flagpole bore the sign "Stay away Niggers." "I didn't put it up there," insisted the principal, "and I'm not going to take it down." ©Bettmann/CORBIS.

Bruce Alger of Dallas, pictured here with his family and a Republican mascot, successfully ran for Congress in 1954, aligning himself with President Eisenhower. Alger ultimately reversed course, abandoning his support for Eisenhower's "modern Republicanism." In 1958, federal funding of the school milk program passed in the House of Representatives by a vote of 348 to 1, with Alger casting the sole vote against "socialized milk." Courtesy of the Dallas Morning News Archives.

Lyndon Johnson embraces Henry Wade, conservative Democrat and popular district attorney of Dallas County. Running for Bruce Alger's congressional seat in 1956, Wade raised the race issue, challenging Alger's and the Republican Party's claim that theirs was a "platform of peace." "We don't have peace in . . . Mansfield, Texas," Wade said. Three days earlier, a white mob had attempted to prevent the enrollment of three black students at Mansfield High School. Wade's remarks and other pressures accounted for Alger's abandonment of "gradualism." Courtesy of the Dallas Morning News Archives.

Just four days before the 1960 presidential election, Congressman Bruce Alger and a crowd of Dallas Republican women stood outside the Adolphus Hotel in downtown Dallas waiting for the arrival of Lyndon B. Johnson, US senator from Texas and running mate of the Democratic presidential nominee, John F. Kennedy. Johnson and his wife claimed they were shoved and spat upon by the protestors. The incident received national attention, reinforcing the popular association of Dallas with violent extremism. A fiasco for both the Nixon-Lodge ticket and the Dallas Republican Party, it likely ensured Kennedy's victory. Courtesy of the Dallas Morning News Archives.

John Tower sits with Bruce Alger. Tower, a former professor, won a special election in 1961 for the seat vacated by Lyndon Johnson to become the first Republican senator from Texas since Reconstruction. At his first meeting of the Senate's Southern Caucus, which Johnson had never attended, the caucus leader, archsegregationist Richard Russell of Georgia, reportedly turned to Tower and said, "I want to welcome Texas back into the Confederacy." Thomas D. McAvoy/LIFE Images Collection/Getty Images.

Supporters greet former general Edwin Walker at Love Field in Dallas in October 1962. Walker resigned from the Army after being "admonished" for distributing John Birch Society material to his troops, and soon after moved to Dallas. Many on the Right hoped Walker would be another Douglas MacArthur, a knight in shining armor who could rally the country. Some even dreamed of his victory over Kennedy for the presidency in 1964. Courtesy of the Dallas Morning News Archives.

Among the archconservative military brass, General Edwin Walker was one of the Kennedy administration's primary targets. When James Meredith became the first African-American to matriculate at the University of Mississippi in October 1962, Walker showed up at the college to protest, along with a crowd of two thousand. Attorney General Robert F. Kennedy sent in five hundred US marshals to restore order. Arrested for inciting a riot, Walker was sent, on Robert Kennedy's orders, for incarceration and observation at a federal mental health facility. Paul Slade/Paris Match Archive/Getty Images.

Attorney General Robert F. Kennedy congratulates US marshals for their work at the University of Mississippi. © Bettmann/CORBIS.

General Edwin Walker (center) and Robert Morris (right), Walker's lawyer and former president of the University of Dallas. Upon hearing of Walker's institutionalization by the Kennedy administration, *National Review* editor William F. Buckley Jr. called his friend Morris and referred him to Thomas S. Szasz, a prominent figure in the antipsychiatry movement on the Right. Morris in turn phoned Szasz, who agreed to help free Walker. Szasz wrote in *Psychiatric Justice*, "Edwin A. Walker was arrested, charged for crimes, and then committed against his will for pretrial psychiatric examination. Without doubt, this is the most widely publicized case ever reported in the American press of an attempt to deny an accused person the right to trial by branding him insane and hence incompetent to stand trial." © Corbis.

A woman looks on with contempt as a black child, with his mother, enters a formerly all-white elementary school in Dallas on the first day of integrated classes in September 1961. Rolls Press/Popperfoto/Getty Images.

Jack Cox strums his guitar while campaigning for Texas governor in 1962. Cox's selection as the Republican gubernatorial nominee testified to the potency of anti–civil rights conservatism in Texas. "Cox had my vote," one Dallasite explained, because he was "the only candidate who is unalterably opposed to the despicable, vicious civil rights bill." Cox came within two percentage points of beating Democrat John Connally to become the first Republican governor of Texas since Reconstruction. Shel Hershorn/LIFE Images Collection/Getty Images.

A mother protests sending foreign aid to Communist countries like Poland and Yugo-slavia at a Dallas event organized by Frank McGehee's National Indignation Convention. Shel Hershorn/Archive Photos/Getty Images.

Demonstrators protest the attendance of Ambassador Adlai Stevenson at a United Nations Day event in Dallas in October 1963. Anti-UN demonstrator Cora Fredrickson struck Stevenson with a placard. The incident reinforced the city's reputation for violent confrontations. President Kennedy was scheduled to visit Dallas in November 1963 to secure amity among warring Democratic factions in Texas and shore up his dwindling support among conservative Democrats. Stevenson urged Arthur Schlesinger to persuade Kennedy to cancel the trip. AP Images.

Policemen grab Robert Hatfield, who approached Adlai Stevenson after the ambassador made a United Nations Day speech in Dallas in October 1963. Hatfield called Stevenson a traitor and spat on him. AP Images.

Protestors await the arrival of President Kennedy at Love Field in Dallas on November 22, 1963. AP Images.

Bruce Alger, John Tower, and Barry Goldwater. In 1960 and 1961, Goldwater campaigned in Texas for Tower, whose own book, *Program for Conservatives*, though more academic, put forward many of the same themes and positions as Goldwater's more popular *The Conscience of a Conservative*. Courtesy of the Dallas Morning News Archives.

Rita Bass, John Tower, and Barry Goldwater. A quintessential moderate conservative Republican, Bass worked to establish the institutional framework of the Dallas Republican Party. In 1963, she was appointed the national canvassing director of the Goldwater campaign. When her husband, Bill Clements, won the gubernatorial election in 1978, Bass became the first Republican first lady of Texas since Reconstruction. Francis Miller/LIFE Picture Collection/Getty Images.

Peter O'Donnell, George H. W. Bush, Frank Cahoon, and John Tower. In 1962, as the newly elected Texas Republican state chairman, O'Donnell publicly encouraged Goldwater to run for president. In February 1963, O'Donnell accepted the position of chairman of the Draft Goldwater Committee and organized its headquarters on Connecticut Avenue in Washington, DC. Whereas O'Donnell was an architect of the GOP Southern Strategy, Bush was one of its artisans, declaring outside Dallas, in Grand Prarie, in an attack against the Civil Rights Act of 1964, "The new civil rights act was passed to protect 14 percent of the people. I'm also worried about the other 86 percent." Courtesy of the Dallas Morning News Archives.

Richard Nixon greets Dallasites. Nixon demonstrated in the late 1960s and 1970s that color-blind rhetoric played far better with suburbanites than overt claims of white supremacy or Barry Goldwater's tirades against the 1964 Civil Rights Act as an infringement of property rights. His electoral strategy appealed to the "forgotten Americans" suffering the consequences of rising crime rates and lacking access to affirmative action or public housing. © Bettmann/CORBIS.

California governor Ronald Reagan shakes hands with Dallas mayor J. Erik Jonnson in 1969. Dallas's electronics and aerospace industry provided a strong base of support for Dallas Republicans. J. Erik Jonnson, president of Texas Instruments from 1951 to 1958, was a prominent Republican. © Bettmann/CORBIS.

Walker's zealotry and obsession with conspiracy theories were so great that at times they crossed the line into paranoia. He questioned former president Eisenhower's loyalty and even defended Robert Welch's assertion that Eisenhower was a Communist. Rejecting as nonsense the argument that Eisenhower wanted "coexistence" with the Soviet Union, Walker accused him of initiating a policy of "conversion" that Kennedy was perpetuating in 1962. "We are converting our advantage to his (the enemy's) advantage."[67] At a press conference at the Baker Hotel, he appeared to channel Joseph McCarthy when he held up what he termed a State Department "blueprint" that supposedly placed American military personnel and weapons under the control of the United Nations. The executive branch and the Supreme Court had been "captured," he said, and the plan now was to "UN-ize" the American soldier. Another time, in a letter to President Kennedy, Walker ridiculed Kennedy for "idle talk and rocking chair action" and implored him to grant the state of Texas all control over its national guard in light of the "government's release of all state and national sovereignty under [the president's] announced program to place all armed forces and weapons under the United Nations."[68]

However conspiratorial and bizarre these views might appear, they pale in comparison to his remarks during a December address, when he described an international Communist conspiracy that, to his mind, had penetrated the highest echelons of government. In an almost pathological, paranoid fantasy, Walker accused the "left-wing" media and Chief Justice Earl Warren of conspiring with Nikita Khrushchev to aid in the election of John F. Kennedy. "The enemy has extended himself into our very midst with the capability to attack our soldiers and our cause from the rear. . . . [Journalist Drew] Pearson and Chief Justice Earl Warren were guests on the Meyer yacht sailing in the Mediterranean waters early last fall. The Meyer family is owner of *Newsweek* and of the left-wing *Washington Post*. It was from this yachting trip that Drew Pearson visited Khrushchev in Moscow, and reported that Khrushchev said he had not released the two American flyers until after the presidential inauguration in January in order to help President Kennedy."[69]

Despite his turn to the extreme right, courting of racists, and poor public speaking, some far-right Dallasites wanted Walker to run for public office. One Dallas member of the John Birch Society, Tibor Laky, suggested nominating "Gen. Walker as Candidate for Congressman-at-Large in 1962—for Senator replacing Sen. Yarborough in 1964. . . . He could win by a landslide."[70] Others had higher expectations. They dreamed of his election in 1962 as the first Republican governor of Texas since Reconstruction, followed by victory over Kennedy for the presidency in 1964.[71]

When Walker expressed interest in running for Texas governor in 1962, both Bruce Alger and John Tower concluded that it was a terrible idea. The two men met with Walker and discouraged any run for office, whether as a Democrat or a Republican.[72] Like Buckley, Alger and Tower recognized the general's shortfalls, including his extremist positions, poor speaking skills, and lack of stage presence. Alger preferred that Walker remain a silent example for the Right[73] and denounced his subsequent decision to run for governor as a Democrat. According to Alger, Walker "is going to hurt the cause." "I now no longer consider him an effective conservative."[74]

With talk of Walker's potential foray into Texas politics swirling in the rumor mill, the city found itself once again in the national spotlight. Because Walker attracted the national press, his influence was not confined to Dallas. Just as the Adolphus affair shaped public perceptions, even if inaccurate, of Dallas as a hotbed of absolutism and violence, Walker began to shape the perception in the American imagination of the Dallas conservative movement as a bizarre band of nut-jobs.

Walker's appearance before the Senate Preparedness Investigating Subcommittee in April of 1962 affirmed Alger's and Tower's judgment of his shortcomings. The former general's presentation was disorderly and unintelligible.[75] Walker said that "high-ranking US government officials" were part of a "hidden control apparatus" in the grasp of the international Communist conspiracy. Walker, the *Washington Post* observed, was "an exceedingly poor spokesman for the radical right." One reporter said, "Walker might be trouble but he won't be. By the grace of God, he is the worst speaker in the United States." As one leading Dallas Republican put it, Walker, far from being their white knight, was the "dud of the year."[76]

By the spring of 1962, Walker's supporters fell into the ultraconservative camp, with those in the more respectable moderate camp steering clear of his activities. Yet Walker did more than help define where conservatives in Dallas stood individually. For moderate conservatives navigating his controversies sharpened their hand for politics and taught them which positions to keep and which to jettison.[77] Walker's extremism led to a resurgence of moderate conservative Republicanism in Dallas. Respectable moderate conservatives responded by working to drum him out of the conservative movement. Alger, who had veered away from his ultraconservative stance since the emergence of Walker in Dallas, received a great deal of correspondence disparaging his public criticism of Walker. One Walker supporter wrote Alger that "if they [the Communists] can get *you*, and John Tower, and Goldwater, and our great Senator Strom Thurmond to discount General Walker, they have his destruction made." Showing how opinion of Walker served to distinguish between ultraconservative and moderate Republicans, the same person threatened, "If Mr. Tower and Mr. Goldwater keep on knocking him, and keep on knocking other good Americans like Robert Welch of the John Birch Society, they are going to be wanting votes in their next campaign."[78] William Brinson, another Walker supporter, protested that the "censuring of patriots by you and Senator Tower is a matter of great concern. It should not be at this time of great danger."[79] Once again, then, ultraconservatism helped define a more moderate Republicanism, as Bruce Alger and Tower publically criticized Walker as a reactionary, were assailed by Walker's ultraconservative supporters, and found themselves legitimated in the process.

Attorney General Kennedy v. General Walker

Although most were willing to consign Walker to history's ashcan by the spring of 1962, at least three men were not so inclined. One was President Kennedy, who worked to ensure that Fletcher Knebel's book *Seven Days in May*, about a military coup in which the villain was a fictionalized Edwin Walker, became a motion picture.[80] The second was Lee Harvey Oswald, who called Walker "the most dangerous man in America" and, one month before assassinating Kennedy, fired a single shot that shattered a window of the general's Turtle Creek home but missed Walker. The third was Robert Morris, who demonstrated once again how ultraconservatives framed the terms of debate for moderate conservatives. The Walker episode of 1962 had a tremendous ideological and political impact on Morris. Especially as Walker's antics grew more unpredictable, Morris's association with Walker made the former's future in politics more precarious.

Walker appeared again on the national scene when James Meredith, an Air Force veteran, attempted to become the first African-American to enroll at the University of Mississippi in Oxford. With the prospect of federal troops being sent in by President Kennedy growing increasingly likely, Walker went on the radio to back Governor Ross Barnett's resistance, urging his followers, "Bring your flags, your tents and skillets! It's time!"[81] In Oxford, a crowd of two thousand gathered on the lawn in front of the administration building, yelling "Go to hell, JFK" and hurling rocks and bricks at the federal marshals. As Kennedy monitored the situation from the White House, he said of Walker, "Imagine that son of a bitch having been commander of a division."[82] Some reports held that Walker actively incited rioting and others that he discouraged it; either way, his presence steeled a hostile crowd and contributed to the violence.[83] Arrested for inciting a riot, Walker was sent, at the behest of Attorney General Robert Kennedy, on a government airplane for incarceration and observation at a federal mental health facility in Springfield, Missouri.[84] The American Civil Liberties Union protested that the federal government had violated Walker's rights to due process by failing to hold him overnight in Mississippi to appear before a judge with an attorney present the following morning.[85] One Texan called Walker's institutionalization "unlawful reconstruction number two" and concluded that the president and his brother, the attorney general, "should be the ones tried for mental capacity."[86]

Walker's institutionalization affected attitudes toward psychiatry on the Right for years to come and became a cornerstone of the budding antipsychiatry movement led by Dr. Thomas S. Szasz. In contrast to another radical psychiatrist of the era, R. D. Laing—who had attacked the psychiatric profession from the Left and posited that the family and other Western institutions engendered mental illness—Szasz assailed psychiatry from the Right and became a darling of conservatives like William F. Buckley Jr.[87] Having read of Walker's institutionalization, Buckley called his friend Robert Morris and referred him to Szasz. Morris phoned Szasz, who agreed to journey to Dallas to speak with the general's lawyers and help free Walker.[88] A professor of psychiatry at the

State University of New York, Szasz was also a prolific and gifted writer. Like Erving Goffman's *Asylums*, a damning indictment of hospitalization's demoralizing impact on mental patients, and Michael Foucault's *Madness and Civilization*, which presented insanity as a Western social and cultural construct, Szasz's biting commentary railed against psychiatry as a machination of state power.[89] In the original essay for his most famous and controversial work, *The Myth of Mental Illness*, Szasz wrote, "The concept of illness, whether bodily or mental, implies *deviation from some* clearly *defined norm*."[90] He then argued that the disease-illness model did not apply to mental illness because there existed no generally accepted standards of what constituted mental health. Psychiatrists, he maintained, were abusing their craft by controlling the discourse of mental health. Consequently, the possibilities for abusing the language of mental health for political gain were enormous.

The strange case of General Walker was the best possible evidence for Szasz's case. Szasz wrote in *Psychiatric Justice*, "Edwin A. Walker was arrested, charged for crimes, and then committed against his will for pretrial psychiatric examination. Without doubt, this is the most widely publicized case ever reported in the American press of an attempt to deny an accused person the right to trial by branding him insane and hence incompetent to stand trial."[91] Szasz wrote again of the Walker episode in Buckley's *National Review*. In Walker's case, observed Szasz, a high-profile figure with friends in high places had been subjected to involuntary imprisonment after a doctor who had never even met him, from nearly a thousand miles away, made a medical evaluation based entirely upon selected news reports. Ordinary Americans who lacked Walker's influence and found themselves in a similar situation might, in Szasz's view, suffer an even worse fate.[92]

In Dallas, Szasz spent a "long afternoon and evening" with Morris presenting his view that psychiatry was a threat to civil liberties, particularly for those on the Right. "Psychiatry is despotism in the service of the Therapeutic State, rationalized as 'progressive' science and 'compassionate' medical care," wrote Szasz.[93] Whoever held state power often controlled what constituted psychiatric fitness, Szasz observed. "Before the Civil War," he told Morris, "proslavery physicians in the South diagnosed black slaves who tried to escape to the North as mentally ill, 'suffering from drapetomania.'" "In the Walker case, pro-integration psychiatrists in the North diagnosed white segregationists as mentally ill, 'suffering from racism.'"[94]

The Radicalization of Robert Morris

Under the influence of three notable events—President Kennedy's disarmament proposal, the Supreme Court's ban on school prayer, and Walker's incarceration in a psychiatric facility for political activity—Robert Morris came to abandon his moderate conservatism and turn increasingly reactionary. Morris was literally color-blind (and had been prohibited from enlisting in the Navy during World War II for that reason). Although he could not see the color red, he had a keen eye for detecting Communists. From 1951 to 1953 and from 1956 to 1958, Morris had served as the chief counsel for Senator Pat McCarran's Internal Security Subcommittee and gained a reputation as an indefatigable fighter of Communism. Yet he was no ultraconservative Republican in 1961, when he moved to Dallas and accepted the position of president of the fledgling University of Dallas. At that time he implored President Kennedy to appoint as secretary of state Richard Nixon, hardly a favorite among ultraconservative Republicans, because of the former vice president's foreign policy experience. Morris's statements and columns, which appeared regularly in the *Dallas Morning News*, displayed all the qualities of a moderate conservative Republican. He often spoke in the traditionalist conservative language of Edmund Burke, lamenting that the United States had not learned "the treasures of our civilization" and had failed "to comprehend the nature of its dedicated enemy, international Communism." "We simply don't know what the score is," he complained.[95] Even so, his pronouncements contained none of the apocalyptic rhetoric or anti-intellectualism that characterized the ultraconservatives.

In fact, Morris's tenure as president of the University of Dallas brought him into a world of respectable intellectual conservatism. The faculty, on the whole, believed in original sin, embraced absolute truths, and instilled in their students an appreciation for classic primary texts and such conservative traditionalists as Richard Weaver and Russell Kirk. In the early 1960s, Willmoore Kendall, William F. Buckley's mentor at Yale University, whose primary legacy in the intellectual tradition of American conservatism was (as historian George Nash observed) to "Americanize contemporary conservatism by pointing conservatives back to their own past," joined the University of Dallas faculty, contributing to the college's ethos of cultural conservatism.[96] A fascinating figure, Kendall resigned his position in Yale University's political science department, convinced Yale to purchase his tenure rights, and moved from Connecticut to find fulfillment at the University of Dallas. Students adored the man they called "St. Willmoore" and wore shirts proclaiming "Kendall for King." "At Dallas," Kendall observed, "I can be Moses back from the 40 years of his preparation, among his people—I found myself sinking into the local accent, which was mine 40 years ago, as a weary man sinks into a warm bath." After arriving in Dallas, he wrote cheerfully to a friend that he had broken free from the Atlantic seaboard and the "land of the Buckleys."[97] Frederick Wilhelmson, a "passionate Catholic traditionalist," in historian Patrick Allitt's words, already sat on the faculty of UD. As president, Morris relished teaching courses in Greek and associated with respectable intellectual conservatives, such as English professor Louise Cowan, who as a graduate student of Donald Davidson at Vanderbilt University had begun to champion the Southern Agrarian tradition.[98] In her contributions to *National Review*, Cowan decried "the growing technological revolution, the consequent turn away from the land, and the loss of the community."[99]

Morris's book *No Wonder We Are Losing* clearly illustrates that, at least in the 1950s, Morris was far from a conspiracy theorist imagining furtive collusions and government machinations behind every setback in foreign policy. To be sure, he believed that Communism was a "revolutionary movement whose ultimate aim is world domination," but at this point in his public career, Morris distinguished differences between, as he put it, "the Communists and those manipulated by them." Unlike the ultraconservative Republicans who generally thought that perfidious public officials purposely gave away China, Cuba, and Eastern Europe, Morris, as late as 1961, held that "egregious errors" rather than conscious conspiracy accounted for "Soviet conquests," which were now occurring "at an accelerated pace."[100] Torpid and "indifferent" American policymakers had failed to react aggressively to the warnings of the recent past.[101] "The lessons . . . we should have learned from the fall of mainland China were ignored completely when the Soviets struck slyly in

Cuba," he wrote, concluding that "the nerve endings of those officials in Washington whose duty it was to alert the nation and to galvanize us to action seemed completely dead" and "the fault is in our national will."[102]

In the 1950s, Morris might have blamed Communist expansion on errors of judgment and "the national will," but by the early 1960s, he had embraced conspiracy theories. Just as the John Birch Society drove Mary Ann Collins to the right, the Walker case nudged Robert Morris into the ultraconservative camp. Combined with other factors (President Kennedy's deficit spending, along with his disarmament proposal and the Supreme Court decision on school prayer), this issue set off a cascade resulting in Morris's adoption of the belief that Kennedy was planning a "merger" with the Soviet Union and ceding national sovereignty to a world government controlled by the United Nations. "Today," Morris wrote, "containment has been replaced by a new policy, announced in 1961, and now being vigorously implemented." "Pacific merger with the Soviet Union under the direction of the United Nations is our new national policy."[103]

World government, Morris clarified, meant erecting a great international monolith that would entail "international control of all phases of Human endeavor," the end of the "common law heritage," the end of free enterprise, and "education of all men over the world."[104] He argued that "what the government erroneously calls 'disarmament' . . . is not disarmament at all but a transfer of our military and judicial power to what is euphemistically called a 'strengthened U.N.' This, in essence, is world government." By 1963, Morris concluded that Kennedy's desire for world government even accounted for his affinity for deficit spending. Liberal planners in Washington inflated the deficit, Morris essentially said, because they believed that "there is to be no day of reckoning" once the merger has occurred. "This race toward fiscal infinity is running apace. Obviously, the planners feel that this upcoming state of merger is going to solve all our problems all at once."[105]

The upcoming merger, Morris suggested, also explained the court's decision to ban school prayer. Washington planners, he said, "are working to socialize the United States to make the prospect of merger with us more palatable for Khrushchev." "There are forces at work," he explained, "striking God from our institutions, our legislative halls, and our schools, so that these will conform to the framework of the United Nations, the umbrella for the proposed merger, which proscribes all references to God."[106] Yet it was the Walker case, in particular, that solidified his journey to right-wing extremism because the example of Walker demonstrated to Morris how this fantastical "merger" would proceed: Kennedy, he concluded, would use the power of the government and mental health institutions to silence the military in preparation for the merger with the Soviet Union. The second episode of the Walker case involved a "dangerous precedent": "A United States citizen in the future may wish to protest the action of the federal government in something other than overriding the authority of the State of Mississippi. He may wish, for instance, to protest being merged under the banner of the United Nations with Mr. Khrushchev as his leader. If he engages in peaceable assembly to raise his voice in protest, he could be rushed off to a federal prison hospital, ordered held for psychiatric observation, denied bail, denied a public trial, and denied even the writ of habeas corpus."[107] Dan Smoot echoed Morris's sentiments. "The new mental health laws being written by state legislatures ... make it easier for bureaucrats, and political enemies, and selfish relatives to get someone committed as a 'mentally ill' person and thus get them out of the way." "The fountainhead" for the "propaganda about the need for mental health programs" has been the UN, Smoot claimed. The fact that Morris's statements now reflected themes similar to those of Dan Smoot illustrate the extent to which Morris had come to embrace ultra-conservative Republican positions.[108]

Bass Blasts Disarmament

At the same time Morris was undergoing an ideological makeover, another bellwether in Dallas politics, Rita Bass, was also experiencing a transformation. In the late 1950s, Rita Bass had been a moderate Republican celebrating free markets, promoting low taxes, and advocating an enervated federal government. While her husband, Richard "Dick" Bass, and his brother, Harry Bass were important contributors to moderate Dallas Republicanism, Rita was an even more potent force. She eschewed the dogmatism of the ultraconservative Republicans and concentrated on the nuts and bolts of Republican politics. Her work in the

1950s typified a movement culture established by Dallas housewives that balanced political activism, child-rearing, and domestic duties. If the 1950s were about the importance of the Republican Club women in building the party's institutional structure, Rita Bass exemplified women's move, in 1960s Dallas, into the party structure itself. According to Bass, she hadn't had time to join a Republican Club, which met year-round, because "I was raising four children and I was involved in the community so I was just mainly working . . . a few months prior to the election time. I had a lot of friends and acquaintances . . . that were that type of volunteer."[109] Instead, she focused her energy on goals associated with moderate conservative Republicans: establishing the party's institutional framework, recruiting better candidates, inspiring greater voter participation, and establishing ancillary conservative organizations.

In her ideology, Bass also embodied moderate conservative Republican ideals. She denounced "cradle-to-the-grave governmental security" and called "socialized medicine or Federal aid to education" "[robbing] Peter to pay Paul." She believed that a workingman was "a partner with his employer."[110] Like many other moderate Republicans, Bass held that the bedrock of free markets and individualism was Christianity. "My duty as a Christian, as an American citizen, and as a wife and mother (was) to work daily at preserving individual freedom," she declared.[111] Advocating weak labor, lower taxes, "constitutional government," and the "private competitive market," Bass's brand of conservative Republicanism reflected the concerns of many on the Right with keeping and increasing their wealth.[112]

The relatively centrist faiths that predominated in Rita Bass's hometown of Newton, Kansas, accounted, at least in part, for her moderate conservative Republicanism. A member of the Episcopal Church, Bass, like many expatriate Kansans, treated home, family, and church as central features of her life. Born Rita Joan Crocker, she came from a family of Republican politicos: her grandfather and great-uncle served in the Kansas state legislature, and her father was a Republican chairman in McCullough County. In 1941, at the age of ten, she and her family moved from Newton to Texas's Hill Country. She actively worked for Eisenhower and the Young Republicans as a student at the University of Texas. After graduation, she moved to Dallas, married oilman Dick Bass, and became involved in Dallas Republican Party politics. By 1958, she was serving as a precinct chairman. Complementing moderate Republican H. N. Mallon's work for the Dallas Council of World Affairs, Rita Bass was active in the council's women's group, which entertained the wives of the predominantly male speakers.[113]

Rita Bass's politics changed when she encountered the ideas of Robert Morris. Just as Edwin Walker had edged Morris into the reactionary camp, so Morris's radicalization had an effect on Bass, particularly on the issue of nuclear disarmament. As we have seen, Morris made the conspiratorial assertion that the Kennedy administration's disarmament program entailed dismantling the nation's armed forces and substituting "rule of the world and ourselves by a 'U.N. Peace Force.'" Morris moved in the same circles as Bass.[114] Having read Morris's *Disarmament: Weapon of Conquest*, Bass became an activist and joined "80 Women from Dallas," an organization opposed to disarmament. The organization's president, Jean Jones, called it a "study group" to examine "all available information concerning the United States disarmament program."[115]

Bass and the "80 Women" soon became fastidious fact-collectors and spent their days collecting, reprinting, and distributing pieces (such as op-eds by Morris and pamphlets like the State Department's *Freedom from War*) from their Dallas-based clearinghouse. In late October 1962—in the immediate aftermath of the Cuban Missile Crisis—"80 Women" heard Morris make his case that disarmament was a furtive plan to surrender political sovereignty to a United Nations peace force. Bass took copious notes. "Our disarmament program is not disarmament at all," she wrote. "It is transfer of power from [the] US to [the] Soviet Union."[116] The chairman of the Irving Freedom Forum, along with *Dallas Morning News* editorial writer Kenneth Thompson, joined Bass and the "80 Women."[117] From the Highland Park town hall, the group sent telegrams to the White House with the policy suggestion that "the John Foster Dulles Policy of Massive Retaliation is the only honorable way for us to enforce peace." On the question of general disarmament, they exhorted the president: "Display the courage you once demonstrated for your country by withdrawing."[118] Letters from members of "80 Women" grew increasingly doom-laden. One portentous letter from a member of the group's steering committee read, "It is my firmest conviction that, if we do not reverse the course of this nation by the end of 1964, we will never again have a reasonable hope of preserving freedom for ourselves or our children."[119] "We must," the organization declared, "brave the calculated risk of atomic holocaust if we prefer death to surrender."[120]

The disarmament issue championed by Morris and Bass often rendered inscrutable the distinction between ultraconservative and moderate Republican politics. Historically a far-right fringe group, Dallas-based CIVICS, the Conservative Independent Voters Information Coordinating Services, also picked up the cause and opposed the disarmament plan, which turned "our means of defense . . . over to the enemy—the U.N."[121] Prompted by "80 Women," William Herbert Hunt (son of H. L. Hunt) requested that Wayne Poucher, the voice of Hunt's ultraconservative radio program *Life Line*, write an editorial calling the disarmament program "the sinking of our security." "It is all part of a plot of the Mistaken to take away . . . our freedom as individuals and independence as a nation. Foiling this plot is the greatest work that Constructives can do in this hour of our country's greatest danger," observed Poucher.[122] While established ultraconservatives vehemently opposed the measure as a recipe for "world government," more established party leaders followed in lockstep. Barry Goldwater opined that the disarmament proposal "borders on treason." During the 1962 gubernatorial campaign, Republican nominee Jack Cox charged that President Kennedy wanted to turn over the armed forces to the United Nations and assailed his disarmament proposal as "an open invitation to surrender."[123] Robert Morris continued his preoccupation with the disarmament issue until losing to George H. W. Bush in the Republican primary for US Senate in 1964.[124] In that campaign, Morris observed that the most important issue was the "convergence policy of the State Department which is designed to merge the United States with Russia."[125] H. L. Hunt wrote in July 1963, "The U.S. may be negotiating its early demise at the nuclear test-ban conference in Moscow." Exaggerating the effect of the Arms Control and Disarmament Act of 1961, Hunt wrote in a letter to the editor in October 1963, "If the disarmament authorized by this law were put into effect there may be no Air Force Academy, no West Point, no Annapolis, no private firearms—no defense!"[126] Just weeks before the assassination of President Kennedy, the commentators of

Hunt's radio program *Life Line* were asserting over the air that America's commander-in-chief had circumvented Congress, established a dictatorship, and was controlled by Moscow. On the morning of the president's Dallas visit, *Life Line*'s commentator predicted that Americans would soon be denied firearms to protect themselves from their leaders. Dallasites listening to the radio on the morning of November 22, 1963, heard a *Life Line* commentator state that in the Soviet Union, "no firearms are permitted the people because they would then have the weapons with which to rise up against their rulers."[127]

Parasol Politics

Highlighting just how thoroughly ultraconservative ideology had permeated Dallas politics, the most bizarre criticism of disarmament policy occurred in Dealey Plaza at the very moment of President Kennedy's assassination. At 12:30 p.m. on November 22, 1963—just as Lee Harvey Oswald fired three shots into the presidential limousine—Louis Steven Witt was standing on the sidewalk of Elm Street as the motorcade passed. Witt was doing something that many of us would consider peculiar. He carried a large black umbrella, opened wide, as the sun shone brightly in the Texas sky. In Abraham Zapruder's famous twenty-six-second film capturing the assassination, Witt's umbrella can be seen just as the limousine, having briefly been obstructed by a freeway sign, reappears and President Kennedy suddenly grasps for his throat. In the years following the tragedy, assassination theorists produced outlandish accounts of what Witt—the Umbrella Man, as they named him—was doing. Some posited that he was a signalman for the supposedly numerous gunmen in Dealey Plaza that day. Others speculated that the umbrella itself fired a dart, rendering the president frozen for the kill shot. In fact, Witt's umbrella exemplified a common form of protest by the far right. It was meant to disparage any foreign policy that involved compromise with the Soviets by invoking the memory of British prime minister Neville Chamberlain (who always carried an umbrella) and the failed policy of appeasement that he championed against Hitler at the Munich Conference in 1938.[128]

Umbrella protests first began in England after Chamberlain arrived home from the conference carrying his trademark accessory. Wherever

Chamberlain traveled, the opposition party protested his appeasement at Munich by displaying umbrellas. Throughout the 1950s and 1960s, Americans on the far right adopted the practice, employing umbrellas to criticize leaders they believed were appeasing the enemies of the United States. Some politicians refused to use them for that reason. Vice President Richard Nixon banned his own aides from carrying umbrellas when picking him up at the airport for fear of being photographed and charged as an appeaser.[129] Returning from the Geneva Conference in 1955, President Eisenhower had to give a speech in the pouring rain because Nixon had prohibited presidential assistants from carrying umbrellas.[130] Campaigning against Adlai Stevenson, Eisenhower's opponent in 1952 and 1956, Nixon declared, "If the umbrella is the symbol of appeasement, then Adlai Stevenson must go down in history as the Umbrella Man of all time."[131] When the Berlin Wall was constructed in 1961 and President Kennedy did not send American troops to tear it down, German students, as well as many Americans, sent him umbrellas.[132] Upon returning home after having established new cultural and commercial ties with China in the 1970s, President Richard Nixon was met with umbrella-wielding students, who shared William F. Buckley's assertion that Nixon had "sold out" by meeting with the leaders of the Communist dictatorship.

Louis Steven Witt later said that the real target of his protest in Dallas had been Joseph P. Kennedy Sr., the US ambassador to England at the time of the Munich agreement, whose support of Chamberlain was well known. Appearing before the House Select Committee on Assassinations in 1978, Witt explained that being a "conservative-type fellow" and, having heard from a work colleague that the umbrella was a "sore spot" for President Kennedy (because his father had been criticized intensely), he had wanted "to heckle the President's motorcade" and thought the umbrella would do the job.[133]

Witt's explanation is plausible, but what really matters is how others *understood* his actions that morning. If we consider the historical context—Dallas's status as a redoubt of the far right and the flurry of newspaper articles in Ted Dealey's *Dallas Morning News* comparing Kennedy to Chamberlain and the 1963 Test Ban Treaty to the Munich agreement—it is likely that Witt's umbrella was at least perceived by the crowd around him as a protest of President Kennedy's nuclear disarmament policy. "Kennedy acts like Neville Chamberlain," observed one letter to the editor in March 1963.[134] Another reader wrote in August 1963 that the "dissolution of the British Empire started at Munich with Neville Chamberlain, that of the United States in January, 1961, with the Kennedy regime."[135] Another Dallasite, W. E. Parks, wrote in 1963, "The nuclear-test-ban treaty . . . is the Chamberlain-Hitler 'peace in our time' pact' with a new cast and new lines."[136] In an editorial on September 9, 1963, the *Dallas Morning News* drew what it called "parallels between the Munich agreement and the current U.S.-British-Soviet test-ban treaty." Suggesting that John F. Kennedy was another Neville Chamberlain, who appeased dictators, the *News* observed that there "is no more encouragement today for believing that the Soviets have changed their aggressive intentions than there was to believe the Nazis had changed their goals in 1938."[137] The incident illustrates the potency and ubiquity of far right ideas in Dallas in 1963. Elements of this worldview extended into different aspects of everyday behavior, sometimes even when ordinary moments turned into extraordinary events.

Bruce Alger, Mary Ann Collins, Robert Morris, and Rita Bass responded to the growing influence of such far-right institutions as the John Birch Society and its two primary spokesmen, Robert Welch and Edwin Walker, the latter himself a Dallasite. In the wake of the scandalous protest that greeted Lyndon and Lady Bird Johnson at the Adolphus Hotel in November 1960, many Americans were convinced that Dallas deserved a reputation as a "city of hate." Bruce Alger, who had been at the center of the incident, came to realize that his city and party were becoming dangerously associated with the reactionary extremism of the John Birch Society, with its hierarchical leadership and predilection for conspiracy theories, and shifted back to more moderate Republicanism. While Alger still aligned himself with the racial views of some of the most intolerant ultraconservatives, the Birch Society pushed him toward the mainstream, albeit briefly. The ascent of the John Birch Society in Dallas was a watershed moment for other Dallas Republicans because it forced many to define where they stood. The organization and the controversial figures associated with it represented a challenge to the status of the Dallas Republican Party—not only as an ideologically coherent force but also as a politically viable movement. The Birch Society pushed some individuals from the ledge of ultraconservative politics back into the camp of moderate Republican politics. But at the same time, ultraconservative Repubicans influenced some former moderates to become more reactionary. The martyrdom of General Edwin Walker following his institutionalization, as well as the appeal to anti-Communist sentiments through charges of left-wing conspiracies involving the Kennedy administration, served to push former moderates like Mary Ann Collins, Robert Morris, and Rita Bass to the far right. The legacy of ultraconservative Dallas politics was both a strengthened conservative mainstream and a radicalized fringe fraught with anxiety over state control, Communist appeasement, and world government.

6 Architects and the Artisans of the Southern Strategy

Wharton Whiz Kid

Peter O'Donnell embodied a new brand of smart and savvy political leadership in the postwar New South. As journalist Theodore White put it, this new generation was made up of "men between thirty and forty years old, city people, well-bred, moderate segregationists, efficient, more at ease at suburban cocktail parties than when whiskey-belting in courthouse chambers."[1] O'Donnell became convinced in the late 1950s that the Republican Party needed to identify itself as the anti–civil rights party in the South, and Alger's 1956 victory over Henry Wade taught him that rebranding the GOP was possible. If Alger was the progenitor of the GOP's Southern Strategy, O'Donnell was its chief strategist, masterminding for Republican candidates a plan to make the GOP the preferred choice in Dixie. Both participated in making the lasting legacy of the Dallas Republican Party its contribution to developing the Southern Strategy for the national Republican Party.

In the late 1950s, the vast majority of Southerners loathed the Republican Party because of its historical legacy as the party of Lincoln. Southerners still wanted no part of a party that had been established in 1854 for the purpose of promoting nonslave labor and stopping the spread of slavery into the American West. O'Donnell wanted to counter this Southern antipathy by reinventing the party's image in the region. While certainly no racist himself, he helped steer the party in a direction that would win elections by appealing to untapped white resentment, starting with the Dallas Republican Party, then moving on to the Texas Republican Party and, finally, the national Republican Party. The new GOP would champion issues dear to both fiscal conservatives and segregationists: states' rights, lower taxes, and less government regulation. "The problem of government today," O'Donnell submitted in 1958, "is to prevent the federal government from encroaching upon states' rights and intervening in every aspect of the private lives of our citizens."[2]

The son of a well-to-do cotton broker, O'Donnell excelled at the University of Pennsylvania's Wharton School of Business. He used his steel-trap mind and organizational acumen in the business world, profiting handsomely from investments in oil and gas properties. When he joined the Republican Party in 1954 he had no particularly strong political bent, but his interest in politics grew, and in 1956 he became a Highland Park precinct chairman. In 1958 he managed Bruce Alger's reelection campaign, during which the candidate battled an urban renewal proposal, arguing that it "means forced integration in public housing."[3] After this successful campaign, O'Donnell's star rose. His aggressive campaign style and organizational genius won him the position of Dallas County Republican chairman, which had been vacated by Maurice Carlson. "A hot potato," the *Dallas Morning News* quipped, "was thrust into cool hands."[4] O'Donnell's organizational philosophy focused on picking races that Republicans could win. At the same time he continued to stake out his staunch segregationist and pro–states' rights vision for a new Republican Party in Dallas and beyond. Championing states' rights while promising to "enlist dependable workers" and "build up the Republican organization," O'Donnell carved out an image that combined a "whites only" image that appealed to Southern reactionaries with an image of businesslike efficiency that spoke to moderate conservatives.[5] He was, after all, a respectable member of the Dallas business establishment, actively involved with Southwestern Medical School and on the board of directors of the Dallas Council on World Affairs.[6] Together Bruce Alger and Peter O'Donnell nudged their party toward the disaffected conservatives and segregationists who felt abandoned by the Democrats and were natural GOP constituents.

As early as 1959, Maurice Carlson, O'Donnell's predecessor as Dallas County Republican chairman, had been advising Republicans on the national scene to apply throughout the South the racial strategy that had worked for Bruce Alger in Dallas in 1956. Upon learning that Vice President Richard Nixon would be visiting Dallas in October 1959, Maurice Carlson provided the leading contender for the 1960 Republican nomination with a detailed summary of Texas politics. Foreshadowing the Southern Strategy Nixon would adopt in his 1968 campaign, Carlson advised the vice president to convince white voters that he was antagonistic toward African-Americans. "Negroes," Carlson observed, "are regimented under NAACP. If the Whites think the Negroes are against you, it will help under the old rule of birds of a feather."[7] There can be no doubt Nixon was listening. Not only was it likely the vice president wrote "excellent job" on Carlson's memorandum, Charlie McWhorter, Nixon's assistant, observed that "the VP had been quite pleased with a report he received prior to his visit to Texas. This report had been prepared by Maurice Carlson, the Dallas County Chairman. The VP said that he would like to get the same kind of report for every state he visited."[8]

The new racial strategy forged by O'Donnell and Carlson profoundly influenced not only established politicians like Nixon but also newcomers, especially Dallas Republican John Tower, whose surprising victory in the US Senate race was built on the momentum that conservatives developed in Dallas County in the 1960 presidential race, when 63 percent of Dallas County supported Richard Nixon for president, despite John Kennedy's victory in Texas overall.

The Little Giant

John Tower, a little-known professor of political science, ran for the US Senate from Texas, first unsuccessfully in 1960 against Lyndon Johnson and then successfully in 1961 in a special election to fill the vacant senate seat of the new vice president.[9] With his victory, Tower became the first Republican senator from Texas since Reconstruction. Tower embraced wholeheartedly Alger and O'Donnell's ultraconservative stance on race. As early as 1952, he had spoken of Reconstruction as a burden to the development of a modern Republican Party. After President Eisenhower sent federal troops to enforce desegregation in Arkansas in 1957, the diminutive and domineering Tower observed that "the Little Rock imbroglio has damaged the Republican Party in the South, and has probably set us back in our organizational efforts here." "We are badly crippled," he lamented.[10] By the following year, Tower was echoing Alger's defiance of the Republican president's stand at Little Rock's Central High. As chairman of the state party's Platform and Resolutions

Committee, Tower wrote in the 1958 platform that "the gradual solution for problems relating to desegregation in Texas [should] be left to the people, the school boards, and the courts, within this state."[11]

At the 1960 Republican National Convention in Chicago, Tower led the drive by the Goldwater wing for a more prosegregationist plank on civil rights. According to Dallas lawyer William Burrow, Tower believed that "the civil rights issue is part of the worldwide revolutionary trend, with the riots in Tokyo, Mexico, the Congo, South Africa, and Cuba and the sit-downs in the United States all of the same pattern."[12] A member of the Civil Rights Subcommittee, Tower was chosen by the Southern members of the platform committee to serve as their floor leader. While Tower was in Chicago slogging through committee hearings, his nemesis, Governor Nelson Rockefeller, who supported a strong civil rights plank, was in his penthouse on New York's Fifth Avenue courting Richard Nixon, the likely presidential nominee and the only man who could determine with any finality the contents of the platform. The agreement forged by Nixon and Rockefeller became known as the "Pact of Fifth Avenue" and included a strong civil rights plank. The platform committee ultimately embraced the spirit of the Nixon-Rockefeller accord and advocated voting rights for African-Americans along with other reforms. Yet political scientist Karl Lamb's exhaustive study of the civil rights plank concluded that Tower secured four substantial concessions for Southerners, fighting proposed language that included favorable references to sit-in demonstrations and the establishment of a permanent Fair Employment Practices Commission. Tower, Lamb found, "became the chief spokesman for the southern viewpoint in negotiations with Mr. Nixon's representatives and later with Mr. Nixon himself."[13] According to Nixon, Tower's performance at the convention was "statesmanlike," and he "tremendously increased his stature in the party." Buoyed, Tower resigned his professorship at Midwestern University to run as the Republican candidate for Lyndon Johnson's Senate seat, capturing a respectable 42 percent of the electorate.

With the election of John Tower to the US Senate, the politics of race was gradually pushing the Party of Lincoln into the arms of the segregationists. When Tower attended his first meeting of the Senate's Southern Caucus (Johnson had never attended), the caucus leader, archsegregationist Richard Russell of Georgia, reportedly turned to him and said, "I want to welcome Texas back into the Confederacy."[14] According to historian David Farber, Tower's victory "made the case that at least in Texas the Republican Party had replaced the Democratic Party as the anti–civil rights party."[15] Tower's victory also further testified to Peter O'Donnell's organizational skills, precipitated his rise to the position of state party chairman, and elevated his stature in national Republican circles. O'Donnell, who served as Tower's chief strategist during both campaigns and went to work in Washington as the senator's first administrative aide, was elated by the win and eager to secure the election of the first Republican governor of Texas since Reconstruction.

Then Came Little Rock

Jack Cox of nearby Stephens County was Peter O'Donnell's "personal choice" to be the gubernatorial nominee in 1962. O'Donnell actively promoted his candidate, and when Cox secured the nomination, O'Donnell served as his campaign manager. The Cox nomination further reinforced the GOP's image, at least in Texas, as an anti–civil rights, pro–states' rights party.[16] "Cox had my vote," one Dallasite explained, because he was "the only candidate who is unalterably opposed to the despicable, vicious civil rights bill." In 1957, Cox had served as executive director of Freedom in Action (FIA), which was a linchpin between the Republican Party and conservatives disturbed with the burgeoning civil rights movement. For many, FIA served as an introduction to headier activity in the GOP. Founded in 1955 by Judge Elwood Fouts of Houston, FIA only admitted recruits who had received the approval of an existing member. According to Cox, the organization sought to forge an alliance between "States' righters' and free-enterprisers" and to "prevent dictatorship by the Supreme Court and labor bosses."[17]

Membership had flagged in 1956, but when President Eisenhower decided to send federal troops to Little Rock in 1957, interest in FIA skyrocketed. In the grand ballroom of Dallas's Statler Hilton on the night of October 30, 1957, Freedom in Action sponsored a dinner for Texas conservatives. While organizers had expected 150 attendees, hundreds of conservatives waited in line trying to get tickets. "It couldn't have happened a few months ago," one conservative commented after the spectacle. "The spirit wasn't there. You couldn't have collected so many conservative political leaders from all parts of Texas to sit down at six dollars a plate and talk about the vanishing rights of the states. Then came Little Rock. Suddenly everybody began to talk."[18] By 1958 FIA had hundreds of members in all 254 Texas counties, with organizations in 40 Texas counties and full-time offices in Dallas, Austin, San Antonio, and Corpus Christi.[19]

In a sign that the Dallas GOP was becoming the party associated with opposition to civil rights, several members of FIA became active leaders in the Republican Party. Though initially nonpartisan, by the late 1950s, FIA was predominantly a vehicle for Republicanism in Dallas. The organization produced candidates like Jack Cox and Billy Naughton, who was Bruce Alger's campaign manager in 1962. Naughton received his "political education" in the group's "seminars on free enterprise," and by 1962 he listed his occupation as "capitalist" for poll tax purposes. FIA had also encouraged its members to register as Republican voters: in a January 1959 meeting of the Highland Park Republican Women's Club, a representative of Freedom in Action presented a program for selling poll taxes to register voters for the GOP.[20]

The nomination of a man as closely identified with states' rights as Jack Cox led John Connally, Cox's Democratic opponent, to stake out a racial strategy of his own. Connally played on long-standing Southern prejudices against the Republican Party. To be sure, Connally was Lyndon Johnson's mentee and knew about working both sides of the aisle. While telling liberal Texans that the Republican Party "talks about principles, but they preach prejudice," he also reminded conservative Texans that "the last time a Republican governor was elected in Texas, it was under Federal supervision and at the point of federal bayonets."[21] Cox ran the campaign as an ultraconservative. The *Dallas Morning News* estimated that at least 90 percent of Edwin Walker's backers in the Democratic primary voted in the general election for Cox.[22]

Cox won Dallas County but took only 45 percent of the vote statewide to Connally's 47. Nonetheless, the fact that he came so close testifies that his racial strategy worked, foreshadowing its broader implementation. The *Dallas Morning News* crowed, "Cox gave the GOP ticket the momentum it needed in Dallas County—now the bulwark of

Barry Goldwater–John Tower Republicanism in Texas and maybe in the nation."[23]

Wild about Barry

From the vantage point of most Dallas Republicans in early 1963, Barry Goldwater represented the brightest hope for national conservative Republicanism since the death of Robert Taft in 1953. Annoyance with the New Deal, particularly the National Industrial Recovery Act's wage and price controls, which interfered with the management of his family's department store, led to Goldwater's first foray into politics as a member of the Phoenix city council. A successful candidate for the United States Senate in 1952, Goldwater assailed President Truman's New Deal. Campaigning for reelection in 1958, he attacked "labor bosses" and unions with even more ferocity than in 1952. The Arizona senator's views echoed those of many North Texas businessmen. Enclosing a thousand-dollar check, Fort Worth oilman W. A. Moncrief wrote to Goldwater that Walter Reuther, the president of the United Auto Workers, was "the most powerful and dangerous man in America today." Seven months later, Goldwater made a similar point. Reuther, he said, was "a more dangerous menace than the sputniks or anything that the Russians might do."[24]

Goldwater's 1960 book, *Conscience of a Conservative*, ghostwritten by Brent Bozell, had a powerful impact on many Dallas Republicans, including Catherine Colgan. "Many of us were very impressed with Barry Goldwater," she recalled. His "line of thinking" and "personal values" "made a lot of sense to us."[25] Goldwater's message and worldview also inspired numerous Democrats, many of whom attended "resignation rallies," where they renounced their old party affiliation and declared their allegiance to the Republican Party.[26]

In Texas the "Goldwater phenomenon" originated from Dallas County, where GOP leaders like Peter O'Donnell, John Tower, and Harry and Rita Bass galvanized the drive to elect the Arizona Republican. In 1960 and 1961, Goldwater had stumped in Texas for Tower, whose own book, a *Program for Conservatives*, while somewhat academic, contained many of the same themes and positions as Goldwater's book. In July 1963 Harry Bass said, "We're working now toward the goal of replacing one-term

Governor Connally and one-term President Kennedy with well-qualified fiscally responsible men who will be, of course, Republicans." Bass epitomized the optimism that many Dallas conservatives felt: "With Goldwater heading the ticket, we can expect to elect a Republican senator to Ralph Yarborough's seat, at least three more congressmen, and thirty-five or forty more representatives in Texas."[27]

Goldwater's most fervent champion, however, was O'Donnell, who injected his infectious enthusiasm and trademark organizational mastery into the movement. Moreover, he contributed significantly to Goldwater's use of the Southern Strategy and his consequent victory in five Deep South states in 1964. As the newly elected Republican state chairman in 1962, O'Donnell publicly encouraged Goldwater to run for president and secured the Texas Republican state committee's passage of a measure praising *Conscience of a Conservative* as "an affirmative philosophy and program."[28] As early as the fall of 1962, Texas was firmly ensconced in the Goldwater camp.[29] So sure was O'Donnell that Texas, as one campaign sign read, was "wild about Barry," that he left Dallas in February 1963, accepted the position of chairman of the Draft Goldwater Committee, and organized its headquarters on Connecticut Avenue in Washington, DC. O'Donnell was "the natural choice" and "the ideal man," according to F. Clifton White, the former chairman of the Young Republicans. "I couldn't see how Barry Goldwater—or any other leading Republican in his right mind—could possibly thumb his nose at Peter O'Donnell."[30] Rita Bass accepted O'Donnell's invitation to join him in Washington and became the national canvassing director. With White serving as national director of the committee, O'Donnell and John Grenier began the task of rounding up potential Southern delegates for Goldwater.[31] By the time the committee held its first press conference, O'Donnell and White had already lined up Draft Goldwater chairmen in thirty-three states and had nationwide Republican support from precinct chairmen to national committeewomen.[32]

Part of what made Goldwater so appealing to O'Donnell was his early affinity to the Southern Strategy. In the early 1960s, the national Republican Party stood at a crossroads on racial issues. George Hinnan, Governor Nelson Rockefeller's advisor, called race the "Great Republican issue," one that divided the party. He noted that segregationist discourse was on the rise among party leaders, and "Barry has been falling increasingly for it." Hinnan outlined the reasoning of these new converts: "Their theory is that by becoming more reactionary than even the Southern Democratic Party, the Republican Party can attract Southern conservatives who have been Democrats, and by consolidating them with the conservative strength in the Middle West and Far West, the Republicans can offset the liberalism of the Northeast and finally prevail."[33] Rockefeller himself bemoaned as "completely incredible" the Southern strategists' plan of "writing off" the black vote.[34] Hinnan was correct in his perception: Following Nixon's defeat in 1960, Goldwater told Atlanta Republicans that the GOP, despite receiving 36 percent of the African-American vote that year, is "not going to get the Negro vote ... so we ought to go hunting where the ducks are."[35] With that, Goldwater headed South in search of some ducks.

Goldwater empathized with the South because his own philosophy drew on the argument that the Constitution protected property rights and restricted democracy in order to preserve privilege. From John C. Calhoun and other slave-owning politicians of the antebellum Old South to their conservative disciples of the New South, the region emphasized the role of the Constitution in curbing federal power. Goldwater subscribed to Calhoun's understanding of the Constitution as a restrictive document that protected property rights and sanctified the power of the states over the federal government.[36] "Our right of property," Goldwater said, "is probably our most sacred right."[37] Goldwater's narrow definition of liberty as it applied mainly to property owners allowed him to embrace "freedom" even as he ignored the plight of African-Americans at midcentury and railed against the 1964 Civil Rights Act for ineluctably giving rise to "a federal police force of mammoth proportions."[38]

It was therefore no accident that, in historian David Farber's words, "Goldwater played in the South." His vision of liberty distinctly paralleled that of slave owners who had regarded slaves as their property.[39] Skeptical that every individual would be able to comport himself responsibly, Goldwater consistently supported rich over poor, employer over employee, and white over black. His vision of a restrictive Constitution caused him to attack the existing Supreme Court and champion a return to the antilabor, probusiness, segregationist courts of the Gilded

Age. He revered freedom yet attacked the *Brown v. Board of Education* decision, arguing that it was "not based on law" because it represented a direct violation of Southern traditions of white entitlement and black exclusion.[40] Defending his conception of the protections the Constitution offers against this kind of court interference, Goldwater said, "I am firmly convinced—not only that integrated schools are not required—but that the Constitution does not permit any interference whatsoever by the federal government in the field of education."[41] From assailing stronger labor laws to rejecting federal aid for education to battling colonial independence movements, he vehemently took on any reform that promoted egalitarian causes or what he perceived as the redistribution of wealth and property from privileged whites to the underprivileged and nonwhites.[42]

During the first press conference for the Draft Goldwater Committee, O'Donnell addressed the media and declared that the national Republican Party ought to pursue an intentional Southern Strategy. Because Goldwater was the only candidate who could successfully execute such a strategy, the Arizona senator ought to be the party's nominee. "The key to Republican success," O'Donnell argued, "lies in converting a weakness into a strength and becoming a truly national party." The phrase "converting a weakness into a strength" meant securing the once solidly Democratic South for a Republican candidate. In his book about Goldwater's campaign for the presidency, *Suite 3505*, F. Clifton White cleared up any doubt over what O'Donnell meant by including after that crucial phrase this parenthetical remark: "(the paucity of Republican votes in the South)." At this revealing moment in political history, O'Donnell had based his argument on a striking admission. The Southern Strategy was an intentional maneuver on the part of the party to win elections, and Goldwater, with his ability to appeal to racist sentiments in the South, was seemingly the only candidate who could deliver enough Southern votes to ensure a Republican victory.[43]

Republican gains in the South in the 1962 midterm elections—achieved largely through Republican opposition to the Department of Urban Affairs—only bolstered O'Donnell's conviction that Goldwater could win the presidency with appeals to race.[44] William Rusher, publisher for the *National Review* and a former assistant counsel under Robert Morris, agreed that Republicans could beat Kennedy by selecting a candidate opposed to civil rights. Rusher argued against the immorality of racial politics by observing that Southern Democrats had been making appeals to segregationists for decades. While civil rights activists faced off against intractable segregationists, party-builders like O'Donnell were planning a racial strategy for Goldwater and making Republican institutions throughout the South lily-white. The Republican National Committee had dropped all pretense of appealing to minorities when it disbanded its division for minority outreach and established Operation Dixie, which recruited white Southerners to the party. To be sure, Goldwater's allure to middle-class Southerners in the burgeoning Sunbelt drew on class appeals as well as race. Rathering than appealing to the Ku Klux Klan, Goldwater and the GOP tailored their message for moderate Sunbelt suburbanites, who supported "right to work" labor laws, militantly opposed Communism, and assailed welfare policies.[45]

Attesting to the excitement that greeted Goldwater's potential candidacy, nine thousand Americans from forty-four states converged on Washington, DC, on July 4, 1963, and filled the Washington Armory for a rally encouraging the senator to jump into the race. It was Peter O'Donnell's job as the primary organizer and master of ceremonies to pump up the capacity crowd: "We are embarking on a great crusade . . . to put Goldwater in and Kennedy out!"[46] One Washingtonian later declared, "This town's never seen anything like it."[47]

Conservative strategists' increasing optimism and commitment to the Southern Strategy were buoyed by the American public's growing disenchantment with President Kennedy's unequivocal defense of civil rights. In June 1963, President Kennedy had addressed the nation on civil rights, called it a "moral issue," and introduced a substantial civil rights bill to Congress. That summer, his approval rating dove from 70 percent to 55 percent.[48] "Our people are tingling with excitement. I have been receiving long distance calls from all over the nation," O'Donnell declared. "The South will take the lead in making Kennedy a 1-term president." "A year ago it was said that Kennedy was unbeatable. But people are not thinking that way now."[49] With glee, O'Donnell predicted, "if Goldwater can carry the same states that Nixon carried in 1960, and then carry the balance of the Southern States, he will have 320 electoral votes—more than enough to win."[50]

Goldwater himself was less than cooperative. He expressed little enthusiasm for running against Kennedy and throughout 1963 declined to commit himself to the presidential race. Although he never attempted to defuse the grassroots operation by flatly refusing to run, Goldwater remained unaffiliated with the committee that often met furtively in Suite 3505 in New York's Chanin Building. It was "their time and money," he said, although he was reportedly "furious" over the efforts of White and O'Donnell to seek out press coverage.[51]

"If Goldwater doesn't want to make up his mind," O'Donnell said, "we will draft him. And because he might say 'No,' we'll tell him what we're going to do. Won't ask his permission to do it!"[52] O'Donnell was well aware that time was of the essence, that the candidate would need to build the campaign's financial and institutional infrastructure to run competitively against a Kennedy machine that had strong union support.[53] O'Donnell grew increasingly impatient and frustrated with the presumptive candidate's aloofness, but Goldwater refused to sanction fundraising on his behalf and stonewalled even John Tower, who served as O'Donnell's primary intermediary with the Arizona senator. "We're like a wet noodle," O'Donnell complained. "This thing will surprise people if it ever gets started, but right now it isn't started." O'Donnell grew weary of working through Goldwater's aides, who lionized their boss and, like the senator, showed no sense of urgency about announcing for president. After visiting New Hampshire in December 1963, O'Donnell lamented to a Goldwater staffer that "there are serious weaknesses in organization, finance, public relations and advertising, and in my opinion, we stand a great chance of being clobbered."[54]

In addition to these organizational problems, O'Donnell saw Goldwater's extemporaneous speaking style as an issue that might imperil a presidential run. O'Donnell advised Goldwater in a memo to prepare his remarks and avoid "shooting from the hip."[55] This unsolicited advice only further alienated O'Donnell from the senator's inner circle.[56] When Goldwater formally announced his intention to run in January 1964, O'Donnell and White were passed over for all senior positions on the Goldwater for President Committee staff.[57] Rejecting John Grenier's recommendation that O'Donnell be made director of political operations, the campaign offered the job to Lee Edwards, the editor of Young

Americans for Freedom's magazine, *New Guard*.[58] Goldwater did, however, refer to O'Donnell as the "efficiency expert" during public remarks in June 1964 and thanked him for his efforts, saying, "I wouldn't be standing here tonight as a possible nominee of our party for president if it weren't for you."[59]

Although the Goldwater campaign excluded O'Donnell, it nevertheless followed the strategy that had become his trademark and targeted the South with carefully coded appeals to white supremacy. Like some other conservatives, Goldwater exploited white anxieties in the face of the social change and upheaval fomented by the civil rights movement, which many perceived as a "Second Reconstruction." In theory, Goldwater lauded liberty, but in reality, he allied himself with agents of racial separation.[60] Martin Luther King accused Goldwater of "[giving] comfort to the most vicious racists and most extreme rightists in America."[61] Brooklyn Dodger great Jackie Robinson, himself a Republican, remarked that any black person voting for Barry Goldwater "would have a difficult time living among Negroes." William P. Young of Pennsylvania, a black delegate to the Republican Convention in San Francisco's Cow Palace, charged that Goldwater's platform was "attempting to make the party of Lincoln a machine for dispensing discord and racial conflict."[62]

There were three components to Goldwater's version of the Southern Strategy. First, he demonized the Civil Rights Act, which became law in the summer of 1964. Abandoning an earlier attack that claimed the law was unconstitutional, Goldwater now insisted it "dangerously [tread] in the private affairs of men."[63] His opposition earned swift congratulations from O'Donnell, who called the law "vicious," argued that it would create "a federal police state," and declared that "President Johnson has turned his back on Texas to court the liberal extremists and Negro bloc in the North and East."[64] The second component, the film *Choice*, was a much more explicit type of appeal. Although Goldwater prohibited screenings of the film, which he himself called "racist," its production demonstrated that winning the South remained the campaign's chief preoccupation.[65] The third component was an effort to conflate civil rights and civil disorder. Goldwater's subtle argument was that "crime in the streets" resulted from disrespect for authority and waning morals, which in turn derived from liberalism's welfare state. This disregard for authority and social mores crystalized in the civil rights movement's strategy of civil disobedience. By invoking the phrase "law and order," then, Goldwater launched a coded attack on civil rights, playing to the fears of many whites and implicitly promising strong retaliatory measures against those who appeared to threaten white people (particularly women).[66]

The Politics of Law and Order

The politics of law and order had been brewing since at least the summer of 1963. In a memo that June, one Goldwater advisor wrote, "The hostility to the new Negro militancy has seemingly spread like wildfire from the South to the entire country." The president had failed to grasp "the political implications of such a change." "So long as the "tide of rebellion" continued and Goldwater invoked states' rights and argued that "private property must remain inviolate," he had a "serious chance" to beat John Kennedy. The memo suggested that any given category of crime be treated "as a prong of a single fork—a fork labeled 'moral crisis.'" Goldwater, the memo argued, must jab the fork "relentlessly from now until election day."[67]

Goldwater rolled out the discourse of "law and order" in March 1964 in New Hampshire, where he faced a closely contested primary against Nelson Rockefeller and Henry Cabot Lodge. The president, Goldwater declared, ought to "turn on the lights of moral leadership" and the "lights of moral order."[68] His "light-switch" reference identified morality with lightness, whiteness, and civic order (and, by extension, depravity with darkness and the civil rights struggle), connections he made even more explicit that June in Dallas. There, Goldwater specifically identified as criminal behavior the nonviolent resistance campaigns of the civil rights activists. Before a crowd of eleven thousand at the Dallas Memorial Auditorium, Goldwater declared his allegiance to "the principles that look upon violence in the streets, anywhere in this land, regardless of who does it, as the wrong way to resolve great moral questions—the way that will destroy the liberties of all the people."[69]

Goldwater employed the language of law and order to appeal to fears of crime and black militancy while simultaneously blaming social ills on liberalism. He often spoke in terms calculated to evoke fears of black-on-white crime and sexuality, as in the statement "Our women are no longer safe in their homes."[70] In describing Washington, DC, with its high crime rate, as "a place of shame and dishonor," he called into play public awareness of the city's sizable African-American population.[71] Goldwater placed the blame for threats to order squarely with the civil rights movement and the Great Society, President Johnson's set of social and economic reforms. Civil rights, he averred, engendered permissiveness and moral laxity. American liberalism, reaching its crescendo with the Great Society, had banished God from schools and rewarded indolence with social programs. "Government seeks to be parent, teacher, doctor, and even minister," Goldwater lamented. "Rising crime rates" evidenced the "failure" of the liberal strategy of social change.[72]

This strident, racist rhetoric, which originated with the Right, influenced moderates as well. Even temperate public figures like Dwight D. Eisenhower adopted the rhetoric of "law and order," as in this remark at the 1964 Republican Convention in San Francisco: "Let us not be guilty of maudlin sympathy for the criminal . . . roaming the streets with switchblade knife."[73] Roy Wilkins, president of the National Association for the Advancement of Colored Persons, underlined the racist implications of Eisenhower's remark in a strongly worded rebuke: "The phrase 'switchblade knife' means 'Negro' to the average white American."[74] In his own 1964 convention speech, Goldwater tied together Democratic corruption scandals and "violence in our streets" with his plea that law and order "not become the license of the mob and jungle."[75] John Tower also courted segregationist voters by appealing to law and order. At the convention, he observed, "We've come to the point when people can be mauled and beaten and even killed on the streets of a great city with hundreds of people looking on, and doing nothing about it." Placing the blame for this lawlessness with liberal policies, he continued, "We have come to the point where, in many cases, the lawbreakers are treated with loving care . . . while those who uphold and champion the rule of law and order are looked upon in some quarters as suspect."[76]

Rout

In 1964, the country as a whole was not ready for the brand of conservatism that Barry Goldwater embodied and Dallas County voters embraced. Conservative Republicans would have to wait for "future Novembers," as William F. Buckley Jr. put it. But the South was ready. Five of the six states Goldwater won were in the Deep South: Alabama, Georgia, Louisiana, Mississippi, and South Carolina. He took Mississippi with 87 percent of the vote. Whereas Eisenhower had won 40 percent of the nationwide black vote in 1956 and Richard Nixon had garnered 36 percent in 1960, Goldwater took a meager 6 percent in 1964. As historian Michael Flamm concluded, neither perceptions of black violence and crime nor reactions to the rapidity of desegregation in the cities of the Northeast and Midwest were yet strong enough to produce the white voter backlash Goldwater would have needed to win in 1964.[77]

The politics of law and order failed to carry the day in 1964 because the discourse was premature. The assassination of President Kennedy in Dallas in November 1963 had revolutionized the political landscape, and both Goldwater and Congressman Bruce Alger were defeated. The assassination cast a long shadow over both campaigns and over Dallas's identity, reinforcing the city's reputation as a haven for extremism. An incident in which Adlai Stevenson, the US ambassador to the United Nations, was physically abused by an angry mob of Dallasites on October 26, 1963, recalled the day in 1960 when Lyndon Johnson and his wife were accosted at the Adolphus Hotel. A study by Peter O'Donnell conducted a month before the assassination concluded that "neither Republicans nor Democrats identify Goldwater as part of the radical right."[78] That was not the case soon after. By demonstrating that extremism *was* a problem in the body politic, the assassination, although perpetrated by a Marxist, made the identification of Goldwater as a trigger-happy warmonger much more convincing to the public. Some rank-and-file Republicans grew despondent immediately after the tragedy. As Dallas Republican activist Sally McKenzie said, "We all worked our souls out" for Goldwater. "Every bit of that went down the tubes the day that Jack Kennedy was killed in Dallas. I had just finished a door-to-door canvass in my precinct. I went in that night, not that I was being disrespectful of a deceased president, and just tore up the records. It was futile after that."[79]

Goldwater's propensity for "shooting from the hip" provided further fodder for those characterizing him as "trigger-happy." If his promise to grant jurisdiction over tactical nuclear weapons to American command-ers in the field did not scare away voters, his assertion that such weap-ons could be used to defoliate the jungles of Vietnam did.[80] In the final weeks of the campaign Goldwater attempted to remove what O'Don-nell called the "atomic thorn in his heel" with more appeals to law and order. But the "trigger-happy bit," one Dallas conservative Republican noted, hurt Goldwater among American voters. "We had a public rela-tions image hung on us like a dead cat."[81]

With Kennedy's assassination, Lyndon Johnson, a master politician, ascended to the presidency, armed with both a singular understanding of Congress and a mandate to secure his fallen predecessor's legislative program. While Johnson's legislative record had been the most liberal in the nation's history, many Dallasites, Texans, and Americans in the fall of 1964 still regarded the tall Texan as more moderate than his slain predecessor. In a shrewd gesture calculated to garner broad bipartisan support, reinforce his image of steady moderation, and avoid backlash, Johnson identified the 1964 Civil Rights Act as more of a legislative pri-ority for the slain president than for himself. Goldwater, now facing a popular president from Texas instead of an incumbent from Massa-chusetts, was never fully able to execute the Southern Strategy in 1964. Moreover, the assassination had dampened his enthusiasm for the campaign. Goldwater liked Kennedy personally and had relished the op-portunity to run against him.[82] The decision to exclude F. Clifton White and Peter O'Donnell from the campaign also proved unwise. Denison Kitchel, Dean Burch, and Richard Kleindienst—the "Arizona Mafia"— lacked their predecessors' experience, discretion, and organizational wizardry. In the final analysis, Goldwater's running mate, William Miller, probably summed up the election results best: "The American people were just not in the mood to assassinate two Presidents in one year."[83]

Kennedy's assassination contributed to the debacle of the Dallas Republican Party in 1964. All eight Dallas Republicans in the Texas leg-islature were ousted, and Bruce Alger lost his bid for reelection to Con-gress to Democrat Earle Cabell. To be sure, Cabell was a well-financed candidate, a popular mayor who rode the coattails of a president from Texas. Moreover, Cabell made a strong case against Alger's effectiveness as a congressman. Ultimately, the revival of Alger's ultraconservatism—

what many regarded as extremism, especially with Goldwater on the ballot—combined with his Dallas constituents' concern for the city's shattered image, were the most important factors in his defeat.

Alger had modulated his ultraconservative image following the Adolphus incident, but his flirtation with distancing himself from far-right organizations and ideas did not last long. Alger's speeches in 1962 and 1963 contained secular apocalyptic overtones. In his self-proclaimed "one-man campaign against John F. Kennedy," he attacked the administration's distribution of federal money to the nation's cities, calling it a "sure step toward the end of free elections." Aping Senator Joseph McCarthy's 1950 speech in Wheeling, West Virginia, Alger addressed the Petroleum Engineers' Club of Dallas and declared that he held in his hand fifty-five indictments charging the Kennedy administration with coddling Communists. On other occasions, Alger averred that the president was moving the country "closer to dictatorship" and that "the nation cannot survive another four years of the New Frontier policies."[84]

This renewed, more militant ultraconservatism, manifested just as Dallas's image throughout the world was tarnished by the murder of a president, contributed to Alger's loss in 1964. Murdered by Jack Ruby, Lee Harvey Oswald never had his day in court, but Dallas, as A. C. Greene observed, promptly went "on trial."[85] In the days, weeks, and months after the assassination, newspaper and magazine editors descended upon Dallas to dissect its identity and often drew hasty and simplistic conclusions. The outside appraisals, on the whole, concluded that the city of Dallas was culturally bereft, politically autocratic, and socially bankrupt.

Although President Kennedy's killer was a Marxist who had lived in Dallas for only two months, many columnists concluded that the city and its right wing had created an environment that contributed to the assassination.[86] An article in *Fortune* referred to Dallas as the "hate capital of the nation," "a place so steeped in violence and political extremism that school children would cheer the president's death." One newspaper observed, "The hatred preachers got their man. They did not shoot him. They inspired the man who shot him." Another noted that "Mr. Kennedy had prepared a speech which . . . reminded the people of Dallas that . . . America's leadership must be guided by the lights of learning and reason. . . . Dallas's answer, even before that speech was delivered, was to shoot John F. Kennedy."[87] Along with resurrecting the Adolphus and Stevenson incidents, some journalists concluded that the centralized structure of Dallas's Citizens Council inhibited discussion, discouraged dissent, and restricted the intellectual and cultural activity essential to a thriving metropolis.[88] Although many city leaders argued that the assassination "could have happened anywhere," Congressman Alger was the most doctrinaire and hostile in attacking the news media for suggesting that Dallas itself was to blame.[89]

With the city's image under siege, the business community divided its support between Cabell and Alger. Alger garnered support from the oilman Jake Hamon, Dresser Industries' H. N. Mallon, Sun Oil's Tom Hill, and Lone Star Steel's E. B. Germany, while Cabell had the solid backing of the downtown Dallas establishment, including Robert L. Thornton (who founded the Citizens Council), the retailer Stanley Marcus, and John M. Stemmons. In the final analysis, enough business leaders came to the following conclusion: since the federal government already meddled in the life of the city—from civil rights to defense appropriations—Dallas might as well benefit and secure federal money to connect the Trinity River to the Gulf of Mexico, construct a downtown Federal Center, and undertake other projects that would move the city forward. Given concerns over the effect of the city's image on future growth, it made little sense for Dallas leaders to stick with an intractable libertarian ideologue who had come to personify an extremism that frightened the country and appeared to bring out the worst in people.

The assassination also revivified the Democratic Party in Dallas County. Within three months of the tragedy, the North Dallas Democrats, the first local organization working for Democrats on all rungs of the party hierarchy since 1948, was formed. Bill Clark, chairman of the Dallas County Democrats, adopted many of the organizational strategies that Peter O'Donnell had pioneered. Enthusiastic Democratic volunteers went door-to-door and called from numerous phone banks urging Dallasites to vote Democratic, "from the White House to the Court House."[90] Another important factor in Alger's defeat was African-American turnout, which reached 85 percent in some precincts. With Lyndon Johnson committed to the cause of civil rights more vigorously than any predecessor (or successor), thirty-two thousand Dallas black voters chose a straight Democratic ticket; the Democratic proportion of victory in some black precincts was 119 to 1.

Indeed, between 1952 and 1964 the flight of African-Americans from the Republican Party amounted to a seismic shift, and the Dallas Republican Party illustrated that trajectory in microcosm. In 1952, 44 percent of African-American voters nationwide supported Dwight Eisenhower for president, and two years later 67 percent of African-American voters in Dallas County supported Bruce Alger for congressman. But in 1964, only 6 percent of African-American voters nationwide supported Barry Goldwater for president, and locally only 2.4 percent supported Alger.[91]

The Dallas Republican Party's loss of the African-American vote was no fleeting anomaly. Jim Collins, the son of Carr P. Collins and an unsuccessful 1966 GOP congressional candidate from Dallas, performed about as well as Alger had in African-African precincts two years earlier. Despite national Republican chairman Ray Bliss's optimistic appraisal that Collins's support among blacks was "sensational," that it had "exceeded his fondest expectations," and that it showed that blacks were returning to the Republican Party, the actual results in Dallas were nothing for Republicans to celebrate, rising an infinitesimal 0.8 percent to 3.2 percent.[92] Speaking to a Dallas audience in 1968, Richard G. Hatcher, the newly elected black mayor of Gary, Indiana, said that "the Republican Party has in effect turned its back on the black people of this country." The GOP simply did not want black votes, he concluded. The Reverend Ralph Abernathy echoed Hatcher, adding that the 1968 Republican platform and the ticket of Richard Nixon and Spiro T. Agnew "are not an inspiration to black voters."[93]

Despite Alger's and Goldwater's thumping at the polls, they left an important legacy: they had made the case that there was a place for segregationists and states' rights advocates in the Republican Party.[94] Foreshadowing a bright future for the conservative movement, over a million men and women contributed money to Goldwater's campaign in 1964, whereas Richard Nixon had received contributions from only forty-four thousand in 1960.[95] After signing the 1964 Civil Rights bill into law, President Lyndon Johnson told an aide, "I think we just gave the South to the Republicans for your lifetime and mine."[96] Yet Johnson's prognostication was only partially correct. Johnson had given the Deep South another reason to vote against the Democratic Party, but Goldwater gave the region a candidate who was on their side. One Republican from South Carolina expressed the view of many in the region when he observed that although Barry Goldwater was a Westerner, he "could pass for a great Southerner any time, any place."[97] But along with the discovery of a candidate, it took the precedent of Dallas-based, segregationist ultraconservatives like Bruce Alger, John Tower, Jack Cox, Maurice Carlson, and Peter O'Donnell to lay the groundwork for Goldwater's run in 1964 and to demonstrate that national Republicans could finally "whistle Dixie."

Taking Stock, Tacking Leftward

After Dallas Republicans suffered one of the most calamitous losses of any GOP stronghold in the country, the likes of Frank Crowley, Maurice Carlson, Peter O'Donnell, and John Tower led a drive, both locally and nationally, to temper the party's message and tone. Born in Dallas in 1924, Crowley graduated from North Dallas High School in 1941, matriculated at Notre Dame, and served in the Pacific Theater as a first lieutenant in Admiral "Bull" Halsey's renowned Task Force 38. After World War II, Crowley worked as Bruce Alger's "right hand" in Washington, DC, before becoming the second Republican county commissioner ever elected from Dallas County. While Alger was dour, intense, and dogmatic, Crowley was affable, pliant, and eager to please. Running for reelection in 1964, he earned the nickname "the unsinkable." In the months after "the Democrats had beaten the daylights out of them," as the *Dallas Morning News* put it, the gregarious Crowley struck a tone of levity that was welcome in a despondent GOP that was wondering where to turn.

Calling himself "the lone survivor of the Lusitania," Crowley soon became a sought-after advisor on the question of what the party needed to do to win.[98] After distributing "survival kits" to his colleagues at a Dallas GOP gathering in January 1965, he cautioned against both pessimism and dogmatism. He submitted that the party needed to jettison "some of the louder advocates in the party." More important, he admonished the party for conceding large segments of voters—"specifically minority groups"—to the Democrats.[99] In the mid-1960s, Crowley secured the speaking services of Clarence Townes Jr., a black leader in Virginia's Republican Party. Before the Dallas Downtown Republican Women's Club, Townes urged that the party abandon the rhetoric of states' rights because it had cost Goldwater too many black votes. "You just can't ask the Negro to buy that in places like Mississippi," Townes said. Former Republican county chairman Maurice Carlson made essentially the same point. Just prior to Goldwater's defeat, Carlson had contended, "We need leaders who realize that the Republican Party whistling Dixie and marching through Mississippi and Louisiana under the rebel flag urging the restoration of slavery" will only bring defeat.[100]

Peter O'Donnell, with his flexible and discerning mind for political realities, was in complete agreement: the Republican Party needed to revise its extremist image. Having become GOP chairman for the twelve Southern and border states in 1965, O'Donnell called reelecting John Tower to the Senate "the number one goal in 1966."[101] With this aim in mind, he attempted to neutralize the legacy of the Goldwater campaign's extremism by endorsing a formal GOP Policy Committee resolution that rejected such "radical or extremist organization[s]" as the John Birch Society. Following the advice of Crowley, O'Donnell also made it patently clear that such Southern demagogues as George Wallace, whose campaigns for the presidency combined flag-waving, populism, and overt racial appeals, were not welcome in the Dallas or the Texas Republican Party: "Wallace was tearing the country apart. Not only is he pitting race against race, but lower levels of education, income, [and jobs] against persons having higher standards in these groups."[102]

If the consensus among party leaders was that moderation was the necessary path for the late 1960s and early 1970s, the question of exactly how to temper the message remained. O'Donnell's aversion to racial demagoguery did not mean that he encouraged outright abandonment of race as an issue. On the contrary, he exhorted Republicans that "it's up to us to exploit" the issue of civil rights.[103] Reflecting broader trends in the trajectory of the national party, many Dallas Republicans co-opted the message and the language of the civil rights struggle to free themselves from unpopularity and political oblivion.[104]

The Politics of Decency

Like many Republican political leaders nationwide, many Dallas moderate conservative Republicans now acknowledged that, at the very least, the party had been on the wrong side of history in the struggle for civil rights. Many abandoned arguments for white supremacy and claims that the 1964 Civil Rights Act violated property rights, adopting instead an ostensibly color-blind strategy that embraced, at least rhetorically, equality for all. Liberals remonstrated that in practice this meant fighting the "reverse discrimination" of the Equal Rights Amendment, affirmative action, public housing, busing, and benefits that disproportionately affected African-Americans. Conservative Republicans in Dallas and nationwide, liberals averred, simply reversed the liberal argument for fairness and argued that these products of the 1964 Civil Rights Act denied the civil rights of white males.[105] As one white Dallasite said of busing, "It is the broadest abuse of my rights."[106] The *Dallas Morning News* helped to codify and encourage the new rhetoric of fairness, observing in an editorial that "'affirmative action' was a form of reverse racism." The *News* argued against the imposition of racial quotas in hiring practices because they "[could] cause as many injustices as they eliminate."[107] According to the *News*, "busing causes social disruptions that in themselves are detrimental to the goal" of quality education for all. According to detractors, the new strategy attempted to safeguard for a select few the very privileges that it publically promised to all.[108] The rhetoric of color-blind inclusion had as its overriding purpose, or at least led to, continued barriers to the complete participation of women and African-Americans in the civic life of the nation.

Along with some national Republicans, Dallas Republicans Alan Steelman and John Tower proved adept at employing the language of civil rights to safeguard benefits for the privileged and to extend their base throughout Texas. First elected in 1972, Steelman was a Dallas congressman who demonstrated a mastery of color-blind rhetoric. "We are going to put an end to discrimination," he announced, but "I am opposed to busing."[109] Tower co-opted the rhetoric of the civil rights movement in a forceful attack on an open-housing provision of the Civil Rights Act of 1966. He "deplored prejudice and bigotry in any form," he affirmed. "I am in favor of equality of opportunity in housing for all people."[110] Similarly, in regard to busing, Tower opined that "freedom of choice, when it was practiced as the old 'separate-but-equal doctrine,' was an intolerable suffering. It was disallowed for that reason. Real freedom of choice in a school system that equalizes opportunity remains the best principle."[111] Using language resembling that of civil rights activists of the early 1960s, Tower in 1971 declared forced busing wrong because people of any "race, creed, or color should be treated equally." In 1975, he called the practice "immoral, undemocratic, [and] inherently racist."[112]

During the presidential elections of 1968 and 1972, Republican Richard Nixon merged this color-blind rhetoric of civil rights with a "law and order" discourse. His electoral strategy appealed to the "forgotten Americans" suffering the consequences of rising crime rates and lacking access to affirmative action or public housing. According to Nixon, this "silent majority" of middle-class suburban home owners paid their taxes, mowed their lawns, funded their neighborhood schools, and comported themselves with propriety, and thus deserved safer communities and freedom from forced busing. Nixon called for "greater opportunity for all Americans, justice for all, renewed respect for law, and peaceful resolution of conflicts that mar society."[113] This rhetoric proved more effective than it had in 1964 because the continual barrage of race riots and student protests that appeared on televisions across America in the intervening years had exacerbated middle-class suburban anxieties about violent crime and societal breakdown. National Republicans charged that Democrats and liberals were the real extremists. Incessant violence revealed the limitations of liberalism: the Democrats' solutions to the chaos consisted solely of more government programs, and since these policies were seen as having produced the breakdown in the first place, it was easy for those who opposed them to argue for the moral bankruptcy of liberal ideology.[114]

As Nixon demonstrated, color-blind rhetoric played far better with suburbanites than overt claims of white supremacy or Goldwater's tirades against the 1964 Civil Rights Act as an infringement of property rights. Middle-class suburbanites, not just in Dallas County but throughout the United States, could embrace its affinity for home ownership, neighborhood schools, residential class distinctions, minimal diversity, and a new focus on the rights of taxpayers. By the late 1960s, racial demagoguery was unsettling to such voters, but they would not tolerate anybody encroaching on rights to which they felt entitled. The political advantage of this discourse, then, was that, while preserving the rights and privileges that had long been a priority for the white businessmen and professionals in the Republican Party, it cast a wider net and secured a new set of suburban voters for the GOP in the 1960s and 1970s.[115]

"Color-blind" rhetoric, with its claims of reverse discrimination, proved palatable to working-class white men throughout the country who, having enjoyed bountiful employment opportunities during the years when segregation was legal and women did not compete alongside them in the workplace, had come to see a pathway to the middle class through employment as a birthright. In disproportion to women and black men, white men had enjoyed, become accustomed to receiving, and used as a springboard to a better life benefits like college education (in many cases financed through the GI Bill). Many were amenable to the argument that affirmative action and other policies threatened their access to these advantages and thus constituted reverse discrimination.[116]

Having adopted color-blind language, Dallas Republicans increasingly appealed to Mexican-Americans in the late 1960s and 1970s. More than any other GOP politician of his era, John Tower attempted to attract Mexican-Americans into the party. He succeeded beyond anybody's expectations. Stressing, during his successful 1966 reelection campaign, that the ethnocultural heritage of Mexican Americans was consonant with GOP values, Tower received the support of the League of United Latin American Citizens (LULAC) and other Mexican-American organizations in South and Central Texas. Unfulfilled promises made by the Democratic Party to this growing cohort of the Texas population contributed to his strong showing of 40 percent of the Mexican-American vote in 1966. Disenchanted with the conservative wing of the Democratic Party and their lack of access to the institutional structure in Democratic politics, Tejanos por Tower and Mexican-American Republicans of Texas (MART) backed Tower in 1972. That year, Tower did even better with Mexican-American voters and received 45 percent.[117]

The new color-blind strategy proved a boon to Republican candidates. First, using rhetoric that incorporated the language of civil rights allowed elected officials to appear nondiscriminatory in their present actions. The career of Jim Collins provides a case in point. Collins, who had run unsuccessfully for Congress in 1966, been elected in 1968 as a moderate Dallas conservative, and began to take on ultraconservative positions once in office, said in 1970, "Most parents do not oppose busing because of racial animosity, but because they believe in the concept of the neighborhood school—an educational tradition of this nation."[118] On another occasion, he introduced a "Freedom from Quotas" bill, which aimed to prohibit affirmative action under the Civil Rights Act of 1964.[119] According to Collins, quotas were repugnant because they discriminated "on the basis of race, color, religion, or sex."[120] The fact that some African-Americans subscribed to color-blind rhetoric and converted to the GOP legitimated such individual denials of prejudice. Second, color-blind rhetoric offered politicians a clever, if cynical, way to gloss over their own histories of aligning themselves with voices of intolerance and "standing at the schoolhouse door" in resistance to a more egalitarian world.[121] Speaking to Dallas Republicans in 1970, Frances Fairbanks of Colorado, the first African-American to head a State Federation of Republican Women, epitomized this assault on memory when she offered this revisionist view of her party: "From the beginning . . . the Republican Party has stood for fair employment and equal rights."[122] Third, beyond sanitizing their own pasts, conservative Republicans could act as if the broader national legacy of injustice toward people of color did not exist, as if the present were a "clean slate" and an even playing field existed for all Americans, obviating any need for redistributive policies.

A final advantage to denouncing affirmative action, low-income housing, and busing—and labeling them reverse discrimination—was the impact this rhetoric had on conservative attitudes. Such language stoked antipathy toward a range of entitlement programs born during the New Deal, the Fair Deal, the New Frontier, and the Great Society. The result was resentment toward government programs that provided succor in old age as well as protections for workers and safeguards against indigence.[123]

The color-blind language of civil rights was not only a rhetorical strategy; it both reflected and accommodated a new political reality. Throughout the long civil rights era, some conservative and ultraconservative Republicans in Dallas and across the country were changing their hearts and minds about race. Many Republicans softened their positions and tone on matters of race and civil rights, some even regretting past opposition to desegregation and other causes of social justice. Ironically, during the late 1960s and 1970s—when Catholics like Frank Crowley and Fred Agnich were running the Dallas Republican Party—the most important confession from a Dallas Republican came from a Baptist minister, W. A. Criswell. Criswell, who in 1956 had assailed the *Brown v. Board of Education* decision as a "denial of all that we believe in," reversed course in 1968 and called his former position a "colossal mistake." "I have enlarged my sympathies and my heart during the past few years," he said. Moderate segregationists likely discerned that Criswell's transformation on race and his powerful new role as president of the Southern Baptist Convention did not bode well for their cause. Yet his new stance did indeed augur well for the color-blind doctrine.[124]

Criswell's most famous congregant, Billy Graham, and the neo-Pentecostal or charismatic movement of the 1960s helped forge a softer color-blind discourse. Discouraging the adoption of any more civil rights laws, Graham argued that the federal government had already done what it could on race. Along with disparaging those who wanted the courts to intervene more directly on questions of civil rights, Graham observed that only individual competition in the marketplace and personal spiritual renewal through Christ would extirpate the last vestiges of racial prejudice. Only Christian love, not government coercion, could create a postracial America.[125]

If Graham pioneered the color-blind doctrine among religious leaders, the neo-Pentecostal or charismatic movement boosted its viability and credibility. The charismatic movement grew popular in the 1960s among the middle and upper-middle classes in Northern Texas and throughout many entrepreneurial communities of the Southwest. Charismatics held that the gifts of the Holy Spirit—speaking in tongues, faith healing, and prophecy—were extended not only to the first Christians but to present-day Christians as well. Previously, Assemblies of God churches had had a monopoly on glossalia, or the spiritual gift of speaking in tongues, but many charismatics remained in their Baptist, Presbyterian, or Episcopal denominations. Charismatics fostered the color-blind doctrine by extending their personal morality to the wider world and working to attack poverty and racism.[126] Championing the therapeutic powers of the Holy Spirit, Pat Robertson was one of the most successful charismatic messengers in the 1970s. With a commercial station in Dallas by 1973, Robertson's Christian Broadcasting Network stressed God's ability to cure not only individual illness but the country's racial divide.[127]

In part because color-blind language sometimes did represent an earnest change of heart on the question of race, claims that Democrats and Republicans "essentially switched positions on civil rights issues"—the latter adopting racial conservatism and the former supporting civil rights—overstate the historical record.[128] Some Republicans, in Dallas and nationwide, expressed genuine remorse for their former failure to embrace the cause of the civil rights movement. Moreover, liberal and moderate Republicans from the North and the Midwest often resisted the racial conservatism of southern GOP campaigns in the early 1960s. For instance, congressional Republicans like Everett Dirksen were instrumental in passing the Civil Rights Act of 1964 and the Voting Rights Act of 1965—the most important civil rights legislation of the twentieth century. Finally, the Democratic Party continued to field successful segregationist candidates well into the late 1960s, as the gubernatorial elections of Alabama's Lurleen Wallace and Georgia's Lester Maddox attest. "Backlash politics was still fluid," observed historian Joseph Crespino, "not the domain of any one party."[129]

On the other hand, there is compelling evidence that the GOP was abandoning, albeit not completely, its heritage as the party of Radical Reconstruction, Abraham Lincoln, and black male suffrage and office-holding. In their campaigns, GOP liberals and moderates never matched the unity and coordination of Republican racial conservatives. Moreover, blacks largely abandoned their support for GOP presidential candidates in 1964 and have never returned to the party.

GOP racial conservatism not only accounted for black opposition but contributed greatly to white southern support for Republican presidential candidates, also by 1964.[130] As this book has shown, the GOP Southern Strategy was more explicitly racial in motivation and implementation than historians have understood. Dallas's lasting legacy is its contribution to developing that strategy for the national Republican Party: Bruce Alger's decision to "play the race card" gave rise to a strategy that was honed by O'Donnell, embraced by other Dallas Republicans, and bequeathed to the national party by 1964.

Republicans' use of color-blind discourse as a political strategy for holding onto an ultraconservative and segregationist base without alienating moderates makes a strong case that the GOP was, at the very least, moving away from being the party of Lincoln. Having tested the more extreme ideological waters of Dallas, the national GOP went on to refine its Southern Strategy, fine-tuning its image and message to appear increasingly inclusive. The resounding losses Senator Goldwater and Congressman Alger experienced in 1964 convinced Peter O'Donnell, Republican county commissioner Frank Crowley, and Maurice Carlson that the older stratagem of thinly veiled appeals to right-wing and racist sentiments would no longer work. In place of antiquated arguments invoking states' rights, the defense of racial hierarchies, and property rights, a color-blind language of justice for all emerged. The party tailored its appeal to those who formerly identified themselves as workers or members of ethnic or faith-based groups (including Catholics and, to a lesser extent, Jews). Conservative Republicans in Dallas and nationwide embraced the new color-blind message and co-opted the liberal argument for fairness, contending that affirmative action, public housing, busing, and other products of the 1964 Civil Rights Act denied the civil rights of middle-class white people. Thus while publically promising privileges to all, the color-blind strategy actually protected the benefits already claimed by the privileged.

Epilogue: Revival

Dallas's Reunion Arena, home to the Dallas Mavericks basketball team, was a fitting location for the annual meeting of the iconoclastic Religious Roundtable. On August 21, 1980, Ronald Reagan, the Republican presidential nominee, addressed fifteen thousand people there. The roundtable's founder, James Robison, a Dallas-based Baptist preacher, was among the most prominent representatives of a new generation of conservative evangelical Christians who were abandoning their long-standing reluctance to become involved in politics. W. A. Criswell, Jerry Falwell, and Pat Robertson also sat on the main stage next to Reagan. President Jimmy Carter, himself an evangelical Christian, had declined an invitation to the nonpartisan event.

Robison spoke immediately before Governor Reagan, declaring that "not voting is a sin against Almighty God!" Robison testified to those assembled that he was "sick and tired about hearing about all the radicals and the perverts and the liberals and the Communists coming out of the closet! It's time for God's people to come out of the closet, out of the churches, and save America!"[1] Reagan won the day when, following Robison, he declared, "I know you can't endorse me because this is a nonpartisan meeting, but I endorse you." Reagan had made an emotional appeal to the Christian Right. He went on to compare the persecution that Jesus Christ predicted for all Christians with the state in which his audience found itself, "persecuted together by Democrats and liberals."[2] But he brought down the house when he said of the Bible, "All the complex and horrendous questions confronting us have their answer in that single book." Robison later said that on the day Reagan was elected president, "God gave us grace."[3]

The influence of ultraconservatism had ebbed in Dallas in the years after the Goldwater rout, but a new contingent of ultraconservative evangelical Republicans concerned with promiscuity, pornography, homosexuality, and drug use arrived on the scene and had a significant influence on local, state, and national GOP politics after 1976.[4] To be sure, increased engagement in political activities among evangelical Christians was a national phenomenon, but politically ultraconservative evangelicals from Dallas were central to igniting this trend. Most evangelical Christians had not encouraged participation in politics since the 1920s, emphasizing the importance of personal salvation over political action. Against this backdrop, the political engagement of W. A. Criswell in the 1950s had been groundbreaking, and now, in the 1980s, many evangelical Christians were beginning to place a higher priority on political reform. They were now a larger, more coherent movement and had formed their own institutions. The profligacy of the counterculture, the greater frequency of abortions, a decline in church attendance, and swelling divorce rates impelled many evangelical Christians in Dallas and across the nation to become more active in GOP politics.[5] The Supreme Court's decision in *Roe v. Wade*, a case filed in Dallas, beckoned even more evangelicals to join the ranks of a Republican Party that was increasingly committed to anti-abortion platforms.[6]

At the start of the 1970s, there was little indication that evangelical Christians—in Dallas or nationwide—would turn to politics with greater interest. Reflecting the introspective ethos of the time, evangelical Christians in Dallas gave more attention to activities that promoted spiritual growth and saving one soul at a time. In the 1970s, Dallas's bulging suburbs increasingly became home to evangelical Christians who attended the numerous megachurches dotting the region. Building churches, witnessing to potential members, and engaging in missionary activity all trumped championing political causes or electing candidates to office. In June 1972, at least a hundred thousand young people attended Explo '72 in Dallas. Sponsored by Bill Bright's Campus Crusade for Christ and called the "Christian Woodstock" or "Godstock," the event drew many young evangelicals, including a future Arkansas governor, Mike Huckabee. Attendees took part in evangelical training sessions, listened to sermons from Billy Graham, and danced to music from Johnny Cash, Larry Norman, Kris Kristofferson, and others. While approximately 75 percent of those attending identified themselves as politically conservative, they were far more interested in saving souls than the world.

A best-selling book from 1970, *The Late Great Planet Earth* by Dallas Theological Seminary graduate Hal Lindsey, inspired the event's name, which conjured up images of fiery destruction and illustrated the evangelical Christian focus in the early 1970s on personal salvation rather than political reform. There was little point in engaging in politics when one was living through the earth's last days. Jesus Christ's imminent return made the obvious priority saving as many souls as possible before the Rapture of his church.[7]

Francis Schaefer was central in bringing about the most significant return of evangelical Christians to politics since the 1920s. In 1976, Schaefer wrote *How Should We Then Live*, explicitly arguing that proliferating pornography, accelerating abortion rates, the prohibition of prayer in public school, and other examples of "secular humanism" were the work of Satan on earth. It was the mission of evangelical Christians to save the country from Satan by taking back their government.[8] But Schaefer was a reclusive intellectual theologian living on a mountaintop in Switzerland. His clarion call would not have been distributed so extensively without an infusion of oil money from the Dallas-based Hunt family. While H. L. Hunt had largely disappeared from public view by the early 1970s, his son Nelson Bunker Hunt had become politically vocal. After helping make Explo '72 possible through a generous infusion of funds, the rotund international oilman bankrolled a documentary film adaptation of *How Should We Then Live*. A phenomenal success, the film convinced thousands of evangelical Christians that a culture war was afoot and they had an obligation to take the fight to Satan by abandoning any past reluctance to engage in politics.[9]

Taking a cue from Schaefer, politically conservative evangelical leaders like Jerry Falwell, Tim LaHaye, and Pat Robertson grew increasingly willing to become involved in political affairs in the late 1970s.[10] Always more open to engaging political issues than his contemporaries, W. A. Criswell eagerly spoke out on such secular matters as the Equal Rights Amendment (ERA), homosexuality, and evolution. He led the purge of liberal and moderate factions in the Southern Baptist Convention and stepped up his involvement in GOP politics as well. Likely comforted by

President Gerald Ford's close relationship with Francis Schaefer, who Garry Wills called the president's "own private Billy Graham," Criswell endorsed Ford in 1976.[11] In 1980, Criswell would support Ronald Reagan for president. By the end of the 1970s, the rising popularity of Dallas-based James Robison—a handsome and fiery Baptist preacher who vilified feminists and the movements for women's and homosexual rights—evinced a growing contentiousness among the Christian Right in Dallas.[12] H. L. Hunt praised Robison as "the most effective communicator I have ever heard." In 1979, Robison called the assassination of Harvey Milk, the openly gay member of San Francisco's board of supervisors, God's punishment. "A homosexual is in the same class with a rapist, a bank robber, or a murderer," he said.[13] Robison gained national headlines when his Dallas radio station, WFAA, took him off the air for his inflammatory diatribes against homosexuals. Jerry Falwell, one of the founders of the Moral Majority, which fostered evangelical political activism, rushed to his aid, calling him "the prophet of God for our day" and vowing, "We will die for our right to preach." Having become increasingly interested in politics since his show's cancellation, Robison became executive director of the Religious Roundtable, a more ecumenical counterpart to the Moral Majority, albeit with many of the same leaders. Its executive board included Jerry Falwell, Pat Robertson, and W. A. Criswell.

Conservative evangelicals in Dallas were well represented throughout the late 1970s by Republican congressman Jim Collins, who had drifted into the ultraconservative camp since his election in 1968. Nelson Bunker Hunt and his half-brother Ray Hunt were major donors to Collins and helped him earn a $160,000 profit by encouraging Collins to buy silver when Nelson and another brother, William Herbert Hunt, were attempting to corner the global market for this commodity in the late 1970s. In his early years in Congress, Collins employed the color-blind language that was winning over moderate conservative voters, but soon his rhetoric became not only ultraconservative but also full of (secular) doomsday scenarios. Denouncing the nation's growing deficit and moral decline, he predicted that "if we don't get a balance in this country in ten years, we will turn this country into a socialist nation."[14] His father, Carr Collins, had convinced Dallas laymen to bring Criswell to their city. One of the first congressmen to introduce a constitutional amendment to allow voluntary prayer in public schools, Collins's main preoccupation throughout his legislative career was ending the practice of forced busing, which he provocatively called "a form of slavery, if there ever was one."[15] Unlike many national and local men and women of the Right who, whether for political, personal, or other reasons, embraced the civil rights movement as a necessary social movement, by the end of the 1970s Collins was portraying it as a national tragedy.[16] In the early 1980s, Collins opposed the extension of the 1965 Voting Rights Act because, according to him, "it constituted the most significant federal intervention in the South since Reconstruction."[17]

Evangelical Christians were not the only source of conservative Republican support throughout North Texas in the 1970s. Socially conservative Catholics and economically conservative Republicans also embraced positions that boded well for Reagan in 1980. In 1970, Frederick Wilhelmson, a Catholic professor of philosophy at the University of Dallas and a member of the Sons of Thunder, which advocated civil disobedience to protest abortion rights, organized students to break into a Dallas Planned Parenthood office. When the Dallas police arrested Wilhelmson and his students, they were praying their rosaries and holding signs reading "Viva il Papa" and "Stop Fascist Genocide." While using tactics more militant than many in the pro-life movement, Wilhelmson and his students embodied the passion that many on the Republican Right brought to the abortion debate.[18]

While some professors fought abortion, others agitated for fiscal fitness. Before running successfully for Congress, Richard "Dick" Armey, a professor of economics at North Texas State from 1972 to 1983, impressed upon many of his students the virtues of the free market. In particular, he championed economist James M. Buchanan's public choice theory, which rejected the concept of the public interest as a farce and held that government bureaucrats would always accrue power for their own gain. Armey also touted Austrian-school intellectual Ludwig von Mises's economic ideas, which left little room for government intervention. Mises himself was no stranger to North Texas. After leaving the presidency of the University of Dallas, Robert Morris established the University of Plano in the late 1960s and recruited Mises as a visiting scholar.[19]

The activities of these North Texas activists dovetailed with resurgent conservative activism on the national stage in the 1970s. The decade saw the foundation of new conservative intellectual organizations that decried the nation's sordid culture and weak economy. Catholic Phyllis Schlafly, already popular among Goldwater supporters for her best-selling tract *A Choice Not an Echo*, combatted the Equal Rights Amendment by founding STOP ERA. The amendment, she argued, would end long-standing traditions like female exemption from the military draft. With financial support from Colorado's Joseph Coors, scion of his family's brewing business, and Pittsburgh's Richard Mellon Scaife, successor to the Mellon fortune, Paul Weyrich, a conservative Catholic from Wisconsin, formed the Heritage Foundation. Other contributors to the spread of conservative economic ideas in the 1970s included Robert Bartley's *Wall Street Journal* and the Business Roundtable, comprising the nation's top CEOs.[20]

With these organizations and institutions infusing conservatism with new energy and legitimacy on a national scale, Dallas Republicans were buoyed in 1978 by the election of the first Republican Texas governor since Reconstruction, and set their sights on winning back the White House. Rita Bass's second husband, Bill Clements (a Dallasite and moderate conservative Republican), won the gubernatorial election in 1978 by appealing to evangelicals and with the support of Ronald Reagan, who had won 67 percent of the vote in the 1976 Texas Republican primary. In 1980, Reagan courted evangelicals throughout Texas, paying special attention to Dallas and making the city a centerpiece for his Reagan Revolution.[21] In the summer of 1980, the Reagan campaign made half a million pro-Reagan brochures available to the fifteen thousand evangelicals attending a Christian bookselling convention in Dallas.[22] Reagan's August 1980 endorsement of the Religious Roundtable's activities helped him gain the support of the religious Right, which became an important member of the coalition in his landslide victory in November.

Having reached its apogee in GOP politics, Dallas hosted the Republican National Convention in 1984. Prominent among the factors that had improved Dallas's image since the Kennedy assassination and made this event possible were the city's winning football team and its TV presence. The Dallas Cowboys were "America's team" thanks to their success on the field, which included five Super Bowl appearances and a pair of championships during the 1970s, and the national popularity of such icons as Tom Landry and Roger Staubach—both outspoken Republican conservatives and Reagan backers. The city, or at least its TV incarnation, had also become familiar to a nation that was captivated by the devilish antics of J. R. Ewing, the lead character of the country's most popular television program in the early 1980s, *Dallas*.

W. A. Criswell's sermons at the 1984 Republican Convention and at his church on the following Sunday powerfully demonstrated evangelical Christians' commitment to politics. Criswell—whose biblical defense of segregation in 1956 had influenced Bruce Alger and had wider implications for the future GOP—delivered the benediction after President Reagan accepted the Republican nomination for the second time. On the Sunday after his benediction, Criswell spoke at First Baptist Church on the subject of homosexuality: "In our lifetime we are scoffing at the word of God . . . and opening up society and culture to the lesbian and sodomite and homosexual . . . and now we have this disastrous judgment . . . the disease and sin of AIDS."[23] This trenchant antigay rhetoric evoked the harsh racist tirades that proliferated before color-blind discourse displaced it in Dallas Republican circles. Like one of J. R. Ewing's unscrupulous deals or the Dallas Cowboys' "Doomsday Defense," the vituperative rhetoric of the Dallas ultraconservatives in the 1950s and 1960s had its intended effect: to shock and awe.

The shrill rhetoric of "Nut Country" reverberates today throughout many regions of America. In scenes that reminded David Broder of the maltreatment of Lyndon Johnson and his wife at the Adolphus Hotel in 1960, angry Tea Party protesters in 2009 hurled racist and antigay slurs at members of Congress in town hall meetings and lambasted President Barack Obama's healthcare reform as "socialized medicine."[24] Some congressmen received death threats. The congressional district of Gabrielle Giffords appeared in the crosshairs of a rifle scope in a campaign ad. While there is no indication that the would-be assassin who later shot Giffords was motivated by the propaganda, the campaign material certainly did not contribute to a healthy political discourse.

Many Americans today avidly embrace the conspiracism of "Nut Country." Between Barry Goldwater's loss in 1964 and his own death in 2008, William F. Buckley Jr. checked the far right's predilection for conspiracy theory.[25] Today, however, Republican leaders patronize Tea Party rallies that warn of President Obama's plan to implement martial law. The shock jocks of conservative talk radio—Glenn Beck and Michael Savage—fire up their daily listeners with conspiracy-tinged explanations of contemporary events. Birthers, who are convinced that Obama was born in Kenya rather than Hawaii, heartened the Republican Party, which after its success in the 2010 midterm elections grew even more intransigent in its commitment to obstruct Obama's inaugural call for a "new era of responsibility" and postpartisanship.

Today's far right embraces absolutism and opposes any efforts to find middle ground. Braced by newly elected members affiliated with the Tea Party, congressional Republicans in 2011 refused to raise the debt limit (a long-standing formality) unless the president agreed to deep spending cuts. The country narrowly prevented an unprecedented default on government bonds and the accompanying economic implications when Congress reached an agreement. As of 2014, many far-right Republicans whose ideology would likely receive the approbation of H. L. Hunt and Dan Smoot remain prominent leaders in Congress and call for ever greater deficit reductions. Many are generously funded, celebrated by their constituencies, and appear to have bright futures in the Republican Party. They inveigh regularly against the constitutionality of the Federal Reserve and the progressive income tax, and offer market-based alternatives to government programs that have granted security to millions of Americans for decades. As the summer of 2011 attested, the far right's willingness to place principle before the fiscal solvency of the nation and the health of the global economy is uncontestable. But potential economic collapse is only one consequence of a Republican Party manacled by a far-right faction. The partisan wrangling and gridlock that results from a dysfunctional Republican Party make it impossible to deal thoughtfully with threats to the environment, rising inequality, gun violence, an emboldened Russia, terrorism, and other issues that could derail all hope of a second American century and of the nation's continuing to be what Abraham Lincoln called mankind's "last best hope."

Few contemporary leaders of either party today dare to repudiate such domestic extremism. President Kennedy had intended to forcefully denounce Dallas ultraconservatism on November 22, 1963. Had his motorcade safely made it to the Trade Mart, he would have told the citizens of Dallas that there will "always be dissident voices heard in the land. . . . But today other voices are heard in the land—voices preaching doctrines wholly unrelated to reality, wholly unsuited to the Sixties, doctrines which apparently assume that words will suffice without weapons, that vituperation is as good as victory and that peace is a sign of weakness." "We can hope," Kennedy would have said, "that fewer people will listen to nonsense."[26] Today the American people could certainly use a strong dose of the same advice.

Acknowledgments

At last, I have the opportunity to offer thanks to the individuals who have made this book possible. The archivists and librarians at the Dallas Public Library, the John Hay Library at Brown University, the DeGolyer Library at Southern Methodist University, the Cushing Memorial Library and Archives at Texas A&M University, the Dwight D. Eisenhower Presidential Library, the Blakley Library and Lower Level Archives at the University of Dallas, the John F. Kennedy Presidential Library, and Southwestern University were all extremely helpful. At the University of Chicago Press, Timothy Mennel, Joel Score, Nora Devlin, and Levi Stahl helped me navigate the publishing process. Meg Grier graciously granted me access to copies of the transcripts used for her book, *Grassroots Women*.

A supportive community of scholars deserves my deepest gratitude for listening to my ideas and reading and commenting on portions of the manuscript at various stages. They include Donald Critchlow, Darren Dochuk, Robert Fairbanks, Kevin Kruse, Michelle Nickerson, Andrew Preston, and Bruce Schulman. I want to thank friends and professors from my time as a graduate student at Boston College, including Ian Delahanty, Gráinne McEvoy, Seth Meehan, John Spiers, Clayton Trutor, Heather Cox Richardson, Mark Gelfand, Seth Jacobs, Lynn Johnson, Kevin Kenny, Devin Pendas, Sarah Ross, and David Quigley, who all offered unwavering support and insightful criticism. Clayton Trutor graciously perused and edited several versions of the text and also supplied many laughs. In Paul Herron, I found great insight, great conversation, and a great friend. My sister-in-law Elizabeth Quinn, Virginia Quinn, and Judith Robey gave the manuscript valuable edits. Katherine Calzada, Ilka Kostka, Crissy McMartin-Miller, Patrick Plunkett, Karl Reynolds, Mahtab Rezvani, Balazs Szelenyi, Erik Voss, Natasha Watson, and other new colleagues at NU Global in the College of Professional Studies at Northeastern University generously provided encouragement as well as essential advice on teaching history to international students.

I want to thank my Providence College professors, Richard J. Grace and Margaret M. Manchester, and Weymouth High School teachers, Jack Decoste, George Ghiorse, and Gail Shields, all of whom encouraged my love of history and writing. I also need to thank all my pals, including Howie Bean, Kevin Botelho, Jim Carnell, Dave Chepiga, Jay Combs, Stefan Koenig, Michael O'Connor, Phirum Peang, and Clayton Trutor, who keep me smiling and laughing.

My greatest intellectual debt is owed to Cynthia Lynn Lyerly, James O'Toole, and Patrick Maney. As has been the case with many of her graduate students, Professor Lyerly brought out my best. The best coach I've ever had, Lynn turned me into an historian. Professor O'Toole offered invaluable advice about the craft of writing and supported me from the earliest stages of the project. Professor Maney offered his keen insight into the politics of the Midwest and the South.

My family deserves the most praise. My wonderful in-laws provided not only weekly child-care, but also encouragement and incessant kindness. The Quinn and Houston families supplied unflagging support, constructive critiques, and delicious meals at many family gatherings. The Boice, Carnell, and Miller families have supported my love of history throughout my lifetime. I especially want to thank my parents, whose love knows no bounds. My wife has endured the greatest burden of living with this project. I shall enjoy spending a lifetime repaying that debt. I dedicate this book to my wife Katie and son Jack.

Notes

Introduction

1. Revelation 13:3: "And I saw one of his heads as it were wounded to death; and his deadly wound was healed: and all the world wondered after the beast."

2. In the Rapture, Jesus Christ calls his true believers, who disappear into thin air and enter heaven. The ensuing chaos, which includes the vanishing of all the world's infants, heralds the beginning of the Tribulation, the seven-year reign of the Antichrist. During that interval, Jews return to Israel to rebuild their temple and the Antichrist assembles his armies for the final battle of Armageddon. With the exception of 144,000 who convert to Christianity, all Jews succumb to the Antichrist. Jesus Christ returns again, defeats the Antichrist, and inaugurates a thousand-year reign that ends on Judgment Day. William C. Martin, *With God on Our Side: The Rise of the Religious Right in America* (New York: Broadway Books, 1996), 48; Michael Phillips, *White Metropolis: Race, Ethnicity, and Religion in Dallas, 1841–2001* (Austin: University of Texas Press, 2006), 49; Paul Boyer, *When Time Shall Be No More: Prophecy Belief in Modern American Culture* (Cambridge, MA: Belknap Press, 1992), 13; "The Early Crusades, 1950–1969," episode 1 of *With God on Our Side: The Rise of the Religious Right in America*, VHS, distributed by PBS Home Video (Lumiere Productions, 1996); United Press International. *Four Days; The Historical Record of the Death of President Kennedy* (New York: American Heritage, 1964).

3. Don E. Carleton, *Red Scare! Right-Wing Hysteria, Fifties Fanaticism, and Their Legacy in Texas* (Austin: Texas Monthly Press, 1985), 93.

4. Robert G. Sherrill, "H. L. Hunt: Portrait of a Super-Patriot," *Nation*, February 24, 1964, 185, 186–91.

5. Harry Hurt, *Texas Rich: The Hunt Dynasty from the Early Oil Days through the Silver Crash* (New York: W. W. Norton, 1981), 27–28, 69, 91; *Dallas Morning News*, February 17, 1972; Heather Hendershot, *What's Fair On the Air: Cold War Right-Wing Broadcasting and the Public Interest* (Chicago: University of Chicago Press, 2011).

6. Terminology in a study of American conservatism presents questions fraught with challenge and opportunity. I have divided Dallas Republicans into two groups: the more temperate and pragmatic "moderate conservative Republicans," concerned with organizing and building institutions, and the more reactionary and ideological "ultraconservative Republicans." Some scholars have eschewed the terms "ultraconservative" and "ultraconservatism" (which in this book are used interchangeably

with "ultraconservative Republican" and "ultraconservative Republicanism"), but I believe they capture the ethos of these individuals and avoid the condescending connotation of such terms as "Radical Right," "Rampageous Right," "Fanatical Right," and even "right-winger." While the ideology of many of those I tag as "moderate conservative Republicans" may seem to be immoderate, they were, compared to the "ultraconservative Republicans," and in the context of the place and the time, nearly centrist.

7. Darwin Payne, *Initiative in Energy: Dresser Industries, Inc., 1880–1978* (New York: Simon & Schuster, 1979), 187–88; *Dallas Morning News*, February 6, 1952.

8. H. N. Mallon to Prescott S. Bush, March 24, 1953, box 530, folder D, Central Files, General Files, Dwight D. Eisenhower Presidential Library, Abilene, KS; Mallon to Stanley Marcus, January 7, 1955, box 250, folder 4, Stanley Marcus Papers, DeGolyer Library, Southern Methodist University, Dallas, TX.

9. John Lawrence to Bruce Alger, January 22, 1960, box 7, folder 16; J. C. Freeman to Alger, February 17, 1959, box 7, folder 17; Neil Mallon to Alger, February 20, 1959, box 7, folder 17—all in Bruce Alger Papers, Dallas Public Library, Dallas, TX.

10. See Richard Hofstadter, *The Paranoid Style in American Politics, and Other Essays* (Chicago: University of Chicago Press, 1979); Daniel Bell, "The Dispossessed" and "Interpretations of American Politics," in *The Radical Right*, ed. Daniel Bell (Garden City, NY: Anchor Books, 1964), 1–45, 47–73; Seymour Martin Lipset and Earl Raab, *The Politics of Unreason: Right-Wing Extremism in America, 1790–1977* (New York: Harper and Row, 1978); Arnold Forster and Benjamin R. Epstein, *Danger on the Right: The Attitudes, Personnel, and Influence of the Radical Right and Extreme Conservatives* (New York: Random House, 1964). On backlash, see Dan T. Carter, *The Politics of Rage: George Wallace, the Origins of the New Conservatism, and the Transformation of American Politics* (New York: Simon & Schuster, 1995); Dan T. Carter, *From George Wallace to Newt Gingrich: Race in the Conservative Counterrevolution, 1963–1994* (Baton Rouge: Louisiana State University Press, 1996); Thomas Byrne Edsall and Mary D. Edsall, *Chain Reaction: The Impact of Race, Rights, and Taxes on American Politics* (New York: Norton, 1991).

11. John A. Andrew, *The Other Side of the Sixties: Young Americans for Freedom and the Rise of Conservative Politics* (New Brunswick, NJ: Rutgers University Press, 1997); Michael Bowen, *The Roots of Modern Conservatism: Dewey, Taft, and the Battle for the Soul of the Republican Party* (Chapel Hill: University of North Carolina Press, 2011); Donald T. Critchlow, *The Conservative Ascendancy: How the GOP Right Made Political History* (Cambridge, MA: Harvard University Press, 2007); Patrick Allitt, *The Conservatives: Ideas and Personalities throughout American History* (New Haven, CT: Yale University Press, 2009); Gregory L. Schneider, *Cadres for Conservatism: Young Americans for Freedom and the Rise of the Contemporary Right* (New York: New York University Press, 1999); Lisa McGirr, *Suburban Warriors: Origins of the New American Right* (Princeton, NJ: Princeton University Press, 2001); Matthew D. Lassiter, *The Silent Majority: Suburban Politics in the Sunbelt South* (Princeton, NJ: Princeton University Press, 2006); Stephen P. Miller, *Billy Graham and the Rise of the Republican South*

(Philadelphia: University of Pennsylvania Press, 2009); Mary C. Brennan, *Turning Right in the Sixties: The Conservative Capture of the GOP* (Chapel Hill: University of North Carolina Press, 1995); Catherine E. Rymph, *Republican Women* (Chapel Hill: University of North Carolina Press, 2006). For a more comprehensive examination of the historiography on American conservatism, see Kim Phillips-Fein, "Conservatism: A State of the Field," *Journal of American History* 98 (December 2011): 723–43. For examples of exceptions to this emphasis on "mild mannered" conservatism, see Michelle M. Nickerson, *Mothers of Conservatism: Women of the Postwar Right* (Princeton, NJ: Princeton University Press, 2012); Darren Dochuk, *From Bible Belt to Sunbelt: Plain-Folk Religion, Grassroots Politics, and the Rise of Evangelical Conservatism* (New York: W. W. Norton, 2011); Jonathan M. Schoenwald, *A Time for Choosing: The Rise of Modern American Conservatism* (New York: Oxford University Press, 2001); Nancy MacLean, *Freedom Is Not Enough: The Opening of the American Work Place* (New York: R. Sage, 2006); Hendershot, *What's Fair On the Air*; Rick Perlstein, *Before the Storm: Barry Goldwater and the Unmaking of the American Consensus* (New York: Nation Books, 2009).

12. Michelle Nickerson and Darren Dochuk, eds., *Sunbelt Rising: The Places of Space, Place, and Region* (Philadelphia: University of Pennsylvania Press, 2011), 18; Dochuk, *From Bible Belt to Sunbelt*, 329–32, 274–76; Miller, *Billy Graham*, 134–35; Micaela Anne Larkin, "Southwestern Strategy: Mexican Americans and Republican Politics in the Arizona Borderlands," in *Barry Goldwater and the Remaking of the American Political Landscape*, ed. Elizabeth Tandy Shermer (Tucson: University of Arizona Press, 2013), 66–86; McGirr, *Suburban Warriors*; Lassiter, *Silent Majority*; Matthew Dallek, *The Right Moment: Ronald Reagan's First Victory and the Decisive Turning Point in American Politics* (New York: Free Press, 2000); MacLean, *Freedom Is Not Enough*; Joseph Crespino, *In Search of Another Country: Mississippi and the Conservative Counterrevolution* (Princeton, NJ: Princeton University Press, 2007); Nancy MacLean, "Neo-Confederacy versus the New Deal: The Regional Utopia of the Modern American Right" in *The Myth of Southern Exceptionalism*, ed. Matthew D. Lassiter and Joseph Crespino (New York: Oxford University Press, 2009), 308–30. Scholars like Jack Bass, Walter DeVries, and Alexander Lamis traced the conception of the Southern Strategy to the 1960s. Bass and De Vries, *The Transformation of Southern Politics: Social Change and Political Consequence since 1945* (New York: Basic Books, 1976), 23–32; Lamis, *The Two-Party South* (New York: Oxford University Press, 1984); Joseph A. Aistrup, *The Southern Strategy Revisited: Republican Top-Down Advancement in the South* (Lexington: University Press of Kentucky, 1996), 6–12. See also Edward G. Carmines and James A. Stimson, *Issue Evolution: Race and the Transformation of American Politics* (Princeton, NJ: Princeton University Press, 1989). For a different perspective, emphasizing how voting laws and economic factors influenced partisan change, see David Lublin, *The Republican South: Democratization and Partisan Change* (Princeton, NJ: Princeton University Press, 2004); Byron E. Shafer and Richard Johnston, *The End of Southern Exceptionalism: Class, Race, and Partisan Change in the Postwar South* (Cambridge, MA: Harvard University Press, 2009).

13. McGirr, *Suburban Warriors*; Crespino, *In Search of Another Country*; Nickerson, *Mothers of Conservatism*; Kevin Kruse, *White Flight: Atlanta and the Making of Modern Conservatism* (Princeton, NJ: Princeton University Press, 2005); Lassiter, *Silent Majority*; Elizabeth Tandy Shermer, *Sunbelt Capitalism: Phoenix and the Transformation of American Politics* (Philadelphia: University of Pennsylvania Press, 2013); Nickerson and Dochuk, *Sunbelt Rising*; Dochuk, *From Bible Belt to Sunbelt*.

14. Sean P. Cunningham, *Cowboy Conservatism: Texas and the Rise of the Modern Right* (Lexington: University Press of Kentucky, 2010), produced an exceptional study of the GOP in Texas. For examples of studies that have addressed the role of the Dallas Right to some extent, see Nickerson, *Mothers of Conservatism*; Dochuk, *From Bible Belt to Sunbelt*; Hendershot, *What's Fair on the Air*; and Phillips, *White Metropolis*.

15. Boyer, *When Time Shall Be No More*, ix, 13; Phillips, *White Metropolis*, 50; Chandler Davidson, *Race and Class in Texas Politics* (Princeton, NJ: Princeton University Press, 1990), 213; McGirr, *Suburban Warriors*, 10, 161, 167; Joel Gregory, *Too Great a Temptation: The Seductive Power of America's Super Church* (Fort Worth, TX: Summit Group, 1994), 282–83; Hofstadter, *Paranoid Style*, 3–40; Oran P. Smith, *The Rise of Baptist Republicanism* (New York: New York University Press, 1997), 40–41; George Norris Green, "The Far Right Wing in Texas Politics, 1930's–1960's" (PhD diss., Florida State University, 1966); William R. Glass, *Strangers in Zion: Fundamentalists in the South, 1900–1950* (Macon, GA: Mercer University Press, 2001), 107–17; Joel A. Carpenter, *Revive Us Again: The Reawakening of American Fundamentalism* (New York: Oxford University Press, 1997) 20; George M. Marsden, *Fundamentalism and American Culture* (New York: Oxford University Press, 2006), 123; John D. Hannah, *An Uncommon Union: Dallas Theological Seminary and American Evangelicalism* (Grand Rapids, MI: Zondervan, 2009).

16. Stanley Marcus, *Minding the Store: A Memoir* (Boston: Little, Brown, 1974), 249; Herbert S. Parmet, *George Bush: The Life of a Lone Star Yankee* (New York: Scribner, 1997), 92.

17. Richard Reeves, *President Kennedy: Profile of Power* (New York: Simon & Schuster, 1993), 661; William Manchester, *The Death of a President, November 20–November 25, 1963* (New York: Harper & Row, 1967).

18. *Battle Line*, August 1964, box 13, folder 33, Alger Papers.

19. William E. Leuchtenburg, *The White House Looks South: Franklin D. Roosevelt, Harry S. Truman, Lyndon B. Johnson* (Baton Rouge: Louisiana State University Press, 2007), 269; Geoffrey M. Kabaservice, *Rule and Ruin: The Downfall of Moderation and the Destruction of the Republican Party, from Eisenhower to the Tea Party* (New York: Oxford University Press, 2012), 132; Bill Minutaglio and Steven L. Davis, *Dallas 1963* New York: Twelve, 2013); Patricia Evridge Hill, *Dallas: The Making of a Modern City* (Austin: University of Texas Press, 1996), 169.

20. Kabaservice, *Rule and Ruin*, 104; Joseph Crespino, *Strom Thurmond's America* (New York: Hill and Wang, 2012).

21. Timothy N. Thurber, *Republicans and Race: The GOP's Frayed Relationship with African-Americans, 1945–1974* (Lawrence: University Press of Kansas, 2013), 3–4.

22. No Republican presidential candidate has received more than 15 percent of the African-American vote since 1964.

Chapter 1

1. Kenneth Bridges, *Twilight of the Texas Democrats: The 1978 Governor's Race* (College Station: Texas A&M University Press, 2008), 2; Randolph B. Campbell, *Grass-Roots Reconstruction in Texas: 1865 to 1880* (Baton Rouge: Louisiana State University Press, 1997), 24.

2. Kristi Throne Strickland, "The Significance and Impact of Women on the Rise of the Republican Party in Twentieth-Century Texas," (PhD diss., University of North Texas, 2000), 125.

3. Conservative Democrats dominated Texas politics during the first half of the twentieth century. Between 1938 and 1958, what historian George Norris Green called the "establishment," "a loose-knit aristocracy of the Anglo upper classes," held the office of Texas governor. These conservative Democrats— governors W. Lee O'Daniel (1939–1941), Coke Stevenson (1941–1947), and Allan Shivers (1949–1957)—received the support of economizing businessmen and advocated sparse regulation, minimal social services, light taxation, segregation, and a nonunionized workforce. Clifton McCleskey, *The Government and Politics of Texas* (Boston: Little, Brown, 1972), 109; Green, *The Establishment in Texas Politics: The Primitive Years, 1938–1957* (Norman: University of Oklahoma Press, 1979); Campbell, *Grass-Roots Reconstruction*, 379–92; Bridges, *Twilight of the Texas Democrats*, 2; Sean P. Cunningham, *Cowboy Conservatism: Texas and the Rise of the Modern Right* (Lexington: University Press of Kentucky, 2010), 13–15; Randolph B. Campbell, *Gone to Texas: A History of the Lone Star State* (New York: Oxford University Press, 2003), 287–89; David W. Blight, *Race and Reunion: The Civil War in American Memory* (Cambridge, MA: Belknap Press/Harvard University Press, 2001).

4. Bridges, *Twilight of the Texas Democrats*, 8.

5. Mike Kingston, Sam Attlesey, and Mary G. Crawford, *The Texas Almanac's Political History of Texas* (Austin, TX: Eakin Press, 1992), 88; Richard Kraemer, Ernest Crain, and William Earl Maxwell, *Understanding Texas Politics* (New York: West Publishing, 1975), 26–28.

6. Historian Mike Davis argues that city myths are "the paramount axis of cultural conflict" and were often employed by elites to establish hegemony. Davis, *City of Quartz: Excavating the Future in Los Angeles* (London: Verso, 1990), 23; Patricia Evridge Hill, *Dallas: The Making of a Modern City* (Austin: University of Texas Press, 1996).

7. Holland McCombs, "The Dynamic Men of Dallas," *Fortune*, February 1949, 98–103, 162–66. See also Ted Jones, *Dallas: Its History, Its Development, Its Beauty; Points of Interest and a Map of the City* (Dallas: Lamar & Barton, 1925), 7; Chris Cravens, "Edwin A. Walker and the Right Wing in Dallas, 1960–1966" (Master's thesis, Southwest Texas State University, 1991), 21.

8. Harvey J. Graff, *The Dallas Myth: The Making and Unmaking of an American City* (Minneapolis: University of Minnesota Press, 2008), 50, 68.

9. By the late 1950s, Dallas-based Neiman Marcus was selling his-and-hers Jaguars, and his-and-hers private planes appeared in its 1960 Christmas catalog. But even these luxury items paled in comparison to the full-scale replica of Noah's Ark—replete with exotic animals—that the store made available to its wealthy clientele. Bryan Burrough, *The Big Rich: The Rise and Fall of the Greatest Texas Oil Fortunes* (New York: Penguin Press, 2009), 254, 260. John Bainbridge, *The Super-Americans: A Picture of Life in the United States, as Brought into Focus, Bigger than Life, in the Land of the Millionaires—Texas* (Garden City, NY: Doubleday, 1961), 17–18; Green, "Far Right Wing," 278–80.

10. Michael Phillips, *White Metropolis: Race, Ethnicity, and Religion in Dallas, 1841–2001* (Austin: University of Texas Press, 2006), 5; Hill, *Dallas.*

11. Martin V. Melosi, "Marketing the Metroplex" in *Sunbelt Cities: Politics and Growth since World War II*, ed. Richard M. Bernard and Bradley R. Rice (Austin: University of Texas Press, 1983), 163; Char Miller and Heywood Sanders, eds., *Urban Texas: Politics and Development* (College Station: Texas A & M University Press, 1990), 19; Bradley R. Rice and Richard M. Bernard, "Introduction," in Bernard and Rice, *Sunbelt Cities*, 12.

12. James Howard, *Big D Is for Dallas: Chapters in the Twentieth-Century History of Dallas* (Austin, TX, 1957), 64–74.

13. Tom Lee McKnight, *Manufacturing in Dallas: A Study of Effects* (Austin: Bureau of Business Research, University of Texas, 1956), 8, 18.

14. McKnight, *Manufacturing in Dallas*, 168.

15. Rice and Bernard, "Introduction," in Bernard and Rice, *Sunbelt Cities*, 12.

16. McKnight, *Manufacturing in Dallas*, 63; Robert B. Fairbanks, "Dallas in the 1940s: The Challenges and Opportunities of Defense Mobilization," in Miller and Sanders, *Urban Texas*, 145–46.

17. Hill, *Dallas.*

18. Rice and Bernard, "Introduction," 12.

19. Fairbanks, "Dallas in the 1940s," 141–43.

20. McKnight, *Manufacturing in Dallas*, 32.

21. Fairbanks, "Dallas in the 1940s," 150.

22. McKnight, *Manufacturing in Dallas*, 43–44; Darwin Payne, *Big D: Triumphs and Troubles of an American Supercity in the 20th Century* (Dallas: Three Forks Press, 1994), 274.

23. Stanley H. Brown, *Ling: The Rise, Fall, and Return of a Texas Titan* (New York: Atheneum, 1972), 7, 33; McKnight, *Manufacturing in Dallas*, 43–44.

24. Graff, *Dallas Myth*, xix; Phillips, *White Metropolis*, 2. See also Michael Hazel, *Dallas: A History of "Big D"* (Austin: Texas State Historical Association, 1997), 8–9; Philip Lindsley, *A History of Greater Dallas and Vicinity*, 2 vols. (Chicago: Lewis Publishing, 1909), 1:62–63; Randolph B. Campbell, *An Empire for Slavery: The Peculiar Institution in Texas, 1821–1865* (Baton Rouge: Louisiana State University Press, 1989); Campbell, *Gone to Texas*; Melosi, "Marketing the Metroplex," 163; Robert B. Fairbanks, *For the City as a Whole: Planning, Politics, and the Public Interest in Dallas,*

Texas, 1900–1965 (Columbus: Ohio State University Press, 1998), 11; Payne, *Big D*, 5, 273; Numan V. Bartley, *The New South, 1945–1980* (Baton Rouge: Louisiana State University Press, 1995), 134; "Voting Record, Bruce Reynolds Alger, Republican, Texas—5th District, 1955–1956," box 2, folder 6, "Voting Record Files, 1955–1956," Bruce Alger Papers, Dallas Public Library, Dallas, TX; McCleskey, *Government and Politics of Texas*, 89–90; Lisa McGirr, *Suburban Warriors: Origins of the New American Right* (Princeton, NJ: Princeton University Press, 2001), 29.

25. Green, "Far Right Wing," 267.

26. McCleskey, *Government and Politics of Texas*, 88; Theodore H. White, "Texas: Land of Wealth and Fear," *Reporter*, June 8, 1954, 34.

27. Green, *Establishment in Texas Politics*, 200.

28. Lon Tinkle, *Mr. De: A Biography of Everette Lee DeGolyer* (Boston: Little, Brown, 1970).

29. Howard, *Big D*, 91–96.

30. With TI paving the way, Dallas became the epicenter of the state's electronics industry. In 1958, Jack Kilby, an engineer at TI, constructed the world's first integrated circuit, an invention that revolutionized electronics. Campbell, *Gone to Texas*, 408.

31. D. W. Meinig, *Imperial Texas: An Interpretive Essay in Cultural Geography* (Austin: University of Texas Press, 1969), 48, 64.

32. Jack Temple Kirby, *Rural Worlds Lost: The American South, 1920–1960* (Baton Rouge: Louisiana State University Press, 1987), 275–308.

33. Ben F. Johnson, *Arkansas in Modern America, 1930–1999* (Fayetteville: University of Arkansas Press, 2000), 116.

34. Walter L. Buenger, *The Path to a Modern South: Northeast Texas between Reconstruction and the Great Depression* (Austin: University of Texas Press, 2001).

35. Brand Whitlock, *Forty Years of It* (New York: D. Appleton and Company, 1925), 27; Eugene H. Roseboom and Francis P. Weisenburger, *A History of Ohio* (New York: Prentice Hall, 1934); Zane L. Miller, *Boss Cox's Cincinnati: Urban Politics in the Progressive Era* (New York: Oxford University Press, 1968); Bernard Sternsher, "The Harding and Bricker Revolutions: Party Systems and Voter Behavior in Northwest Ohio, 1860–1982," *Northwest Ohio Quarterly* 50 (Summer 1987): 91–111; Alexander P. Lamis and Mary Anne Sharkey, *Ohio Politics* (Kent, OH: Kent State University Press, 1994), 5–11. On Taft, see James T. Patterson, *Mr. Republican; A Biography of Robert A. Taft* (Boston: Houghton Mifflin, 1972); William Smith White, *The Taft Story* (New York: Harper, 1954). On Bricker, see Karl B. Pauly, *Bricker of Ohio: The Man and His Record* (New York: G. P. Putnam's Sons, 1944).

36. James H. Madison, *The Indiana Way: A State History* (Bloomington: Indiana University Press, 1986), 218–30, 295–302, 303; Richard J. Jensen, *The Winning of the Midwest: Social and Political Conflict, 1888–1896* (Chicago: University of Chicago Press, 1971); Paul Kleppner, *The Cross of Culture: A Social Analysis of Midwestern Politics, 1850–1900* (New York: Free Press, 1970); Leonard Joseph Moore, *Citizen Klansmen: The Ku Klux Klan in Indiana, 1921–1928* (Chapel Hill: University of North

Carolina Press, 1991); Michael Paul Poder, "The Senatorial Career of William E. Jenner" (PhD diss., University of Notre Dame, 1976); Dale R. Sorenson, "The AntiCommunist Consensus in Indiana, 1945–1958" (PhD diss., Indiana University, 1980); William B. Pickett, "The Capehart Cornfield Conference and the Election of 1938: Homer E. Capehart's Entry into Politics," *Indiana Magazine of History* 73 (December 1977): 251–75; Robert E. Burns, *Being Catholic, Being American: The Notre Dame Story, 1934–1952* (Notre Dame, IN: University of Notre Dame Press, 2000), 431–36.

37. Richard Kirkendall, *A History of Missouri*, vol. 5, *1919 to 1953* (Columbia: University of Missouri Press, 1986), 217–23, 280–84, 343–53.

38. Robert Wuthnow, *Red State Religion: Faith and Politics in America's Heartland* (Princeton, NJ: Princeton University Press, 2011).

39. Michael O'Brien, *Rethinking the South: Essays in Intellectual History* (Baltimore: Johns Hopkins University Press, 1988); Geoffrey Blodgett, *The Gentle Reformers: Massachusetts Democrats in the Cleveland Era* (Cambridge, MA: Harvard University Press, 1966); Andrew R. L. Cayton and Susan E. Gray, *The American Midwest: Essays on Regional History* (Bloomington: Indiana University Press, 2001), 1–26.

40. Rice and Bernard, "Introduction," 14.

41. "Voting Record, Bruce Reynolds Alger, Republican, Texas—5th District, 1955–1956," box 2, folder 6, "Voting Record Files, 1955–1956," Alger Papers. Nationwide, median family income was $3,216.

42. Cayton and Gray, *American Midwest*, 1–26.

43. McGirr, *Suburban Warriors*, 1–53.

44. Stanley Marcus, *Minding the Store: A Memoir* (Boston: Little, Brown, 1974), 177.

45. Fairbanks, *For the City as a Whole*, 235.

46. Cravens, "Edwin A. Walker," 22–23; Warren Leslie, *Dallas: Public and Private: Aspects of an American City* (Dallas: Southern Methodist University Press, 1998), 152–64; "The Legacy of Citizen Robert," *Texas Monthly*, July, 1985.

47. "Lynn Landrum vs. the Modern World," *D Magazine*, September 1987.

48. *Dallas Morning News*, January 12, July 12, 1940; Green, "Far Right Wing," 120–27, 133; Martin Dies, *The Trojan Horse in America* (New York: Dodd, Mead & Company, 1940), 128; Hill, *Dallas*.

49. Cravens, "Edwin A. Walker," 22–23; Leslie, *Dallas, Public and Private*, 152–64; Green, "Far Right Wing," 155, 286; Saul Friedman, "Tussle in Texas," *Nation*, February 3, 1964, 114–17.

50. Bainbridge, *Super-Americans*, 326–28.

51. Ibid.

52. *Dallas Morning News*, October 2, 1960.

53. Robert Wuthnow, *Rough Country: How Texas Became America's Most Powerful Bible-Belt State* (Princeton, NJ: Princeton University Press, 2014), 123, 128, 236, 247–48.

54. *Dallas Morning News*, October 2, 1960.

55. Sarah Posner, *God's Profits: Faith, Fraud, and the Republican Crusade for Values Voters* (Sausalito, CA: Polipoint Press, 2008), 45.

56. Posner, *God's Profits*, 1–50; D. R. McConnell, *A Different Gospel* (Peabody, MA: Hendrickson Publishers, 1995), 55–74.

57. *Dallas Morning News*, November 5, 1955, December 21, 1949.

58. *Dallas Morning News*, October 23, 1951.

59. Ibid. In Matthew 25:14–30, three servants are given talents (money). While two of the servants trade and make more money, the other servant buries the talent in the ground.

60. *Dallas Morning News*, October 2, 1960.

61. *Dallas Morning News*, March 8, 1950, October 2, 1960.

62. Evelyn Oppenheimer and Bill Porterfield, *The Book of Dallas* (Garden City, NY: Doubleday, 1976), 143–45.

63. *Dallas Morning News*, October 2, 1960.

64. *Dallas Morning News*, July 31, 1948.

65. *Dallas Morning News*, April 18, 1960.

66. Harry Hurt, *Texas Rich: The Hunt Dynasty from the Early Oil Days through the Silver Crash* (New York: W. W. Norton, 1981), 188.

67. Bainbridge, *Super-Americans*, 329–30.

68. Billy Keith, *W. A. Criswell: The Authorized Biography* (Old Tappan, NJ: Revell, 1973), 157.

69. Oppenheimer and Porterfield, *Book of Dallas*, 145.

70. Keith, *W. A. Criswell*, 40.

71. Ibid., 17–34.

72. Collins was apparently returning a favor. During the Great Depression, he had asked for Criswell's assistance in directing the Greater Baylor Financial Campaign. Criswell, who felt a debt of gratitude toward his alma mater, filled in for Collins, who was ill, by delivering the address at the drive's launch in Fort Worth. Ibid., 42, 57–74; Campbell, *Gone to Texas*, 393. Collins, a fundamentalist Protestant, got rich by peddling Crazy Crystals, a quack panacea for the digestive system that was ultimately banned by the Pure Food and Drug Administration.

73. W. A. Criswell, *Standing on the Promises: The Autobiography of W. A. Criswell* (Dallas: Word Publishing, 1990), 184–85.

74. Oran P. Smith, *The Rise of Baptist Republicanism* (New York: New York University Press, 1997), 40–41.

75. Keith, *W. A. Criswell*, 83. See also Leon McBeth, *The First Baptist Church of Dallas: Centennial History, 1868–1968* (Grand Rapids, MI: Zondervan, 1968), 327.

76. Chandler Davidson, *Race and Class in Texas Politics* (Princeton, NJ: Princeton University Press, 1990), 212; Keith, *W. A. Criswell*, 94.

77. W. A. Criswell, *Did Man Just Happen?* (Grand Rapids, MI: Zondervan, 1957); McBeth, *First Baptist Church*, 327, 339.

78. Carol Estes Thometz, *The Decision-Makers: The Power Structure of Dallas* (Dallas: Southern Methodist University Press, 1963), 27–58, 63–68; Fairbanks, "Dallas in the 1940s," 141–43; Leslie, *Dallas, Public and Private*, 49–67.

79. J. Morgan Kousser, *Shaping of Southern Politics: Suffrage Restriction and the Establishment of the One-Party South, 1880–1910* (New Haven, CT: Yale University Press, 1974), 11–44, 139–45, 246–65; C. Vann Woodward, *Origins of the New South: 1877–1913* (New Orleans, 1951), 322–23; Morton Keller, *Affairs of State: Public Life in Late Nineteenth Century America* (Cambridge, MA: Belknap Press/Harvard University Press, 1977), 454–56, 527–28; Alexander Keyssar, *The Right to Vote: The Contested History of Democracy in the United States* (New York: Basic Books, 2000), 107–16; V. O. Key Jr., *Southern Politics in State and Nation* (New York: A. A. Knopf, 1949).

80. Cunningham, *Cowboy Conservatism*, 15–16; Campbell, *Gone to Texas*, 329–38.

Chapter 2

1. *Dallas Morning News*, February 26 and 27, 1962; P. W. Gifford to Freedom Forum Advisory Board, April 3, 1962, box 1, folder 21, Rita Crocker Clements Papers, Texas A&M University, College Station, TX.

2. 1962 Freedom Forum Ronald Reagan Program, 1962; "Freedom Forum Report by Rita Bass," February 9, 1962—both in box 1, folder 21, Clements Papers.

3. P. W. Gifford to Freedom Forum Advisory Board, April 3, 1962, box 1, folder 21, Clements Papers.

4. Robert Wuthnow, *Red State Religion: Faith and Politics in America's Heartland* (Princeton, NJ: Princeton University Press, 2011), xi, 5–6, 8, 15, 22, 52, 61, 67, 109; James H. Madison, *The Indiana Way: A State History* (Bloomington: Indiana University Press, 1986), 185; Richard Kirkendall, *A History of Missouri*, vol. 5, *1919 to 1953* (Columbia: University of Missouri Press, 1986), 317; George W. Knepper, *Ohio and Its People* (Kent, OH: Kent State University Press, 2003), 163–70.

5. Michael Phillips, *White Metropolis: Race, Ethnicity, and Religion in Dallas, 1841–2001* (Austin: University of Texas Press, 2006), 150; Arnold Forster and Benjamin R. Epstein, *Danger on the Right: The Attitudes, Personnel, and Influence of the Radical Right and Extreme Conservatives* (New York: Random House, 1964).

6. Patrick Allitt, *Catholic Intellectuals and Conservative Politics in America, 1950–1985* (Ithaca, NY: Cornell University Press, 1993), 63.

7. *Dallas Morning News*, August 23, 24, and 26, 1960; 1961 Freedom Forum program, box 1, folder 21, Clements Papers.

8. *Dallas Morning News*, September 20, 1960.

9. *Dallas Morning News*, September 22, 1960.

10. *Dallas Morning News*, October 19, 1961.

11. Allitt, *Catholic Intellectuals*, 1–118.

12. *Dallas Morning News*, December 7 and 18, 1960.

13. Allitt, *Catholic Intellectuals*, 1–48.

14. *Dallas Morning News*, February 12, 1961.

15. Allitt, *Catholic Intellectuals*, 1–118.

16. J. C. Oehler to Bruce Alger, November 3, 1954, box 1, folder 6; "Washington Report by Congressman Bruce Alger," January 12, 1957, box 3, folder 7, "Speeches-Speech Material, 1957"; Bruce Alger speech at Chamber of Commerce banquet,

January 28, 1955, Dallas Texas, box 3, folder 28, "Alger Speech File, 1954–1958"—all in Bruce Alger Papers, Dallas Public Library, Dallas, TX.

17. *Dallas Morning News*, March 15, October 23, 1958. In October 1958, the AFL-CIO denounced the FIA and the White Citizens Council in an initial draft of a report condemning segregation and calling for equality in civil rights.

18. *Dallas Morning News*, November 25, 1958.

19. *Dallas Morning News*, March 14, 1958.

20. David M. Oshinsky, *A Conspiracy So Immense: The World of Joe McCarthy* (New York: Free Press, 1983), 449.

21. Unidentified constituent to Bruce Alger, April 6, 1961, box 10, folder 1, Alger Papers.

22. *Dallas Morning News*, April 20, 1961.

23. Allitt, *Catholic Intellectuals*, 62–120.

24. Dallas County GOP Newsletter, October 28, 1954, box 1, folder 7, Alger Papers.

25. The literature on the New Deal is voluminous. For earlier Whiggish appraisals emphasizing continuity with progressive traditions, see Carl Degler, *Out of Our Past: The Forces That Shaped Modern America* (New York: Harper and Row, 1956); William Leuchtenburg, *Franklin Roosevelt and the New Deal, 1932–1940* (New York: Harper and Row, 1963); and Arthur M. Schlesinger Jr., *The Age of Roosevelt*, 3 vols. (Boston: Houghton Mifflin, 1957–1960). For appraisals asserting that the New Deal represented a break from the past, see Richard Hofstadter, *The Age of Reform: From Bryan to FDR* (New York: Alfred A. Knopf, 1955); David Kennedy, *Freedom from Fear: The American People in Depression and War, 1929–1945* (New York: Oxford University Press, 1999), 623; Fred I. Greenstein, *The Hidden Hand Presidency: Eisenhower as Leader* (New York: Basic Books, 1982), 50; Alonzo Hamby, *Liberalism and Its Challengers* (New York: Oxford University Press, 1985), 122, 124–25; and Stephen E. Ambrose, *Eisenhower: Soldier and President* (New York: Simon & Schuster, 1990), 545.

26. Jennifer Burns, *Goddess of the Market: Ayn Rand and the American Right* (Oxford: Oxford University Press, 2009; David Farber, *The Rise and Fall of Modern American Conservatism* (Princeton, NJ: Princeton University Press, 2010), 68–69; John B. Judis, *William F. Buckley, Jr., Patron Saint of the Conservatives* (New York: Simon & Schuster, 1988), 132–80.

27. Edward Cain, *They'd Rather Be Right: Youth and the Conservative Movement* (New York: Macmillan, 1963), 269.

28. On Alger's support for natural law, see Reverend Martin T. Jenson to Bruce Alger, September 15, 1955, box 2, folder 3, "Congratulatory Letters, 1955," Alger Papers. For letters between Rand and Alger, see Ayn Rand, *Letters of Ayn Rand* (New York: Penguin Books, 1997), 605–6. Rand vehemently objected to Alger's apparent assertion of atheism's "illegality."

29. Bruce Alger speech, Washington, DC, June 16, 1955, box 3, folder 28, "Alger Speech File, 1954–1958," Alger Papers; Judis, *William F. Buckley, Jr.*, 132–80; Allitt, *Catholic Intellectuals*, 72–76.

30. Bruce Alger speech, Washington, DC, June 16, 1955, box 3, folder 28, "Alger Speech File, 1954–1958," Alger Papers.

31. Friedrich A. von Hayek, *The Road to Serfdom* (Chicago: University of Chicago Press, 1944).

32. Daniel Stedman Jones, *Masters of the Universe: Hayek, Friedman, and the Birth of Neoliberal Politics* (Princeton, NJ: Princeton University Press, 2012), 50–51.

33. George H. Nash, *The Conservative Intellectual Movement in America Since 1945* (Wilmington, DE: ISI Books, 2006), 12–13.

34. Bruce Alger and Roy Edward Colby, *Revolutionary Actions . . . U.S.A. . . . in Retrospect: What to Do Now* (Washington, DC: Citizens Evaluation Institute, 1971), 117–18.

35. Kim Phillips-Fein, *Invisible Hands: The Making of the Conservative Movement from the New Deal to Reagan* (New York: W. W. Norton, 2009), 34–48; Patrick Allitt, *The Conservatives: Ideas and Personalities throughout American History* (New Haven, CT: Yale University Press, 2009), 159–63; Alan O. Ebenstein, *Friedrich Hayek: A Biography* (New York: Palgrave, 2001); Edward Feser, *The Cambridge Companion to Hayek* (New York: Cambridge University Press, 2006); Bruce Caldwell, *Hayek's Challenge: An Intellectual Biography of F. A. Hayek* (Chicago: University of Chicago Press, 2004).

36. Alger and Colby, *Revolutionary Actions*, 2, 117–18.

37. John G. Tower, *A Program for Conservatives* (New York: Macfadden Books, 1962), 13; George Norris Green, *The Establishment in Texas Politics: The Primitive Years, 1938–1957* (Norman: University of Oklahoma Press, 1979), 200.

38. P. W. Gifford to Rita Clements, January 2, 1961, box 1, folder 21, Clements Papers; *Dallas Morning News*, September 21, 1960, October 15, 1960.

39. Jerome L. Himmelstein, *To the Right: The Transformation of American Conservatism* (Berkeley: University of California Press, 1990), 49.

40. Trudy Nichols, "Who's Who in Big D GOP: Jo Kanowsky," *Battle Line*, July 1963, box 13, folder 33, Alger Papers; Mary Ann Collins, interviewed by Meg Grier, Dallas, September 23, 1998.

41. Bruce Alger speech, Sevens Park, Dallas, September 7, 1954, box 3, folder 28, "Alger Speech File, 1954–1958," Alger Papers.

42. *Dallas Morning News*, April 20, 1958; Bruce Alger to Trammell Crow, May 9, 1958, box 4, folder 13, "Urban Renewal—City of Dallas Correspondence, 1958," Alger Papers. Lifelong Dallasite Albert L. Dixon also fretted about federal control. "I am opposed to the states accepting too much federal aid," he said. Dixon to Bruce Alger, January 9, 1955, box 2, folder 3, "Congratulatory Letters, 1955," Alger Papers.

43. Mrs. L. J. Wathen to Bruce Alger, December 30, 1955, box 3, folder 1, "Congratulatory Letters, 1956," Alger Papers.

44. *Dallas Morning News*, April 21, 1958.

45. Reveau Bassett to Bruce Alger, June 3, 1958, box 4, folder 13, "Urban Renewal—City of Dallas Correspondence, 1958," Alger Papers.

46. Dick Smith to Bruce Alger, May 14, 1958, box 4, folder 13, "Urban Renewal—City of Dallas Correspondence, 1958," Alger Papers; *Dallas Morning News*, May 13, 1958

47. Lisa McGirr, *Suburban Warriors: Origins of the New American Right* (Princeton, NJ: Princeton University Press, 2001), 153.

48. Mrs. Richard D. Bass, "TARGET '64, Campaign Activities Committee Report," May 1963, box 25, folder 19, Clements Papers.

49. Ibid.

50. Alvan D. Peabody to Bruce Alger, March 13, 1956, box 3, folder 17, "H.R. 6407—Tax Relief for Small Business," Alger Papers.

51. Michelle Nickerson, "Politically Desperate Housewives: Women and Conservatism in Postwar Los Angeles," *California History* 86, no. 3 (June 2009): 4–21.

52. To be sure, the Midwest's strong manufacturing base was about to experience the effects of deindustrialization and become known as the Rust Belt.

53. Of course, many Republicans who helped to build the party organization were not native Midwesterners. Still, the Midwest made an unmistakable contribution to the party's institutional and ideological foundations. Krueger ran for Dallas city council in 1963. "Abundant Talent Represented On Women's Club Council," *Battle Line*, August, 1964, box 13, folder 33, Alger Papers.

54. Phillips, *White Metropolis*, 150.

55. Clifton McCleskey, *The Government and Politics of Texas* (Boston: Little, Brown, 1972), 88; Theodore H. White, "Texas: Land of Wealth and Fear," *Reporter*, June 8, 1954, 34; M. J. Heale, *American AntiCommunism: Combating the Enemy Within, 1830–1970* (Baltimore: Johns Hopkins University Press, 1990), 153.

56. Taffy Goldsmith, interviewed by Meg Grier, Dallas, June 16, 1999.

57. Trudy Nickels, "Who's Who in Big D GOP: G. N. McDaniel," *Battle Line*, August 1963, box 13, folder 33, Alger Papers.

58. *Dallas Morning News*, December 15, 2007; Alfred M. Leeston, John A. Crichton, and John C. Jacobs, *The Dynamic Natural Gas Industry: The Description of an American Industry from the Historical, Technical, Legal, Financial, and Economic Standpoints* (Norman: University of Oklahoma Press, 1963); John A. Crichton, *The Republican-Democrat Political Campaigns in Texas in 1964* (Author House, 2004).

59. Phillips-Fein, *Invisible Hands*.

60. Their father, Harry Bass, Sr., born sixty miles of Kansas in Eunid, Oklahoma, made his fortune as a drilling contractor in the oil fields of Oklahoma. When he brought his family to Dallas in 1932, the oil industry regarded natural gas as the worthless dregs of processed petroleum to be burned away on site. But Bass disagreed and built a natural gas recycling plant that revolutionized the industry and added to the family's wealth. *Dallas Morning News*, February 19, 1970.

61. *Dallas Morning News*, December 13, 1981; Jeff Bowden, "Largemouth Bass," *D Magazine*, December 1, 2000.

62. *Dallas Morning News*, November 9, 1955.

63. "Campaign Contributions Up to and Including November 15, 1956," box 2, folder 20, Alger Papers; "Statement of Contributions, 1958," box 3, folder 27, Alger Papers; Gwen Pharo, phone interview conducted by Meg Grier, Dallas, June 15, 1999.

64. Our Republican organization, Harry said in a fundraising letter, "exists only because you and thousands of your neighbors have been willing to support it and its candidates—with your vote, with your work, and with your money." "Dear Fellow Conservative" letter from Harry Bass, April 15, 1963, box 25, folder 19, Clements Papers.

65. Martha Martin, "Who's Who In Big D GOP: Harry W. Bass, Jr.," *Battle Line*, July 1963, box 13, folder 33, Alger Papers.

66. He also personified the Dallas "establishment," serving as a member of the Dallas Citizens Council in the 1950s. "Charter, By-Laws, and List of Officers and Members of Dallas Citizens Council," box 83, folder 44, Stanley Marcus Papers, DeGolyer Library, Southern Methodist University, Dallas, TX.

67. Leslie A. Elam, *Harry W. Bass: Memories of His Life* (American Numismatics Society, 1998), 1–65.

68. Martin, "Who's Who in Big D GOP: Harry W. Bass, Jr.," *Battle Line*, July 1963, box 13, folder 33, Alger Papers; *Dallas Morning News*, August 6, 1968.

69. Fred Agnich to Bruce Alger, August 30, 1956, box 2, folder 14, Alger Papers.

70. Mary Ann Collins, interviewed by Meg Grier, Dallas, September 23, 1998.

71. *Dallas Morning News*, March 22, 1967, January 17, 1973.

72. Sally McKenzie, interviewed by Meg Grier, Dallas, October 24, 1997; *Dallas Morning News*, November 23, 1976.

73. While the campaign was not a success, Guillot provided Bush with laughter and a tennis partner at the Brookhollow Country Club in Dallas. Martha Martin, "Who's Who in the Big D GOP: L. E. Guillot," *Battle Line*, October 1964, box 13, folder 33, Alger Papers.

74. "When I was a child," Kanowsky observed, "the importance of everybody in politics was brought to my mind forcibly by my father, probably because he was in business. He made me aware of everything that was going on that had to do with good conservative government." Trudy Nichols, "Who's Who in Big D GOP: Jo Kanowsky," *Battle Line*, July 1963, box 13, folder 33, Alger Papers; Mary Ann Collins, interviewed by Meg Grier, Dallas, September 23, 1998.

75. Taffy Goldsmith, "Who's Who in Big D GOP: Dillard Radke," *Battle Line*, February 1964, box 13, folder 33, Alger Papers.

76. Joan Gaidos, interviewed by Meg Grier, Dallas, August 18, 1999.

77. "Abundant Talent Represented On Women's Club Council," *Battle Line*, August 1964, box 13, folder 33, Alger Papers. Carol Galbraith was another classic example of political socialization. A native of Washington, DC, Galbraith first became involved in Republican Party politics in 1940 while campaigning for Wendell Willkie.

78. Nickerson, "Politically Desperate Housewives."

79. Trudy Nickels, "Who's Who in Big D GOP: G. N. McDaniel," *Battle Line*, August 1963, box 13, folder 33, Alger Papers.

80. "Abundant Talent Represented on Women's Club Council," *Battle Line*, August 1964, box 13, folder 33, Alger Papers.

81. Gwen Pharo, phone interview conducted by Meg Grier, Dallas, June 15, 1999.

82. Taffy Goldsmith, "Who's Who in Big D GOP: Glenna McCord," *Battle Line*, July 1964, box 13, folder 33, Alger Papers; *Dallas Morning News*, November 24, October 28, 1958.

83. John T. Flynn, *The Road Ahead: America's Creeping Revolution* (New York: Devin-Adair, 1949); John E. Moser, *Right Turn: John T. Flynn and the Transformation of American Liberalism* (New York: New York University Press, 2005).

84. *Dallas Morning News*, October 15, 1960.

85. *Dallas Morning News*, May 14, 1957.

86. Michelle Nickerson, *Mothers of Conservatism: Women of the Postwar Right* (Princeton, NJ: Princeton University Press, 2012), 138–39.

87. Ibid.

88. *Dallas Morning News*, April 9, 1963.

89. Gwen Pharo, phone interview conducted by Meg Grier, Dallas, June 15, 1999.

90. Peter O'Donnell, interviewed by Meg Grier, Dallas, January 27, 2000.

91. Mary Lou Wiggins, interviewed by Meg Grier, Dallas, September 25, 1998.

92. *Dallas Morning News*, January 13, 1947.

93. Kristi Throne Strickland, "The Significance and Impact of Women on the Rise of the Republican Party in Twentieth-Century Texas" (PhD diss., University of North Texas, 2000), 123–24.

94. *Dallas Morning News*, January 10, 1947; Catherine E. Rymph, *Republican Women* (Chapel Hill: University of North Carolina Press, 2006), 24. In this capacity, Black served as the female representative from Texas to the Republican National Committee. She served from 1952 to 1960.

95. Rymph, *Republican Women*, 125.

96. *Dallas Morning News*, November 18, 1954.

97. *Dallas Morning News*, October 23, 1953.

98. *Dallas Morning News*, April 22, 1954.

99. *Dallas Morning News*, May 19, 1955.

100. *Dallas Morning News*, May 25, 1955.

101. To establish a state federation of the NFWRCA, prospective applicants needed to establish at least one Republican Woman's Club in 50 percent of the state's counties or 75 percent of state's congressional districts. Strickland, "Significance and Impact of Women," 123.

102. *Dallas Morning News*, April 10, 1954.

103. Dallas County GOP Newsletter, October 28, 1954, box 1, folder 7, Alger Papers; Darwin Payne, *Big D: Triumphs and Troubles of an American Supercity in the 20th Century* (Dallas: Three Forks Press, 1994), 281; Dallas County GOP Newsletter, October 28, 1954, box 1, folder 7, Alger Papers.

104. Mrs. J. F. W. Hannay to Bruce Alger, 1954, box 1, folder 6, Alger Papers.

105. Rymph, *Republican Women*; Rebecca E. Klatch, *Women of the New Right* (Philadelphia: Temple University Press, 1987).

106. Michelle Nickerson, "Women, Domesticity, and Postwar Conservatism," *OAH Magazine of History*, 17 (January 2003): 17–21.

107. Nickerson, "Politically Desperate Housewives."

108. Gwen Pharo, phone interview conducted by Meg Grier, Dallas, June 15, 1999.

109. Taffy Goldsmith, interviewed by Meg Grier, Dallas, June 16, 1999.

110. Peter O'Donnell, interviewed by Meg Grier, Dallas, January 27, 2000.

111. *Dallas Morning News*, August 25, 1967.

112. Nickerson, "Politically Desperate Housewives."

113. Ibid.

114. *Dallas Morning News*, November 24, 1965.

115. Nickerson, "Politically Desperate Housewives."

Chapter 3

1. George Norris Green, "The Far Right Wing in Texas Politics, 1930's–1960's" (PhD diss., Florida State University, 1966), 193–94.

2. H. L. Hunt, *Right of Average* (Dallas: HLH Products), 71.

3. H. L. Hunt, *Old Letters from H. L. Hunt* (Dallas: HLH Products, 1970), 10.

4. Chandler Davidson, *Race and Class in Texas Politics* (Princeton, NJ: Princeton University Press, 1990), 210.

5. Harry Hurt, *Texas Rich: The Hunt Dynasty from the Early Oil Days through the Silver Crash* (New York: W. W. Norton, 1981), 75–103.

6. *Dallas Morning News*, June 10, June 30, and October 10, 1951.

7. Hurt, *Texas Rich*, 27–28, 69, 91; *Dallas Morning News*, February 17, 1972.

8. Hurt, *Texas Rich*, 75–103. H. L. Hunt, *Hunt Heritage: The Republic and Our Families* (Dallas: Parade Press, 1973), 45–74.

9. Green, "Far Right Wing," 7.

10. Heather Hendershot, *What's Fair On the Air: Cold War Right-Wing Broadcasting and the Public Interest* (Chicago: University of Chicago Press, 2011), 65–69; Dan Smoot, *People along the Way: The Autobiography of Dan Smoot* (Tyler, TX: Tyler Press, 1996), 141–86. Fifty-two radio outlets and thirty-one television outlets aired the *Report* in 1961.

11. Davidson, *Race and Class*, 208.

12. J. Evetts Haley, *A Texan Looks at Lyndon: A Study in Illegitimate Power* (Canyon, TX: Palo Duro Press, 1964), 127.

13. Lawrence Wright, "Why Do They Hate Us So Much?" *Texas Monthly*, November 1983.

14. John F. Walvoord, *The Revelation of Jesus Christ: A Commentary* (Chicago: Moody Press, 1966), 122–328; John F. Walvoord, *The Millennial Kingdom* (Findlay, OH: Dunham Publishing, 1959), 249–334; Michael Phillips, *White Metropolis: Race, Ethnicity, and Religion in Dallas, 1841–2001* (Austin: University of Texas Press, 2006), 49; Paul Boyer, *When Time Shall Be No More: Prophecy Belief in Modern American Culture* (Cambridge, MA: Belknap Press, 1992), 13.

15. The *Scofield Reference Bible*, according to historian Paul Boyer, "solidified" dispensationalism "more than any other single work" and sold from 5 to 10 million copies between 1909 and 1967. Boyer, *When Time Shall Be No More*, 97; Mabeth E.

Smoot, "The Dan Smoot Story," *Dan Smoot Report*, special anniversary issue, June 1961, 8; Phillips, *White Metropolis*, 50.

16. *Life Line* became a vital clearinghouse for the Republican Right, denouncing foreign aid, calling for the United States to leave the United Nations, and decrying the removal of God from the public schools. Robert G. Sherrill, "H. L. Hunt: Portrait of a Super-Patriot," *Nation*, February 24, 1964,186–91.

17. J. Dwight Pentecost, *Things to Come: A Study in Biblical Eschatology* (Grand Rapids, MI: Zondervan, 1958); J. Dwight Pentecost, *Prophecy for Today; an Exposition of Major Themes of Prophecy* (Grand Rapids, MI: Zondervan, 1961), 112; John F. Walvoord, *Israel in Prophecy* (Grand Rapids, MI: Zondervan, 1962); Boyer, *When Time Shall Be No More*, 164; John F. Walvoord, "Russia, King of the North—Part I," *Fundamentalist Journal*, January 1984, 37; John F. Walvoord, "The Crisis of This Present Hour," in *The Prophetic Word in Crisis Days* (Findlay, OH: Dunham Publishing, 1961), 15. Nondenominational Dallas Theological Seminary, founded in 1924 by Lewis Sperry Chafer to counter what he perceived as a growing modernist trend in seminaries, contributed some of dispensationalism's most influential and prolific scholars. See William R. Glass, *Strangers in Zion: Fundamentalists in the South, 1900–1950* (Macon, GA: Mercer University Press, 2001), 107–17; Carpenter, *Revive Us Again*, 20; George M. Marsden, *Fundamentalism and American Culture* (New York: Oxford University Press, 2006), 123; John D. Hannah, *An Uncommon Union: Dallas Theological Seminary and American Evangelicalism* (Grand Rapids, MI: Zondervan, 2009).

18. Pentecost, *Prophecy for Today*, 113.

19. Boyer, *When Time Shall Be No More*, 123.

20. Ibid., 139.

21. Ibid., 148.

22. Ibid., 156.

23. Pentecost, *Things to Come*; Pentecost, *Prophecy for Today*; Walvoord, *Israel in Prophecy*; Walvoord, "Russia, King of the North—Part I," 37; Walvoord, "The Crisis of This Present Hour," 15.

24. Pentecost, *Prophecy for Today*, 112.

25. Hunt, *Old Letters*, 8.

26. Ida M. Darden, *The Best of "The Southern Conservative"* (Fort Worth, TX: Author, 1963), 122; *Southern Conservative*, June 1954, June 1959.

27. Hunt, *Old Letters*, 10, 29.

28. *Dallas Morning News*, April 7, 24, 1958; March 18, 19, 20, 21, 22, 1958.

29. Darden, *Best of "The Southern Conservative,"* 193; *Southern Conservative*, January 1951, May 1958.

30. Dan Smoot, "How to Abolish the Federal Income Tax," *Dan Smoot Report* 7, no. 3 (January 16, 1961): 17–24; Dan Smoot, "Repeal the Income Tax," *Dan Smoot Report* 8, no. 11 (March 12,1962): 81–88. Dallasites like Mrs. Tom Leach, Mrs. J. C. Curran, and Mrs. James Hadra also recommended eliminating the income tax altogether. Leach to Bruce Alger, April 3, 1957; Curran to Alger, April 9, 1957; Hadra

to Alger, April 5, 1957—all in box 3, folder 18, "HS Res. 861—Proposed Amendment to the Constitution, 1957," Bruce Alger Papers, Dallas Public Library, Dallas, TX.

31. Mabeth Smoot, "Dan Smoot Story"; Dan Smoot, "The Tragedy of U.S. Membership in the United Nations," *Dan Smoot Report* 9, no. 14 (April 8, 1963): 105–12; Dan Smoot, "Disarmament," *Dan Smoot Report* 9, no. 18 (May 6, 1963): 137–44; Dan Smoot, "Foreign Aid Is Killing America," *Dan Smoot Report* 9, no. 42 (October 21, 1963): 329–36.

32. Dan Smoot, "Impeaching Earl Warren—Part I," *Dan Smoot Report* 7, no. 5 (January 30, 1961): 33–39; Dan Smoot, "World Government, Part I" *Dan Smoot Report* 7, no. 9 (February 27, 1961): 65–72; Dan Smoot, "Foreign Aid, 1961" *Dan Smoot Report* 7, no. 39 (September 25, 1961): 305–12; "Machinery for World Government," *Dan Smoot Report* 7, no. 40 (October 2, 1961): 313–20.

33. Green, "Far Right Wing," 188.

34. John J. Penter to John F. Kennedy, September 22, 1962, box 2910, "Edwin A. Walker Correspondence" folder, White House Central Name File, John F. Kennedy Presidential Library, Boston, MA.

35. Sue B. Fitch to Bruce Alger, March 21, 1957, box 3, folder 23, "Alger Bills—Correspondence," Alger Papers.

36. Erling Jorstad, *The Politics of Doomsday; Fundamentalists of the Far Right* (Nashville, TN: Abingdon Press, 1970), 127–29, 171–72; Sherrill, "H. L. Hunt," 186–91; Hugh F. Pyle, *The Truth about the Church of Christ* (Murfreesboro, TN: Sword of the Lord Publishers, 1977), 51–58; Frank Lambert, *Religion in American Politics: A Short History* (Princeton, NJ: Princeton University Press, 2008), 185.

37. Smoot, *People along the Way*, 77, 82.

38. Smoot, *People along the Way*, 70, 421; Dan Smoot, *The Hope of the World* (Dallas: Miller Publishing, 1958).

39. Boyer, *When Time Shall Be No More*, 97–98; Robert C. Fuller, *Naming the Antichrist: The History of an American Obsession* (New York: Oxford University Press, 1995); Stephen D. O'Leary, *Arguing the Apocalypse: A Theory of Millennial Rhetoric* (New York: Oxford University Press, 1998); Angela M. Lahr, *Millennial Dreams and Apocalyptic Nightmares: The Cold War Origins of Political Evangelicalism* (New York: Oxford University Press, 2007).

40. Mabeth Smoot, "Dan Smoot Story," 8.

41. Hurt, *Texas Rich*, 66; H. L. Hunt, *Early Days* (Dallas: Parade Press, 1973) 13–31; Hunt, *Hunt Heritage*, 1–13; Hunt, *Old Letters*, 61; unidentified reprinted article, "The Facts about Facts Forum," *Providence Journal-Bulletin*, December–January 1953–1954, box 245, folder 9, Stanley Marcus Papers, DeGolyer Library, Southern Methodist University, Dallas, TX; Stanley H. Brown, *H. L. Hunt: A Biography* (Chicago: Playboy Press, 1976), 12–13; Hendershot, *What's Fair On the Air*, 65–66; Sara Diamond, *Spiritual Warfare: The Politics of the Christian Right* (Boston: South End Press, 1989).

42. Smoot, *Hope of the World*, 55.

43. Dan Smoot, *The Invisible Government* (Boston: Western Islands, 1962).

44. J. McCarthy to Robert Welch, October 1963, box 6, "Members letters sent to Welch" folder, John Birch Society Records, Brown University Library, Providence, RI.

45. Hendershot, *What's Fair On the Air*, 26–64; Richard Hofstadter, *The Paranoid Style in American Politics, and Other Essays* (Chicago: University of Chicago Press, 1979), 3–40.

46. Donald T. Critchlow, John Korasick, and Matthew C. Sherman, *Political Conspiracies in America: A Reader* (Bloomington: Indiana University Press, 2008), vii–xii.

47. Arnold Forster and Benjamin R. Epstein, *Danger on the Right: The Attitudes, Personnel, and Influence of the Radical Right and Extreme Conservatives* (New York: Random House, 1964), 3–10; Green, "Far Right Wing," 10; George Norris Green, "Some Aspects of the Far Right Wing in Texas Politics," in *Essays on Recent Southern Politics*, ed. Harold M. Hollingsworth (Austin: University of Texas Press, 1970), 63.

48. *Southern Conservative*, March 1950, January 1951, March 1952, November–December 1953, June 1955; Green, "Far Right Wing," 186.

49. Green, "Far Right Wing," 186.

50. *Southern Conservative*, January 1951, March 1952, February 1959, September 1959; Green, "Far Right Wing," 189.

51. Green, "Far Right Wing," 189.

52. *Southern Conservative*, October 1952, February 1953; Green, "Some Aspects of the Far Right Wing," 63.

53. Donald Janson and Bernard Eismann, *The Far Right* (New York: McGraw-Hill, 1963), 178–79.

54. Allan J. Lichtman, *White Protestant Nation: The Rise of the American Conservative Movement* (New York: Atlantic Monthly Press, 2008), 236.

55. Green, "Far Right Wing," 190.

56. S. T. Darling to Dwight D. Eisenhower, June 25, 1952; undated newspaper clipping—both in box 530, folder D, Central Files, General Files, Dwight D. Eisenhower Presidential Library, Abilene, KS.

57. Mark Fenster, *Conspiracy Theories: Secrecy and Power in American Culture* (Minneapolis: University of Minnesota Press, 1999). Historian Michelle Nickerson found that conspiracy theory served as "rhetorical bullhorns for right-wing women, amplifying female voices." Nickerson, *Mothers of Conservatism: Women of the Postwar Right* (Princeton, NJ: Princeton University Press, 2012), 120–22. See also Michael Barkun, *A Culture of Conspiracy: Apocalyptic Visions in Contemporary America* (Berkeley: University of California Press, 2003); Robert Alan Goldberg, *Enemies Within: The Culture of Conspiracy in Modern America* (New Haven, CT: Yale University Press, 2001).

58. Hendershot, *What's Fair On the Air*, 65–66, 84.

59. Hunt, *Old Letters*, 33.

60. Hofstadter, *Paranoid Style*, 3–38. Also characteristic of ultraconservatives, H. L. Hunt overstated his enemies as omnipotent and omniscient. "The mistaken enemies of freedom," Hunt said, "will maneuver you into awkward positions. You will find yourself uncomfortable until you thoroughly learn the game of words

Mistaken play. False premises will be brought to bear against you. You may find yourself hanging on the verbal ropes." Hunt, *Old Letters*, 20, 57.

61. Critchlow, Korasick, and Sherman, *Political Conspiracies*, vii–xii.

62. Kathryn S. Olmsted, *Real Enemies: Conspiracy Theories and American Democracy, World War I to 9/11* (New York: Oxford University Press, 2009), 8.

63. Ibid., 8.

64. H. L. Hunt, *Alpaca* (Dallas: H. L. Hunt Press, 1960).

65. "McCarthy, Hunt, and Facts Forum." *Reporter*, February 16, 1954, 20–21.

66. *Jeffersonian Democrat* (Austin, TX), September 15, 1936.

67. *Big Spring Daily Herald*, June 8, 1956.

68. The thrust of the doctrine of interposition was to declare *Brown v. Board of Education* unconstitutional on the grounds that it violated state sovereignty. Numan V. Bartley, *The Rise of Massive Resistance* (Baton Rouge: Louisiana State University Press, 1999), 126–27.

69. Dallasite J. H. Roberts wrote the John Birch Society's Robert Welch, asking "if you have any further information as to building products and materials being imported to this country from Communist nations. I have been unable to locate any materials other than matches." The Research Department of the John Birch Society responded that "there are quite a few products being imported from the Soviet bloc. Anyone of your discount houses carries these slave labor goods. There are coat hangers from Yugoslavia, whisk brooms from Hungary, dolls from Poland. By far the biggest commodity being sold in this country is Polish hams. Also, we are sure that Russian crabmeat must be coming into the United States since President Kennedy dropped the ban on it early this year." J. H. Roberts to the John Birch Society, November 1961; Research Department to J. H. Roberts, December 26, 1961—both in box 7, folder "1961," John Birch Society Records.

70. Janson and Eismann, *Far Right*, 112–13.

71. Jeff Woods, *Black Struggle, Red Scare: Segregation and Communism in the South, 1948–1968* (Baton Rouge: Louisiana State University Press, 2004), 6.

72. Green, "Far Right Wing," 183–84.

73. Davidson, *Race and Class*, 126; Walter Davenport, "Savior from Texas," *Collier's*, 116, August 18, 1945, 81.

74. Smoot, "Impeaching Earl Warren—Part I," 35.

75. Dan Smoot, "Unfair Housing," *Dan Smoot Report* 7, no. 4 (January 23, 1961): 25.

76. Ibid., 27.

77. Dan Smoot, "The Mississippi Tragedy," *Dan Smoot Report* 8, no. 41 (October 8, 1962): 327.

78. Smoot, *People along the Way*, 45.

79. Ibid., 34.

80. S. T. Darling to Dwight D. Eisenhower, June 25, 1952; undated newspaper clipping—both in box 530, folder D, Central Files, General Files, Eisenhower Presidential Library.

81. John Owen Beaty, *The Iron Curtain over America* (Dallas: Wilkinson, 1951), 15–59.

82. Stanley Marcus, *Minding the Store: A Memoir* (Boston: Little, Brown, 1974), 184.

83. David W. Reinhard, *The Republican Right since 1945* (Lexington: University Press of Kentucky, 1983), 178; Nancy MacLean, *Freedom Is Not Enough: The Opening of the American Work Place* (New York: R. Sage, 2006), 73; Dan T. Carter, *The Politics of Rage: George Wallace, the Origins of the New Conservatism, and the Transformation of American Politics* (New York: Simon & Schuster, 1995), 218; Donald T. Critchlow and Nancy MacLean, *Debating the American Conservative Movement: 1945 to the Present* (Lanham, MD: Rowman & Littlefield, 2009), 123–39; MacLean, "Neo-Confederacy versus the New Deal," in *Myth of Southern Exceptionalism*, 308–30; John C. Calhoun and Clyde Norman Wilson, *The Essential Calhoun: Selections from Writings, Speeches, and Letters* (New Brunswick, NJ: Transaction Publishers, 1992); Irving H. Bartlett, *John C. Calhoun: A Biography* (New York: W. W. Norton, 1993).

84. Critchlow and MacLean, *Debating the American Conservative Movement*, 137.

85. Smoot, "Impeaching Earl Warren—Part I," 37; Dan Smoot, "The Fourteenth Amendment," *Dan Smoot Report* 9, no. 1 (January 7, 1963): 1–8.

86. Green, "Far Right Wing," 192.

87. Barbara Raderstorf to Robert Welch, August 5, 1963, box 6, "Members letters sent to Welch" folder, John Birch Society Records.

88. Green, "Far Right Wing," 192.

89. *Dallas Morning News*, February 17, 1959.

90. *Dallas Morning News*, March 15, 16, 1955.

91. *Dallas Morning News*, March 17, 22, 1955.

92. Francine Carraro, *Jerry Bywaters: A Life in Art* (Austin: University of Texas Press, 1994), 173–204. *Dallas Morning News*, April 5, 1955.

93. George Germany to Robert Welch, September 1961, box 6, "Members letters sent to Welch" folder, John Birch Society Records.

94. Elizabeth Staples to Robert Welch, June 5, 1958, box 3, "Elizabeth Staples" folder, John Birch Society Records.

95. *Southern Conservative*, April 1952, March, September 1953, February 1954, April, May 1955.

96. Carleton, *Red Scare!*, 154–254.

97. Green, "Far Right Wing," 191.

98. Green, "Some Aspects of the Far Right Wing," 69–80; Green, "Far Right Wing," 227–30.

99. Unidentified individual to John Birch Society, Summer 1961, box 3, "Claude Allen" folder, John Birch Society Records.

100. Hunt, *Old Letters*, 29.

101. Green, "Far Right Wing," 113.

102. Jack Nelson and Gene Roberts, *The Censors and the Schools* (Boston: Little, Brown, 1963), 120–30.

103. *Texas Observer*, June 8, 1962; Nelson and Roberts, *Censors and the Schools*, 120–30; Green, "Some Aspects of the Far Right Wing," 69, 80; Mark Sherwin, *The Extremists* (New York: St. Martin's Press, 1963), 219.

Chapter 4

1. Leon McBeth, *The First Baptist Church of Dallas: Centennial History, 1868–1968* (Grand Rapids, MI: Zondervan, 1968), 245.

2. John W. Storey, *Texas Baptist Leadership and Social Christianity, 1900–1980* (College Station: Texas A&M University Press, 1986), 182–84; *Dallas Morning News*, February 23, 24, 1956.

3. Darwin Payne, *Big D: Triumphs and Troubles of an American Supercity in the 20th Century* (Dallas: Three Forks Press, 1994), 39.

4. William Neil Black, "Empire of Consensus: City Planning, Zoning, and Annexation in Dallas, 1900–1960," PhD diss., Columbia University, 1982, 146–50.

5. Michael Hazel, *Dallas: A History of "Big D"* (Austin: Texas State Historical Association, 1997), 80.

6. Payne, *Big D*, 72.

7. Kenneth Bridges, *Twilight of the Texas Democrats: The 1978 Governor's Race* (College Station: Texas A&M University Press, 2008), 5.

8. Robert B. Fairbanks, "From Consensus to Controversy: Public Housing in Dallas," in *Dallas Reconsidered: Essays in Local History*, ed. Michael Hazel (Dallas: Three Forks Press, 1995), 90; Robert B. Fairbanks, "Dallas in the 1940s: The Challenges and Opportunities of Defense Mobilization," in Miller and Sanders, *Urban Texas*, 143.

9. Numan V. Bartley, *The New South, 1945–1980* (Baton Rouge: Louisiana State University Press, 1995), 160; *Dallas Morning News*, August 13, 1955.

10. Ted Olson, *Crossroads: A Southern Culture Annual 2006* (Macon, GA: Mercer University Press, 2007), 109.

11. Robyn Duff Ladino, *Desegregating Texas Schools: Eisenhower, Shivers, and the Crisis at Mansfield High* (Austin: University of Texas Press, 1996), 41; Numan V. Bartley, *The Rise of Massive Resistance* (Baton Rouge: Louisiana State University Press, 1999), 98; Neil R. McMillen, *The Citizens' Council: Organized Resistance to the Second Reconstruction, 1954–1964* (Chicago: University of Illinois Press, 1971) 104–5.

12. Michael Phillips, *White Metropolis: Race, Ethnicity, and Religion in Dallas, 1841–2001* (Austin: University of Texas Press, 2006), 51; Winthrop D. Jordan, *White over Black: American Attitudes toward the Negro, 1550–1812* (New York: W. W. Norton, 1968), 54–60.

13. In a further testament to his belief in white supremacy, Daniel observed that the descendants of Japheth "were to comprise the great majority of the world's population."

14. Nimrod, Daniel wrote, was a "double-eyed anarchist" who rebelled against "God's plan of segregation of the races." Jesus also sanctioned segregation, according to Daniel. Since Moses had done so and Jesus never objected to anything that

Moses said, "the burden of proof" rested with those who would claim that Jesus was not also a segregationist. Carey Daniel, *God, the Original Segregationist* (Dallas: privately published, 1955), 1–11; Paul Harvey, "Religion, Race, and the Right in the South, 1945–1990," in *Politics and Religion in the White South*, ed. Glenn Feldman (Lexington: University Press of Kentucky), 104–7; Edward J. Blum and Paul Harvey, *The Color of Christ: The Son of God and the Saga of Race in America* (Chapel Hill: University of North Carolina Press, 2012), 215; Lewis V. Baldwin, *The Voice of Conscience: The Church in the Mind of Martin Luther King, Jr.* (Oxford: Oxford University Press, 2010), 156–58.

15. Daniel, *God, the Original Segregationist*, 1–11 (emphases added); Jane Dailey, "Sex, Segregation, and the Sacred after Brown," *Journal of American History* 91, no. 1 (June 2004): 119–44; Blum and Harvey, *Color of Christ*, 215–16; Paul Harvey, *Freedom's Coming: Religious Culture and the Shaping of the South from the Civil War Through the Civil Rights Era* (Chapel Hill: University of North Carolina Press, 2005), 233.

16. Daniel, *God, the Original Segregationist*, 1–11; Stephen R. Haynes, *Noah's Curse: The Biblical Justification of American Slavery* (Oxford: Oxford University Press, 2002), 86; Dailey, "Sex, Segregation, and the Sacred"; Blum and Harvey, *Color of Christ*, 215–216; Paul Harvey, *Freedom's Coming*, 233.

17. *Dallas Morning News*, August 21, 1955. Finsch likely took this from Daniel, *God, the Original Segregationist*. Citing Genesis 11:1, Daniel wrote, "'the whole earth was of one language and one speech.'" Then Nimrod led the building of the Tower of Babel in order to defy segregation: "'LEST, WE BE SCATTERED ABROAD UPON THE FACE OF THE WHOLE EARTH.'" According to Daniel, the United Nations and the builders of the Tower of Babel shared an "amazing parallel" as they both sought the integration of governments as well as races. Haynes, *Noah's Curse*, 86, 119–20; Daniel, *God, the Original Segregationist*, 1–11, 53–54.

18. *Dallas Morning News*, August 29, 1955.

19. *Dallas Morning News*, October 19, 1955.

20. Chandler Davidson, *Race and Class in Texas Politics* (Princeton, NJ: Princeton University Press, 1990), 214.

21. *Dallas Morning News*, February 27, 29; March 3, 4, 8, 18, 24, 1956.

22. Curtis W. Freeman, "Never Had I Been So Blind: W. A. Criswell's 'Change' on Racial Segregation," *Journal of Southern Religion* 10 (2007): 1–12; *Dallas Morning News*, February 24, 1956. By 1968, Criswell had abandoned his earlier belief that the bible supported segregation. "I've changed" Criswell said in a 1968 speech. "I have enlarged my sympathies and my heart during the past few years," he added.

23. *Dallas Morning News*, May 25, 1954; Bartley, *New South*, 160.

24. Bartley, *New South*, 163–66, 188–89; Bartley, *Rise of Massive Resistance*, 144–46.

25. Ladino, *Desegregating Texas Schools*, 41; Bartley, *Rise of Massive Resistance*, 98; McMillen, *Citizens' Council*, 104–5.

26. *Dallas Morning News*, March 6, October 12, 1955; February 28, 1956.

27. *Dallas Morning News*, February 28, 1956.

28. *Dallas Morning News*, June 21, 1956; November 5, 1963.

29. *Dallas Morning News*, October 14, 1956; McMillen, *Citizens' Council*, 265.

30. Tom P. Brady, *Black Monday* (Winona, MS: Association of Citizens' Councils, 1955), 12; McMillen, *Citizens' Council*, 163.

31. Brady, *Black Monday*, 84; Joseph Crespino, *In Search of Another Country: Mississippi and the Conservative Counterrevolution* (Princeton, NJ: Princeton University Press, 2007), 19–25.

32. V. Jacque Voegeli, *Free but Not Equal: The Midwest and the Negro during the Civil War* (Chicago: University of Chicago Press, 1967); Andrew R. L. Cayton and Susan E. Gray, *The American Midwest: Essays on Regional History* (Bloomington: Indiana University Press, 2001); Lana Ruegamer and Emma Lou Thornbrough, *Indiana Blacks in the Twentieth Century* (Bloomington: Indiana University Press, 2000).

33. Settlers from East Texas, which, as Neil Foley notes, "fit comfortably within the cultural and historiographical boundaries of the South, with its history of slavery, cotton, and postemancipation society," also filled Dallas. Foley, *The White Scourge: Mexicans, Blacks, and Poor Whites in Texas Cotton Culture* (Berkeley: University of California Press, 1997), 2.

34. Joseph Crespino, *Strom Thurmond's America* (New York: Hill and Wang, 2012), 6; Crespino, *In Search of Another Country*, 1–110; Michelle Nickerson, "Politically Desperate Housewives: Women and Conservatism in Postwar Los Angeles," *California History* 86, no. 3 (June 2009): 4–21; William Cronon, *Nature's Metropolis: Chicago and the Great West* (New York: W. W. Norton, 1991), 5–8; Thomas J. Sugrue, *The Origins of the Urban Crisis: Race and Inequality in Postwar Detroit* (Princeton, NJ: Princeton University Press, 1996); Kenneth L. Kusmer, *A Ghetto Takes Shape: Black Cleveland, 1870–1930* (Urbana: University of Illinois Press, 1976).

35. George Lewis, *Massive Resistance: The White Response to the Civil Rights Movement* (London: Hodder Arnold, 2006), 80.

36. Ladino, *Desegregating Texas Schools*, 97.

37. *Dallas Morning News*, September 8, 1956.

38. *Dallas Morning News*, September 29, 1956.

39. *Dallas Morning News*, October 10, 1956. See also statements of Charles Durham, Colin Walton, and others in *Dallas Morning News*, October 2, September 23, 1956.

40. Ladino, *Desegregating Texas Schools*, 38.

41. *Dallas Times Herald*, September 2, 1954.

42. Campaign material from 1954, box 1, folder 7, Bruce Alger Papers, Dallas Public Library, Dallas, TX.

43. George Palmer Banitch, "The Ultraconservative Congressman from Dallas: The Rise and Fall of Bruce Alger" (Master's thesis, University of Texas, 2001), 29; Payne, *Big D*, 280–82.

44. Historian Roger M. Olien credited Republican women with Bruce Alger's unprecedented victory. Banitch, "Ultraconservative Congressman," 2001, 33; Mrs. J. F. W. Hannay to Alger, 1954, box 1, folder 6, Alger Papers; Olien, *From Token to Triumph: The Texas Republicans Since 1920* (Dallas: Southern Methodist University

Press, 1982), 140, 141; Judge Whitfield Davidson to Alger, box 3, folder 11, "Letters of Congratulations, 1957," Alger Papers.

45. Payne, *Big D*, 281.

46. Dallas County GOP Newsletter, October 28, 1954, box 1, folder 7, Alger Papers.

47. According to Savage, Hackler was "trying to throw up a smokescreen to conceal his support by two block-voting special interests in Dallas County—the Negroes and the CIO." Newspaper clipping from *St. Louis Post Dispatch*, box 1, folder 8; newspaper clipping from *Dallas Times Herald*, box 1, folder 8—both in Alger Papers. Despite Savage's use of race in the Democratic primary, race was not a factor in the general election between Alger and Savage.

48. Banitch, "Ultraconservative Congressman," 30–39.

49. The liberals' disaffection was in part motivated by their hope that conservative Democrats like Savage would formally switch to the Republican Party and leave the Democratic Party to the liberal wing. Olien, *From Token to Triumph*, 139–41.

50. Bernard Cosman, "Republicanism in the Metropolitan South," (PhD diss., University of Alabama, 1960), 207; Payne, *Big D*, 282.

51. Bruce Alger to Frank Slay, November 12, 1954, box 1, folder 6, Alger Papers.

52. *Dallas Morning News*, June 1, 1955.

53. *Dallas Times Herald*, August 22, 1956.

54. *Richmond News Leader*, November 21, 23, 29, 1955; January 19, 1955; February 2, 1956; Bartley, *New South*, 189. By the spring of 1956, six southern legislatures—in Virginia, Alabama, Georgia, Louisiana, Mississippi, and South Carolina—had secured resolutions supporting interposition.

55. Statement of Congressman Bruce Alger regarding the Southerners' Resolution, March 12, 1956, box 3, folder 28, Alger Papers.

56. Campaign material, box 2, folder 21, Alger Papers.

57. *Dallas Morning News*, September 12, 1956.

58. Unidentified newspaper clipping, box 2, folder 21, Alger Papers.

59. Campaign material, box 2, folder 21, Alger Papers.

60. Olien, *From Token to Triumph*, 133. Leaders of the Radical Republicans during the Reconstruction Era, Stevens and Sumner were passionate advocates for the rights of black people.

61. Frank Slay to Bruce Alger, November 3, 1954; Slay to Alger, August 12, 1955—both in box 1, folder 6, Alger Papers.

62. Homer Massey to Bruce Alger, August 12, 1956, box 3, folder 2, Alger Papers.

63. *Dallas Morning News*, October 25, 1956.

64. "Segregation," box 2, folder 24, Alger Papers; Olien, *From Token to Triumph*, 146; Phillips, *White Metropolis*, 154–56.

65. Campaign material, box 2, folder 21, Alger Papers.

66. An early draft of Alger's statement also quoted from *Plessy*, "if one race be inferior to the other socially, the Constitution of the United States cannot put

them on the same plane." "Statement of Bruce Alger on Segregation," box 2, folder 24; "Segregation," box 4, folder 13—both in Alger Papers.

67. *Dallas Morning News*, May 5, 1958. For Alger's contentious relationship with the civic leaders of the Dallas Citizens Council, see Robert B. Fairbanks, *For the City as a Whole: Planning, Politics, and the Public Interest in Dallas, Texas, 1900–1965* (Columbus: Ohio State University Press, 1998), 220–24.

68. Albert L. Dixon to Bruce Alger, February 26, 1957, box 4, folder 13, Alger Papers.

69. *Dallas Morning News*, January 22, 1960.

70. *Dallas Morning News*, January 23, 1960.

71. *Dallas Morning News*, September 6, 1957.

72. *Dallas Morning News*, September 25, 1958.

73. *Dallas Morning News*, November 14, 1957.

74. *Dallas Morning News*, May 20, 1959; September 25, 27, 1959; October 4, 1959; *New York Times*, September 9, 1954; Bartley, *New South*, 160.

75. Phillips, *White Metropolis*, 154; Sara Diamond, *Roads to Dominion: Right Wing Movements and Political Power in the United States* (New York: Guilford Press, 1994), 75, 77.

76. *Dallas Morning News*, October 14, 1958.

77. Banitch, "Ultraconservative Congressman," 56.

78. H. L. Hunt to "Our Personnel," September 17, 1958, box 4, folder 2, Alger Papers.

79. In August 1957, the Texas legislature passed a law prohibiting desegregation unless it was approved by a school district in a referendum. The law further stymied the implementation of *Brown v. Board of Education*. When Dallas voted in a referendum in 1960, voters supported segregation by a margin of four to one. Judge T. Whitfield Davidson of the United States Fifth Circuit Court of Appeals enjoined Dallas to integrate its schools in September 1961. Bartley, *New South*, 220; Fairbanks, *For the City as a Whole*, 238. For the most complete inquiry into integration in Dallas, see Glenn M. Linden, *Desegregating Schools in Dallas: Four Decades in the Federal Courts* (Dallas: Three Forks Press, 1995). See also W. Marvin Dulaney, "Whatever Happened to the Civil Rights Movement in Dallas, Texas?" in *Essays on the American Civil Rights Movement*, ed. W. Marvin Dulaney and Kathleen Underwood (College Station: Texas A&M University Press, 1993), 76–77.

80. As Steven P. Miller has correctly observed, the "relationship between faith and segregation has garnered no small amount of scholarly back-and-forth." Some historians, such as Andrew W. Manis and Charles Marsh, have stressed the impact of segregationists on politics (as has the present chapter). Others, such as David L. Chappell and Paul Harvey, have argued that biblical defenses of segregation by Southern ministers were uncommon and of negligible importance compared to the condemnations of segregation in black churches, which most agree contributed directly to the dramatic breakthroughs of the civil rights movement. "Southern white ministers," wrote Chappell, "did not contribute much, and showed

little enthusiasm" for segregation. Ministers embracing spiritual segregation "faltered," Harvey observed, first, because belief in the principle was not unanimous and, second, because more moderate counterarguments in the end proved more compelling. On the whole, as Jane Dailey observes, "American historians have subscribed to King's version of the sacred history of the civil rights movement. Most books written about the struggle for racial equality emphasize the central role that religion played in articulating the challenge that the civil rights movement offered to the existing order of segregation. . . . The religiosity of anti-integrationists has not fared so well in the scholarly literature." Miller, *Billy Graham and the Rise of the Republican South* (Philadelphia: University of Pennsylvania Press, 2009), 241. For the argument that segregationist ministers were relatively impotent, see Chappell, *A Stone of Hope: Prophetic Religion and the Death of Jim Crow* (Chapel Hill: University of North Carolina Press, 2004), 3, 8, 318; Chappell, "Disunity and Religious Institutions in the White South," in *Massive Resistance: Southern Opposition to the Second Reconstruction*, ed. Clive Webb (New York: Oxford University Press, 2005), 136–50; Harvey, "Religion, Race, and the Right," 101–24; Chappell, "Religious Ideas of the Segregationists," *Journal of American Studies* 32, no. 2 (1998), 253; Harvey, "God and Negroes and Jesus and Sin and Salvation," in *Religion in the American South: Protestants and Others in History and Culture*, ed. Beth Barton Schweiger and Donald G. Mathews (Chapel Hill: University of North Carolina Press, 2004), 283, 285–91; Mark Newman, *Getting Right with God: Southern Baptists and Desegregation, 1945–1995* (Tuscaloosa: University of Alabama Press, 2001). On the importance of segregationist ministers, see Dailey, "Sex, Segregation, and the Sacred"; Manis, *Southern Civil Religions in Conflict: Civil Rights and the Culture Wars* (Macon, GA: Mercer University Press, 2002); Marsh, *God's Long Summer: Stories of Faith and Civil Rights* (Princeton, NJ: Princeton University Press, 1997); Bill J. Leonard, "A Theology for Racism: Southern Fundamentalists and the Civil Rights Movement, in *Southern Landscapes*, ed. Tony Badger et al. (Tübingen, Germany: Stauffenburg Verlag, 1996), 165–81.

81. Uhen, *From Token to Triumph*, 146; Phillips, *White Metropolis*, 154–56.

Chapter 5

1. Stanley Marcus, *Minding the Store: A Memoir* (Boston: Little, Brown, 1974), 252; George Norris Green, *Establishment in Texas Politics: The Primitive Years, 1938–1957* (Norman: University of Oklahoma Press, 1979), 200.

2. "Bruce Alger Tag Day, October 26, 1958," box 27, folder 19, Rita Crocker Clements Papers, Texas A&M University, College Station, TX.

3. William Leuchtenburg, *The White House Looks South: Franklin D. Roosevelt, Harry S. Truman, Lyndon B. Johnson* (Baton Rouge: Louisiana State University Press, 2007), 288.

4. Alfred Steinberg, *Sam Johnson's Boy: A Close-Up of the President from Texas* (New York: Macmillan, 1968), 543; Robert A. Caro, *The Passage of Power* (New York: Alfred A. Knopf, 2012), 150. Merle Miller, *Lyndon: An Oral Biography* (New York: Putnam, 1980), 271–72; Rowland Evans and Robert D. Novak, *Lyndon B. Johnson: The Ex-*

ercise of Power (New York: New American Library, 1966), 302–4; Robert Dallek, *Lone Star Rising: Lyndon Johnson and His Times, 1908–1960* (New York: Oxford University Press, 1991); *Dallas Morning News*, November 6, 1960.

5. Steinberg, *Sam Johnson's Boy*, 543. "Scared, white-faced, Lady-Bird appeared to be on the verge of tears," observed William Leuchtenburg (*White House Looks South*, 289). Rita Crocker Clements, interviewed by Meg Grier, Dallas, June 14, 1999; Joy Bell, interviewed by Meg Grier, Dallas, August 19, 1999.

6. Warren Leslie, *Dallas, Public and Private: Public and Private: Aspects of an American City* (Dallas: Southern Methodist University Press, 1998), 185.

7. Caro, *Passage of Power*, 150; Steinberg, *Sam Johnson's Boy*, 543.

8. *Dallas Morning News*, November 5, 1960; Alger's response, *Dallas Times Herald*, November 1960, Alger Collection, box 8, folder 12; Leslie, *Dallas, Public and Private*, 186.

9. *Dallas Morning News*, November 5, 1960.

10. *Dallas Morning News*, November 6, 1960.

11. Jonathan Schoenwald, *A Time for Choosing: The Rise of Modern American Conservatism* (New York: Oxford University Press, 2001), 69, 75. See also Sara Diamond, *Roads to Dominion: Right Wing Movements and Political Power in the United States* (New York: Guilford Press, 1994), 51–58. Buckley was referring to *The Life of John Birch*, a biography of the Baptist missionary murdered by the Chinese Communists, and *May God Forgive Us*, in which Welch provided political commentary on the loss of China and Eastern Europe to the Communists.

12. Diamond, *Roads to Dominion*, 53.

13. Rick Perlstein, *Before the Storm: Barry Goldwater and the Unmaking of the American Consensus* (New York: Nation Books, 2009), 110.

14. Robert Welch, *The Politician* (Belmont, MA: Belmont Pubishing, 1964), 224.

15. Ibid., 254–55.

16. Ibid., 15, 202, 204, 215; see also Carl T. Bogus, *Buckley: William F. Buckley and the Rise of American Conservatism* (New York: Bloombury Press, 2011), 176.

17. John Birch Society, *The Blue Book of the John Birch Society* (Boston: Western Islands, 1961), 9–11.

18. Ibid., 147; Schoenwald, *Time for Choosing*, 63, 80.

19. John Birch Society, *Blue Book*, 64; Michelle Nickerson, *Mothers of Conservatism: Women of the Postwar Right* (Princeton, NJ: Princeton University Press, 2012), 138–39.

20. Grier-Clements interview.

21. *Dallas Morning News*, April 16, 1961; J. McCarthy to Robert Welch, September, 1963, box 6, "Members letters sent to Welch" folder, John Birch Society Records, Brown University Library, Providence, RI.

22. *Dallas Morning News*, August 25, 1967; Grier-Collins interview.

23. Grier-Collins interview.

24. Francis X. Gannon to Mrs. Godfrey Collins, July 13, 1960, box 1, folder 38, Clements Papers.

25. *Dallas Morning News*, July 27, 1960; June 18, 1965; August 25, 1967.

26. Robert Morris, interviewed by Sister Frances Marie, Dallas, 1975, "Robert Morris, President" folder, Robert Morris Papers, Blakley Library, Lower Level Archives, University of Dallas, Irving, TX.

27. *Dallas Morning News*, July 27, 1960, June 18, 1965, August 25, 1967.

28. Grier-Collins interview; *Dallas Morning News*, February 7, 1965.

29. Daniel Bell, *The Radical Right* (Garden City, NY: Anchor Books, 1964); Benjamin R. Epstein and Arnold Forster, *Report on the John Birch Society* (New York: Vintage Books, 1966).

30. *Dallas Morning News*, April 16, 1961.

31. Nickerson, *Mothers of Conservatism*, 140.

32. *Dallas Morning News*, April 18, 1961.

33. Schoenwald, *Time for Choosing*.

34. For inquiring letters and their responses, see Bruce Alger to B. G. Massingill, March 21, 1961; Allen B. Cooper to Mary Hornbeck, April 13, 1961; W. E. Frazier to Alger, April 13, 1961—all in box 10, folder 1, Bruce Alger Papers, Dallas Public Library, Dallas, TX.

35. Margaret Charlton to Bruce Alger, April 20, 1961, box 10, folder 1, Alger Papers.

36. Robert J. George to Bruce Alger, April 6, 1961, box 10, folder 1, Alger Papers.

37. Bruce Alger to W. E. Frazier, April 18, 1961, box 10, folder 1, Alger Papers.

38. Bruce Alger to Richard N. Whittle, April 18, 1961, box 10, folder 1, Alger Papers.

39. David Murphy to Bruce Alger, April 8, 1961, box 10, folder 1, Alger Papers.

40. Katie Farrar to Bruce Alger, June 11, 1961, box 10, folder 1, Alger Papers.

41. Richard N. Whittle to Bruce Alger, April 15, 1961, box 10, folder 1, Alger Papers.

42. Richard N. Whittle to Bruce Alger, April 23, 1961, box 10, folder 1, Alger Papers.

43. Richard N. Whittle to Bruce Alger, April 15, 1961, box 10, folder 1, Alger Papers.

44. Robert J. George to Bruce Alger, April 6, 1961, box 10, folder 1, Alger Papers.

45. George Palmer Banitch, "The Ultraconservative Congressman from Dallas: The Rise and Fall of Bruce Alger,"(Master's thesis, University of Texas, 2001), 29; Bruce Alger to Frank McGehee, May 2, 1962, box 14, folder 25, Alger Papers.

46. Shawn Francis Peters, "'Did You Say That Mr. Dean Acheson Is a Pink?': The Walker Case and the Cold War," *Viet Nam Generation* 6, nos. 3–4, (1995): 20.

47. Schoenwald, *Time for Choosing*, 102–4.

48. Perlstein, *Before the Storm*, 146.

49. Chris Cravens, "Edwin A. Walker and the Right Wing in Dallas, 1960–1966" (Master's thesis, Southwest Texas State University, 1991); Bell, *Radical Right*, 526; Curtis Spears to John F. Kennedy, box 2910, "Edwin A. Walker Correspondence"

folder, White House Central Name File, John F. Kennedy Presidential Library, Boston, MA.

50. Donald T. Critchlow, *The Conservative Ascendancy: How the GOP Right Made Political History* (Cambridge, MA: Harvard University Press, 2007), 60.

51. John A. Andrew, *The Other Side of the Sixties: Young Americans for Freedom and the Rise of Conservative Politics* (New Brunswick, NJ: Rutgers University Press, 1997).

52. Darren Dochuk, *From Bible Belt to Sunbelt: Plain-Folk Religion, Grassroots Politics, and the Rise of Evangelical Conservatism* (New York: W. W. Norton, 2011), 234–37; Kent Courtney and Phoebe Courtney, *The Case of General Edwin A. Walker: The Muzzling of the Military Who Warn of the Communist Threat* (New Orleans: Conservative Society of America, 1961), 135.

53. *New York Times*, April 14, 18, and 23, 1961.

54. *Dallas Morning News*, June 4, 13, 1961; Cravens, "Edwin A. Walker," 81.

55. Cravens, "Edwin A. Walker"; Department of Defense Directorate for News Services, 12 June 1961, box 2910, "Edwin A. Walker Correspondence" folder, White House Central Name File, Kennedy Presidential Library; *Dallas Morning News*, June 13, 1961.

56. *Dallas Morning News*, June 10, 1961.

57. Pierre Salinger, *With Kennedy* (Garden City, NY: Doubleday, 1966), 143.

58. Box 2910, "Edwin A. Walker Correspondence" folder, White House Central Name File, Kennedy Presidential Library; Cravens, "Edwin A. Walker," 81.

59. Peters, "'Did You Say That Mr. Dean Acheson Is a Pink?'" 13.

60. George and Jack Salish to John F. Kennedy, May 8, 1961, box 2910, "Edwin A. Walker Correspondence" folder, White House Central Name File, Kennedy Presidential Library.

61. Schoenwald, *Time for Choosing*, 100–123; Peters, "'Did You Say That Mr. Dean Acheson Is a Pink?'"

62. Richard Dudman, *Men of the Far Right* (New York: Pyramid Books, 1962), 57.

63. "Out: Not with a Whimper but a Bang," *National Review*, November 18, 1961, 326.

64. Martha Martin, "American Eagle Weapons for Freedom," address by Edwin Walker, Jackson, MS, December 29, 1961, box 10, folder 23, Alger Papers.

65. Dudman, *Men of the Far Right*, 62; Edwin A. Walker, *Walker Speaks—Unmuzzled! Complete Text of Three Speeches* (Dallas: American Eagle, 1962).

66. Martin, "American Eagle Weapons." In Daniel 3:1–30, Daniel and his friends are thrown into a furnace after failing to bow down to King Nebuchadnezzar's music. They survived unharmed.

67. *Dallas Morning News*, March 21, 1962.

68. Edwin A. Walker to John F. Kennedy, April 22, 1962; Walker to Kennedy, September 26, 1962—both in box 2910, "Edwin A. Walker Correspondence" folder, White House Central Name File, Kennedy Presidential Library.

69. Walker, *Walker Speaks*, 11. On January 26, 1961, Soviet Premier Nikita Khrushchev released two American airmen, Freeman B. Olmstead and John F.

McKone, whose plane was shot down by the Russians over the Barents Sea on July 1, 1960.

70. Tibor Laky to Robert Welch, 1961, box 6, "Members letters sent to Welch" folder, John Birch Society Records.

71. A. G. Hill to Bruce Alger, January 18, 1962, box 10, folder 1, Alger Papers; *Dallas Morning News*, November 13, 1961.

72. Bruce Alger to Rev. Leslie Conrad, Jr., March 13, 1962, box 10, folder 23, Alger Papers.

73. Ibid.; *Dallas Morning News*, February 3, 1962; Oskar Korn to Bruce Alger, February 12, 1962, box 10, folder 23, Alger Papers.

74. Walker's decision to run as a Democrat did not account for Alger's strong opposition. Demonstrating that Walker's controversial positions and speaking deficiencies were at the heart of his reluctance, Alger wrote privately that "poor judgment is the least of his failings." Bruce Alger to A. G. Hill, February 12, 1962, box 10, folder 23, Alger Papers.

75. Critchlow, *Conservative Ascendancy*, 62–63.

76. Cravens, "Edwin A. Walker," 98.

77. Schoenwald, *Time for Choosing*.

78. Bay Bondeson to Bruce Alger, February 14, 1962; M. P. Slay to Alger, February 15, 1962—both in box 10, folder 23, Alger Papers.

79. William E. Brinson to Bruce Alger, February 14, 1962, box 10, folder 23, Alger Papers.

80. William B. Hixson, *Search for the American Right Wing: An Analysis of the Social Science Record, 1955–1987* (Princeton, NJ: Princeton University Press, 1992), 70–71; Niels Bjerre-Poulsen, *Right Face: Organizing the American Conservative Movement 1945–65* (Copenhagen: Museum Tusculanum, 2002), 188.

81. Taylor Branch, *Parting the Waters: America in the King Years, 1954–63* (New York: Simon & Schuster, 1988), 656.

82. Richard Reeves, *President Kennedy: Profile of Power* (New York: Simon & Schuster, 1993), 360.

83. Cravens, "Edwin A. Walker," 115.

84. Critchlow, *Conservative Ascendancy*, 302.

85. Nickerson, *Mothers of Conservatism*, 130.

86. R. B. Cowden to John F. Kennedy, November 21, 1962, box 2910, "Edwin A. Walker Correspondence" folder, White House Central Name File, Kennedy Presidential Library.

87. R. D. Laing, *The Politics of Experience* (New York: Pantheon, 1967); Thomas S. Szasz, *The Myth of Mental Illness: Foundations of a Theory of Personal Conduct* (New York: Hoeber, 1961).

88. Thomas S. Szasz, "The Shame of Medicine: The Case of General Edwin," *Freeman* 59, no. 8 (October 2009). http://www.thefreemanonline.org/columns/the -therapeutic-state/the-shame-of-medicine-the-case-of-general-edwin-walker/ (accessed July 27, 2012).

89. Erving Goffman, *Asylums: Essays on the Social Situation of Mental Patients and Other Inmates* (Garden City, NY: Anchor Books, 1961); Michel Foucault, *Madness and Civilization: A History of Insanity in the Age of Reason* (New York: Pantheon, 1965).

90. Thomas S. Szasz, "The Myth of Mental Illness," *American Psychologist* 15 (1960): 113–18.

91. Thomas S. Szasz, *Psychiatric Justice* (New York: Macmillan, 1965), 178.

92. Thomas S. Szasz, "Psychiatry's Threat to Civil Liberties," *National Review*, March 12, 1963, 191–93.

93. Szasz, "Shame of Medicine."

94. According to Szasz, Morris and his team of lawyers "believed it was obvious that Walker was sane. They wanted me to examine him and say so in court. . . . I reminded the attorneys that a courtroom confrontation concerning his 'sanity' would not be a search for truth or justice (which they well understood). . . . I urged them to avoid unnecessary dramatics and focus on freeing Walker from psychiatric detention as their sole goal. Finally, I persuaded them that in a Mississippi courtroom, I—with a foreign name and a foreign accent—would not be the best possible expert for Walker and talked them out of their plan to have me examine him and engage in a contest of 'expert opinions' about the predictably dire diagnoses of the government's psychiatric experts. Instead, I proposed that they 'nominate' a prominent Dallas university psychiatrist as their defense expert— that is, a local, publicly employed physician who could ill afford to declare Walker insane on the basis of his 'racist' views. Next morning I flew back to Syracuse." Szasz, "Shame of Medicine."

95. *Dallas Morning News*, March 19, 1961.

96. George H. Nash, *Conservative Intellectual Movement in America* (Wilmington, DE: ISI Books, 2006), 385–86. John A. Murley and John Alvis, *Willmoore Kendall: Maverick of American Conservatives* (Lanham, MD: Lexington Books, 2002).

97. Kendall's well-known irascibility probably accounted for the slight. Buckley said that Kendall was the "most difficult human being I have ever known." Nash, *Conservative Intellectual Movement*, 386.

98. On the Southern Agrarians, see Paul V. Murphy, *The Rebuke of History: The Southern Agrarians and American Conservative Thought* (Chapel Hill: University of North Carolina Press, 2001); Mark G. Malvasi, *The Unregenerate South: The Agrarian Thought of John Crowe Ransom, Allen Tate, and Donald Davidson* (Baton Rouge: Louisiana State University Press, 1997); *I'll Take My Stand: The South and the Agrarian Tradition* (Baton Rouge: Louisiana State University Press, 2006).

99. *Dallas Morning News*, January 9, 1965. Louise Cowan, *The Fugitive Group: A Literary History* (Baton Rouge: Louisiana State University Press, 1959).

100. Robert Morris, *No Wonder We Are Losing* (New York: Bookmailer, 1958), 1.

101. Ibid., 196, 199.

102. Ibid., 2, 194, 203.

103. *Dallas Morning News*, November 13, 1963; Robert Morris, *Disarmament: Weapon of Contrast* (New York: Bookmailer, 1963), 20–22, 54–56.

104. Morris, *Disarmament*, 54–56, 66, 70–71.

105. *Dallas Morning News*, September 18, 1963.

106. *Dallas Morning News*, October 4, 1962.

107. *Dallas Morning News*, June 13, 1962, October 9, 1962.

108. Dan Smoot, "The Wages of Socialism," *Dan Smoot Report* 8, no. 42 (October 15, 1962): 333–36.

109. Rita Crocker Clements, interviewed by Meg Grier, Dallas, June 14, 1999

110. Mrs. Richard D. Bass, "TARGET '64," Campaign Activities Committee Report, May 1963, box 25, folder 19, Clements Papers.

111. Notes by Rita Bass on Dallas Freedom Forum, box 1, folder 21, Clements Papers.

112. *Dallas Morning News*, November 4, 1962.

113. *Dallas Morning News*, April 6, 1952; May 18, 1958; January 13, 1973. See also Grier-Clements interview.

114. While Bass was involved significantly in the organization of Dallas's Freedom Forum in 1961, Morris was its headline speaker.

115. It is undeniable that Morris and his ideas incited the women's group. First, the *Dallas Morning News* observed that Morris "alerted the women to disarmament plans." Second, his book *Disarmament: Weapon of Conquest* and the group's "presentation poster" both presented the same argument for taking the matter of disarmament seriously. A letter from "80 Women" reads, "One of the most frequent statements made is this, 'Well, our [US Disarmament Program] proposal is probably just for propaganda. They would never actually do that.' The 'Presentation' brochure has the answer to this in a quote from the disarmament agency director." Morris said the same thing in the chapter "It Is For Real" (*Disarmament*, 45–46); letter of Mrs. George Jones, October 1, 1962, box 1, folder 14, Clements Papers; *Dallas Morning News*, October 31, 1962.

116. Handwritten notes by Rita Bass, "From the Desk of Rita C. Bass, Disarmament by Robert Morris," box 1, folder 14, Clements Papers.

117. *Dallas Morning News*, October 31, 1962.

118. Western Union Telegram to President John F. Kennedy, October 13, 1962, box 1, folder 14, Clements Papers.

119. James W. Woeber to "80 Women from Dallas," March 8, 1963, box 1, folder 14, Clements Papers.

120. Western Union Telegram to President John F. Kennedy, October 13, 1962, box 1, folder 14, Clements Papers.

121. *Dallas Morning News*, April 8, 1963.

122. Wayne Poucher, "What Kind of Disarmament," *Life Line*, December 14, 1962. Hunt preferred the term "constructive" to "conservative." "Conservative," Hunt said, "was an unfortunate word. It denotes mossback, reactionary, and old-fogyism." Heather Hendershot, *What's Fair On the Air: Cold War Right-Wing Broadcasting and the Public Interest* (Chicago: University of Chicago Press, 2011), 44.

123. *Dallas Morning News*, April 27, 1962.

124. Herbert S. Parmet, *George Bush: The Life of a Lone Star Yankee* (New York: Scribner, 1997), 107.

125. *Dallas Morning News*, March 31, 1964.

126. H. L. Hunt, *Old Letters from H. L. Hunt* (Dallas: HLH Products, 1970), 64, 67.

127. Robert G. Sherrill, "H. L. Hunt: Portrait of a Super-Patriot," *Nation*, February 24, 1964,186–91.

128. Attesting to the umbrella's popularity as a sign on the Right in the 1960s, Todd Gitlin writes, "In one corner, right-wingers from Young Americans for Freedom hoisted black umbrellas, intimating that we were Munich-minded equivalents of Neville Chamberlain, and hissed sporadically throughout the evening." Gitlin, *The Sixties: Years of Hope, Days of Rage* (Toronto: Bantam Books, 1987), 99.

129. Richard Reeves, *President Nixon: Alone in the White House* (New York: Simon & Schuster, 2001), 468; Geoffrey M. Kabaservice, *Rule and Ruin: The Downfall of Moderation and the Destruction of the Republican Party, from Eisenhower to the Tea Party* (New York: Oxford University Press, 2012), 100; Neil A. Hamilton, *The 1970s* (New York: Facts On File, 2006), 87.

130. Ira Chernus, *Eisenhower's Atoms for Peace* (College Station: Texas A&M University Press, 2002), 90.

131. Kevin Mattson, *Just Plain Dick: Richard Nixon's Checkers Speech and the "Rocking, Socking" Election of 1952* (New York: Bloomsbury, 2012), 168.

132. Thomas G. Paterson, *Kennedy's Quest for Victory: American Foreign Policy, 1961–1963* (New York: Oxford University Press, 1989), 42.

133. *Dallas Morning News*, September 24, 1978; September 26, 1978.

134. *Dallas Morning News*, March 24, 1963.

135. *Dallas Morning News*, August 12, 1963.

136. *Dallas Morning News*, August 5, 1963.

137. *Dallas Morning News*, September 13, 1963.

Chapter 6

1. Theodore H. White, *The Making of the President, 1964* (New York: Athenaeum, 1965), 136.

2. Peter O'Donnell to Rita Bass, June 2, 1958, box 2, folder 16, Rita Crocker Clements Papers, Texas A&M University, College Station, TX.

3. Robert B. Fairbanks, *For the City as a Whole: Planning, Politics, and the Public Interest in Dallas, Texas, 1900–1965* (Columbus: Ohio State University Press, 1998), 221.

4. *Dallas Morning News*, December 6, 1959.

5. *Dallas Morning News*, December 6, 1959. Martha Martin, "Who's Who in Big D GOP: Peter O'Donnell," *Battle Line*, August 1963, box 13, folder 33, Bruce Alger Papers, Dallas Public Library, Dallas, TX.

6. *Dallas Times Herald*, May 20, 1959.

7. "Analysis of Texas Political Situation," by Maurice Carlson, October 2, 1959, box 47, folder 15, White House Special Files Collection, Richard M. Nixon Presidential Library, Yorba Linda, CA.

8. Memorandum to Bob Haldeman from Charlie McWhorter, January 30, 1960, box 47, folder 15, White House Special Files Collection, Nixon Presidential Library.

9. Adopting the "Alger model," which involved large numbers of female Republican party workers, John Tower proved once again that women were the "organizational sinew" of the GOP. "My election was due," he declared, "to dedicated volunteers and amateurs at the precinct and block level." The *Dallas Morning News* concurred, condescendingly noting, "John Tower can, and does credit much of his victory to doorbell-ringing novices in Republican circles." Roger M. Olien, *From Token to Triumph: The Texas Republicans Since 1920* (Dallas: Southern Methodist University Press, 1982), 143, 203–4; *Dallas Morning News,* June 1, 1961, August 19, 1961.

10. John Tower to Jack Peltson, October 23, 1957, box 4, folder 7, John Tower Papers, Southwestern University, Georgetown, TX.

11. "Biographical Sketch" of John Tower, box 48NA, folder 4, Tower Papers; Paul Casdorph, *A History of the Republican Party in Texas, 1865–1965* (Austin, TX: Pemberton Press, 1965), 214.

12. William Burrow to Leonard Hall, box 51NA, folder 19, Tower Papers.

13. Karl A. Lamb, "Civil Rights and the Republican Platform: Nixon Achieves Control" in *Inside Politics: The National Conventions, 1960,* ed. Paul Tillet (Dobbs Ferry, NY: Oceana Publications, 1962), 55–84; Rick Perlstein, *Before the Storm: Barry Goldwater and the Unmaking of the American Consensus* (New York: Nation Books, 2009), 79–91; Edward G. Carmines and James A. Stimson, *Issue Evolution: Race and the Transformation of American Politics* (Princeton, NJ: Princeton University Press, 1989), 38–39; Unidentified newspaper clipping, box 48NA, folder 15, Tower Papers.

14. *Dallas Morning News,* June 4, 1961.

15. David Farber, *The Rise and Fall of Modern American Conservatism* (Princeton, NJ: Princeton University Press, 2010), 95.

16. *Dallas Morning News,* June 4, 1964.

17. *Dallas Morning News,* November 2, 1957; March 14, 1958.

18. *Dallas Morning News,* November 2, 1957.

19. *Dallas Morning News,* August 24, 1958.

20. *Dallas Morning News,* January 8, 1959.

21. Olien, *From Token to Triumph,* 183.

22. *Dallas Morning News,* April 8, 1962.

23. *Dallas Morning News,* November 7, 1962.

24. Kim Phillips-Fein, *Invisible Hands: The Making of the Conservative Movement from the New Deal to Reagan* (New York: W. W. Norton, 2009), 115–49.

25. Catherine Colgan, phone interview conducted by Meg Grier, Virginia Beach, VA, September 24, 1999.

26. F. Clifton White and William J. Gill, *Suite 3505: The Story of the Draft Goldwater Movement* (New Rochelle, NY: Arlington House, 1967), 158.

27. Martha Martin, "Who's Who In Big D GOP: Harry W. Bass, Jr.," *Battle Line,* July 1963, box 13, folder 33, Alger Papers.

28. Olien, *From Token to Triumph*, 188.

29. Olien, *From Token to Triumph*, 189.

30. Martha Martin, "Who's Who in Big D GOP: Peter O'Donnell," *Battle Line*, August 1963, box 13, folder 33, Alger Papers.

31. While Republican delegates in California ultimately backed Goldwater, as Republican strategist John H. Kessell observed due to the indefatigable efforts of "Goldwater groups in Los Angeles and Orange Counties," the delegates were not secured until June of 1964, when the Arizona senator beat New York governor Nelson Rockefeller, 51.6 percent to 48.4 percent, in the California primary. Kessel, *The Goldwater Coalition: Republican Strategies in 1964* (Indianapolis: Bobbs-Merrill, 1968) 88.

32. Stephen C. Shadegg, *What Happened to Goldwater? The Inside Story of the 1964 Republican Campaign* (New York: Holt, Rinehart and Winston, 1965), 62.

33. Allan J. Lichtman, *White Protestant Nation: The Rise of the American Conservative Movement* (New York: Atlantic Monthly Press, 2008), 246–47.

34. David W. Reinhard, *The Republican Right since 1945* (Lexington: University Press of Kentucky, 1983), 178.

35. Dan T. Carter, *The Politics of Rage: George Wallace, the Origins of the New Conservatism, and the Transformation of American Politics* (New York: Simon & Schuster, 1995), 218.

36. Reinhard, *Republican Right since 1945*, 178.

37. Nancy MacLean, *Freedom Is Not Enough: The Opening of the American Work Place* (New York: R. Sage, 2006), 73.

38. Carter, *Politics of Rage*, 218; Donald T. Critchlow and Nancy MacLean, *Debating the American Conservative Movement: 1945 to the Present* (Lanham, MD: Rowman & Littlefield, 2009), 123–39.

39. Farber, *Rise and Fall*, 89.

40. Perlstein, *Before the Storm*, 48.

41. Joseph Crespino, *Strom Thurmond's America* (New York: Hill and Wang, 2012), 131.

42. *Dallas Morning News*, March 3, 1960, August 7, 1960. Critchlow and MacLean, *Debating the American Conservative Movement*, 123–39; Nelson Lichtenstein, *State of the Union: A Century of American Labor* (Princeton, NJ: Princeton University Press, 2002), 139.

43. White and Gill, *Suite 3505*, 119.

44. Reinhard, *Republican Right since 1945*, 169.

45. Lichtman, *White Protestant Nation*, 246.

46. White and Gill, *Suite 3505*, 184.

47. Martha Martin, "Who's Who in Big D GOP: Peter O'Donnell," *Battle Line*, August 1963, box 13, folder 33, Alger Papers.

48. Lichtman, *White Protestant Nation*, 249.

49. *Dallas Morning News*, May 12, 1963.

50. *Dallas Morning News*, June 18, 1963.

51. Kessel, *Goldwater Coalition*, 42; Shadegg, *What Happened to Goldwater?*, 68.

52. Shadegg, *What Happened to Goldwater?*, 60.

53. White and Gill, *Suite 3505*, 151.

54. Shadegg, *What Happened to Goldwater?*, 63, 68, 93.

55. Goldwater had an "atomic thorn in his heel," observed O'Donnell. Shadegg, *What Happened to Goldwater?*, 273.

56. White and Gill, *Suite 3505*, 225–26.

57. Shadegg, *What Happened to Goldwater?*, 90; White and Gill, *Suite 3505*, 265.

58. Olien, *From Token to Triumph*, 190; Shadegg, *What Happened to Goldwater?*, 176–77.

59. *Dallas Morning News*, June 20, 1964.

60. Critchlow and MacLean, *Debating the American Conservative Movement*, 123–39.

61. MacLean, *Freedom Is Not Enough*, 72.

62. *Dallas Morning News*, June 15, 1964.

63. Lichtman, *White Protestant Nation*, 254.

64. *Dallas Morning News*, June 21, 1964.

65. Perlstein, *Before the Storm*, 254–56.

66. Carter, *Politics of Rage*; Michael W. Flamm, *Law and Order: Street Crime, Civil Unrest, and the Crisis of Liberalism in the 1960s* (New York: Columbia University Press, 2005).

67. Confidential memo by Peter H. Clayton, 6/25/63, "Goldwater President Campaign, 1964," Box 4, Denison Kitchel Papers, Hoover Institution Archives. Michael William Flamm, "'Law and Order': Street Crime, Civil Disorder, and the Crisis of Liberalism," PhD diss., Columbia University, 1998, 74 (http://search.proquest.com/docview/304431458?accountid=9673).

68. "It is impossible to doubt," Walter Lippman wrote in June of 1964, "that Senator Goldwater intends to make his candidacy the rallying point of white resistance." *Dallas Morning News*, June 2, 1964; Michelle Nickerson, *Mothers of Conservatism: Women of the Postwar Right* (Princeton, NJ: Princeton University Press, 2012), 163.

69. *Dallas Morning News*, June 17, 1964.

70. *Dallas Morning News*, October 15, 1964.

71. *Dallas Morning News*, June 17, 1964.

72. Flamm, *Law and Order*, 33.

73. White, *The Making of the President, 1964*, 200.

74. Taylor Branch, *Pillar of Fire: America in the King Years, 1963–65* (New York: Simon & Schuster, 1998), 402.

75. J. William Middendorf, *A Glorious Disaster* (New York: Basic Books, 2008), 303.

76. Sean P. Cunningham, *Cowboy Conservatism: Texas and the Rise of the Modern Right* (Lexington: University Press of Kentucky, 2010), 60–61.

77. Flamm, *Law and Order*, 48–50; Farber, *Rise and Fall*, 116–18.

78. Cunningham, *Cowboy Conservatism*, 58.

79. Meg McKain Grier, *Grassroots Women: A Memoir of the Texas Republican Party* (Boerne, TX: Wingscape Press, 2001), 67–68.

80. White and Gill, *Suite 3505*, 266.

81. *Dallas Morning News*, July 13, 1965.

82. Donald T. Critchlow, *The Conservative Ascendancy: How the GOP Right Made Political History* (Cambridge, MA: Harvard University Press, 2007), 67.

83. Reinhard, *Republican Right since 1945*, 206.

84. George Palmer Banitch, "The Ultraconservative Congressman from Dallas: The Rise and Fall of Bruce Alger," (Master's thesis, University of Texas, 2001), 87–90.

85. Ibid., 107.

86. "The Shame of Dallas," *Saturday Evening Post*, April 11, 1964, 82.

87. *Dallas Morning News*, November 17, 1968.

88. Richard Austin Smith, "How Business Failed Dallas," *Fortune*, July 1964, 156–62, 211, 218; Willie Morris, "What Makes Dallas Different," *New Republic*, June 20, 1964, 20–22.

89. "The Dallas Rejoinder," *Nation*, May 25, 1964, 519.

90. *Dallas Morning News*, November 5, 1964; Saul Friedman, "Tussle in Texas," *Nation*, February 3, 1964, 114–17.

91. *Dallas Morning News*, November 5, 1964.

92. *Dallas Morning News*, November 11, 1966.

93. *Dallas Morning News*, August 19, 1968.

94. Farber, *Rise and Fall*, 79.

95. Ibid., 117.

96. Perlstein, *Before the Storm*, 365.

97. Laura Jane Gifford, "'Dixie Is No Longer in the Bag,': South Carolina Republicans and the Election of 1960," *Journal of Policy History* 19, no. 2 (2007): 214.

98. *Dallas Morning News*, November 11, 1966.

99. *Dallas Morning News*, July 11, 13, 1965.

100. Press release from Maurice I. Carlson, October 17, 1964, box 934, folder 2, Tower papers.

101. *Dallas Morning News*, December 16, 1965.

102. Cunningham, *Cowboy Conservatism*, 108.

103. *Dallas Morning News*, April 12, 1965.

104. *Dallas Morning News*, May 9, 1980.

105. MacLean, *Freedom Is Not Enough*, 225–49.

106. *Dallas Morning News*, July 7, 1971.

107. *Dallas Morning News*, August 24, 1975.

108. *Dallas Morning News*, March 16, 1972.

109. *Dallas Morning News*, December 5, 1974.

110. Cunningham, *Cowboy Conservatism*, 105–6.

111. Ibid., 115–16.

112. Ibid., 157; *Dallas Morning News*, September 23, 1971.

113. Ibid., 108, 94–96.

114. Ibid., 68–75, 94–96; Flamm, *Law and Order*.

115. Joseph E. Lowndes, *From the New Deal to the New Right: Race and the Southern Origins of Modern Conservatism* (New Haven, CT: Yale University Press, 2008), 120–39; Matthew D. Lassiter, *The Silent Majority: Suburban Politics in the Sunbelt South* (Princeton, NJ: Princeton University Press, 2006); Cunningham, *Cowboy Conservatism*, 94–96.

116. MacLean, *Freedom Is Not Enough*, 244–47.

117. Cunningham, *Cowboy Conservatism*, 74, 113, 144–46; Craig Allan Kaplowitz, *LULAC, Mexican Americans, and National Policy* (College Station: Texas A & M University Press, 2005), 197, 202–3.

118. *Dallas Morning News*, April 15, 1970.

119. Paul Burka, "Jim Collins and the Armies of the Faithful," *Texas Monthly*, October 1982, 24–27, 204–18.

120. *Dallas Morning News*, May 9, 1980.

121. MacLean, *Freedom Is Not Enough*, 225–49.

122. *Dallas Morning News*, October 6, 1970.

123. MacLean, *Freedom Is Not Enough*, 225–49, 259–61.

124. Curtis W. Freeman, "Never Had I Been So Blind: W. A. Criswell's 'Change' on Racial Segregation," *Journal of Southern Religion* 10 (2007): 1–12; Barry Hankins, *Uneasy in Babylon: Southern Baptist Conservatives and American Culture* (Tuscaloosa: University of Alabama Press, 2004), 242; Mark Newman, *Getting Right with God: Southern Baptists and Desegregation, 1945–1995* (Tuscaloosa: University of Alabama Press, 2001), 84; Darren Dochuk, *From Bible Belt to Sunbelt: Plain-Folk Religion, Grassroots Politics, and the Rise of Evangelical Conservatism* (New York: W. W. Norton, 2011), 278.

125. Dochuk, *From Bible Belt to Sunbelt*, 279–81; Stephen P. Miller, *Billy Graham and the Rise of the Republican South* (Philadelphia: University of Pennsylvania Press, 2009), 119–54.

126. Scott Billingsley, *It's a New Day: Race and Gender in the Modern Charismatic Movement* (Tuscaloosa: University of Alabama Press, 2008), 1–14, 104–29; Dochuk, *From Bible Belt to Sunbelt*, 281–85; Vinson Synan, *The Holiness-Pentecostal Tradition: Charismatic Movements in the Twentieth Century* (Grand Rapids, MI: William B. Eerdmans, 1997), 183–84; Richard Quebedeaux, *The New Charismatics: The Origins, Development, and Significance of Neo-Pentecostalism* (Garden City, NY: Doubleday, 1976), 157.

127. David Edwin Harrell, *Pat Robertson: A Life and Legacy* (Grand Rapids, MI: William B. Eerdmans, 2010); Pat Robertson and Jamie Buckingham, *Shout It from the Housetops* (Plainfield, NJ: Logos International, 1972); David John Marley, *Pat Robertson: An American Life* (Lanham, MD: Rowman & Littlefield, 2007); Alec Foege, *The Empire God Built: Inside Pat Robertson's Media Machine* (New York: John Wiley & Sons, 1996).

128. Geoffrey M. Kabaservice, *Rule and Ruin: The Downfall of Moderation and the Destruction of the Republican Party, from Eisenhower to the Tea Party* (New York: Oxford University Press, 2012), 104.

129. Kabaservice, *Rule and Ruin*; Crespino, *Strom Thurmond's America*, 195.

130. David Lublin, *The Republican South: Democratization and Partisan Change* (Princeton, NJ: Princeton University Press, 2004), xvi–xvii.

Epilogue

1. Allan J. Lichtman, *White Protestant Nation: The Rise of the American Conservative Movement* (New York: Atlantic Monthly Press, 2008), 344.

2. Sean P. Cunningham, *Cowboy Conservatism: Texas and the Rise of the Modern Right* (Lexington: University Press of Kentucky, 2010), 232.

3. William Martin, "God's Angry Man," *Texas Monthly*, April 1981, 223.

4. Lahr, *Millennial Dreams*, 173–75.

5. Daniel K. Williams, *God's Own Party: The Making of the Christian Right* (Oxford: Oxford University Press, 2010), 115–19.

6. Cunningham, *Cowboy Conservatism*, 156.

7. Paul Eshleman and Norman B. Rohrer, *The Explo Story; A Plan to Change the World* (Glendale, CA: G/L Regal Books, 1972); John G. Turner, *Bill Bright and Campus Crusade for Christ: The Renewal of Evangelicalism in Postwar America* (Chapel Hill: University of North Carolina Press, 2008), 139–51; Angela M. Lahr, *Millennial Dreams and Apocalyptic Nightmares: The Cold War Origins of Political Evangelicalism* (New York: Oxford University Press, 2007), 171–73.

8. Charles Marsh, *Wayward Christian Soldiers: Freeing the Gospel from Political Captivity* (Oxford: Oxford University Press, 2007), 22.

9. Williams, *God's Own Party*, 141.

10. Jerome L. Himmelstein, *To the Right: The Transformation of American Conservatism* (Berkeley: University of California Press, 1990), 97–128.

11. Williams, *God's Own Party*, 141. Demonstrating that many former Republican Goldwater backers from Dallas had moderated their positions since 1964, long-standing Dallas party leaders like Peter O'Donnell and John Tower backed President Ford's nomination in 1976. O'Donnell feared that nominating former California governor Ronald Reagan would lead to a repeat of the rout in 1964. Tower declared glibly, "There's not a chance he [Reagan] can get the nomination." Despite the feeling among party leaders that a Reagan candidacy in 1976 would be "ill-advised," Dallas grassroots Republican activist Gwen Pharo led the drive for Reagan that year, and J. Evetts Haley served as a Reagan delegate at the 1976 Texas state convention. Gilbert Garcia, *Reagan's Comeback: Four Weeks in Texas That Changed American Politics Forever* (San Antonio, TX: Trinity University Press, 2012), 11–119; Chandler Davidson, *Race and Class in Texas Politics* (Princeton, NJ: Princeton University Press, 1990), 201–3; Cunningham, *Cowboy Conservatism*, 155–77.

12. Williams, *God's Own Party*, 182–90.

13. Martin, "God's Angry Man," 223.

14. *Dallas Morning News*, October 17, 1975.

15. Ibid.

16. Hunt started buying silver in the early 1970s, nearly cornered the market by 1979, and encouraged Congressman Collins to invest in the commodity as well.

Collins heeded the advice and made $160,000 from his friend's tip. Davidson, *Race and Class*, 201–3; Harry Hurt, *Texas Rich: The Hunt Dynasty, from the Early Oil Days through the Silver Crash* (New York: W. W. Norton, 1981), 435, 400.

17. *Dallas Morning News*, October 3, 1981; Paul Burka, "Jim Collins and the Armies of the Faithful," *Texas Monthly*, October 1982, 24–27, 204–18.

18. Donald T. Critchlow, *Intended Consequences: Birth Control, Abortion, and the Federal Government in Modern America* (New York: Oxford University Press, 1999), 140.

19. *Dallas Morning News*, November 19, 1965, April 24, 1966.

20. Sean Wilentz, *The Age of Reagan: A History, 1974–2008* (New York: Harper, 2008), 89–95.

21. Carolyn Barta, *Bill Clements: Texan to His Toenails* (Austin, TX: Eakin Press, 1997).

22. Cunningham, *Cowboy Conservatism*, 231.

23. Davidson, *Race and Class*, 216.

24. *Washington Post*, August 13, 2009.

25. Geoffrey M. Kabaservice, *Rule and Ruin: The Downfall of Moderation and the Destruction of the Republican Party, from Eisenhower to the Tea Party* (New York: Oxford University Press, 2012), 388–89.

26. *Dallas Morning News*, November 24, 1963.

Bibliography

Manuscript Collections

Bruce Alger Papers, Dallas Public Library, Dallas, TX
John Birch Society Records, John Hay Library, Brown University, Providence, RI
Earle Cabell Papers, DeGolyer Library, Southern Methodist University, Dallas, TX
Rita Crocker Clements Papers, Cushing Memorial Library and Archives, Texas A&M University, College Station, TX
James Collins Papers, DeGolyer Library, Southern Methodist University, Dallas, TX
Dwight D. Eisenhower Papers, Dwight D. Eisenhower Presidential Library, Abilene, KS
Willmoore Kendall Papers, Blakley Library, Lower Level Archives, University of Dallas, Irving, TX
John F. Kennedy Papers, John F. Kennedy Presidential Library, Boston, MA
Stanley Marcus Papers, DeGolyer Library, Southern Methodist University, Dallas, TX
Robert Morris Papers, Blakley Library, Lower Level Archives, University of Dallas, Irving, TX
Richard M. Nixon Papers, Richard M. Nixon Presidential Library, Yorba Linda, CA
John Tower Papers, Southwestern University, Georgetown, TX

Interviews

University of North Texas Oral History Collection, Women in the Texas Republican Party Oral History Project

Mary Anna Sewalt	Alma Box	Carol Reed
Florence Shapiro	Vivian T. Starks	Barbara Campbell
Jane Guzman	Kay C. Copeland	

Dallas Public Library Oral History Collection
Bruce Alger

Dallas County Republicans, interviewed by Meg Grier

Joy Bell	Taffy Goldsmith
Catherine Colgan	Sally McKenzie
Mary Ann Collins	Peter O'Donnell
Rita Crocker Clements	Gwen Pharo
Joan Gaidos	Mary Lou Wiggins

Secondary Sources

Aistrup, Joseph A. *The Southern Strategy Revisited: Republican Top-Down Advancement in the South*. Lexington: University Press of Kentucky, 1996.

Alger, Bruce, and Roy Edward Colby. *Revolutionary Actions . . . U.S.A. . . . in Retrospect: What to Do Now*. Washington, DC: Citizens Evaluation Institute, 1971.

Allitt, Patrick. *Catholic Intellectuals and Conservative Politics in America, 1950–1985*. Ithaca, NY: Cornell University Press, 1993.

———. *The Conservatives: Ideas and Personalities throughout American History*. New Haven, CT: Yale University Press, 2009.

Ambrose, Stephen E. *Eisenhower: Soldier and President*. New York: Simon & Schuster, 1990.

Andrew, John A. *The Other Side of the Sixties: Young Americans for Freedom and the Rise of Conservative Politics*. New Brunswick, NJ: Rutgers University Press, 1997.

Bainbridge, John. *The Super-Americans; A Picture of Life in the United States, As Brought into Focus, Bigger Than Life, in the Land of the Millionaires—Texas*. Garden City, NY: Doubleday, 1961.

Baldwin, Lewis V. *The Voice of Conscience: The Church in the Mind of Martin Luther King, Jr.* Oxford: Oxford University Press, 2010.

Banitch, George Palmer. "The Ultraconservative Congressman from Dallas: The Rise and Fall of Bruce Alger, 1954–1964." Master's thesis, University of Texas at Arlington, 2001.

Barkun, Michael. *A Culture of Conspiracy: Apocalyptic Visions in Contemporary America*. Berkeley: University of California Press, 2003.

Barta, Carolyn. *Bill Clements: Texan to His Toenails*. Austin, TX: Eakin Press, 1997.

Bartlett, Irving H. *John C. Calhoun: A Biography*. New York: W. W. Norton, 1993.

Bartley, Numan V. *The New South, 1945–1980*. Baton Rouge: Louisiana State University Press, 1995.

———. *The Rise of Massive Resistance*. Baton Rouge: Louisiana State University Press, 1999.

Bass, Jack, and Walter De Vries. *The Transformation of Southern Politics: Social Change and Political Consequence since 1945*. New York: Basic Books, 1976.

Beaty, John Owen. *The Iron Curtain over America*. Dallas: Wilkinson, 1951.

Bell, Daniel. "The Dispossessed." In *The Radical Right*, edited by Daniel Bell. Garden City, NY: Anchor Books, 1964.

———. "Interpretations of American Politics." In *The Radical Right*, edited by Daniel Bell. Garden City, NY: Anchor Books, 1964.

———. *The Radical Right*. Garden City, NY: Anchor Books, 1964.

Bernard, Richard M., and Bradley R. Rice. *Sunbelt Cities: Politics and Growth since World War II*. Austin: University of Texas Press, 1983.

Billingsley, Scott. *It's a New Day: Race and Gender in the Modern Charismatic Movement*. Tuscaloosa: University of Alabama Press, 2008.

Bjerre-Poulsen, Niels. *Right Face: Organizing the American Conservative Movement 1945–65*. Copenhagen: Museum Tusculanum, 2002.

Black, William Neil. "Empire of Consensus: City Planning, Zoning, and Annexation in Dallas, 1900–1960." PhD dissertation, Columbia University, 1982.

Blight, David W. *Race and Reunion: The Civil War in American Memory*. Cambridge, MA: Belknap Press/Harvard University Press, 2001.

Blodgett, Geoffrey. *The Gentle Reformers: Massachusetts Democrats in the Cleveland Era*. Cambridge, MA: Harvard University Press, 1966.

Blum, Edward J., and Paul Harvey. *The Color of Christ: The Son of God and the Saga of Race in America*. Chapel Hill: University of North Carolina Press, 2012.

Bogus, Carl T. *Buckley: William F. Buckley and the Rise of American Conservatism*. New York: Bloombury Press, 2011.

Bowden, Jeff. "Largemouth Bass." *D Magazine*, December 1, 2000.

Bowen, Michael. *The Roots of Modern Conservatism: Dewey, Taft, and the Battle for the Soul of the Republican Party*. Chapel Hill: University of North Carolina Press, 2011.

Boyer, Paul. *When Time Shall Be No More: Prophecy Belief in Modern American Culture*. Cambridge, MA: Belknap Press, 1992.

Brady, Tom P. *Black Monday*. Winona, MS: Association of Citizens' Councils, 1955.

Branch, Taylor. *Parting the Waters: America in the King Years, 1954–63*. New York: Simon & Schuster, 1988.

———. *Pillar of Fire: America in the King Years, 1963–65*. New York, NY: Simon & Schuster, 1998.

Brennan, Mary C. *Turning Right in the Sixties: The Conservative Capture of the GOP*. Chapel Hill: University of North Carolina Press, 1995.

Bridges, Kenneth. *Twilight of the Texas Democrats: The 1978 Governor's Race*. College Station: Texas A&M University Press, 2008.

Brown, Stanley H. *H. L. Hunt: A Biography*. Chicago: Playboy Press, 1976.

———. *Ling: The Rise, Fall, and Return of a Texas Titan*. New York: Atheneum, 1972.

Buenger, Walter L. *The Path to a Modern South: Northeast Texas between Reconstruction and the Great Depression*. Austin: University of Texas Press, 2001.

Burka, Paul. "Jim Collins and the Armies of the Faithful." *Texas Monthly*, October 1982.

Burns, Jennifer. *Goddess of the Market: Ayn Rand and the American Right*. Oxford: Oxford University Press, 2009.

Burns, Robert E. *Being Catholic, Being American: The Notre Dame Story, 1934–1952*. Notre Dame, IN: University of Notre Dame Press, 2000.

Burrough, Bryan. *The Big Rich: The Rise and Fall of the Greatest Texas Oil Fortunes*. New York: Penguin Press, 2009.

Cain, Edward. *They'd Rather Be Right: Youth and the Conservative Movement*. New York: MacMillan, 1963.

Caldwell, Bruce. *Hayek's Challenge: An Intellectual Biography of F. A. Hayek*. Chicago: University of Chicago Press, 2004.

Calhoun, John C., and Clyde Norman Wilson. *The Essential Calhoun: Selections from Writings, Speeches, and Letters*. New Brunswick, NJ: Transaction Publishers, 1992.

Campbell, Randolph B. *An Empire for Slavery: The Peculiar Institution in Texas, 1821–1865*. Baton Rouge: Louisiana State University Press, 1989.

———. *Gone to Texas: A History of the Lone Star State.* New York: Oxford University Press, 2003.

———. *Grass-Roots Reconstruction in Texas: 1865 to 1880.* Baton Rouge: Louisiana State University Press, 1997.

Carleton, Don E. *Red Scare!: Right-Wing Hysteria, Fifties Fanaticism, and Their Legacy in Texas.* Austin: Texas Monthly Press, 1985.

Carmines, Edward G., and James A. Stimson. *Issue Evolution: Race and the Transformation of American Politics.* Princeton, NJ: Princeton University Press, 1989.

Caro, Robert A. *The Passage of Power.* New York: Alfred A. Knopf, 2012.

Carpenter, Joel A. *Revive Us Again: The Reawakening of American Fundamentalism.* New York: Oxford University Press, 1997.

Carraro, Francine. *Jerry Bywaters: A Life in Art.* Austin: University of Texas Press, 1994.

Carter, Dan T. *From George Wallace to Newt Gingrich: Race in the Conservative Counterrevolution, 1963–1994.* Baton Rouge: Louisiana State University Press, 1996.

———. *The Politics of Rage: George Wallace, the Origins of the New Conservatism, and the Transformation of American Politics.* New York: Simon & Schuster, 1995.

Casdorph, Paul. *A History of the Republican Party in Texas, 1865–1965.* Austin, TX: Pemberton Press, 1965.

Cayton, Andrew R. L., and Susan E. Gray. *The American Midwest: Essays on Regional History.* Bloomington: Indiana University Press, 2001.

Chappell, David L. "Disunity and Religious Institutions in the White South." In *Massive Resistance: Southern Opposition to the Second Reconstruction*, edited by Clive Webb, 136–50. New York: Oxford University Press, 2005.

———. "Religious Ideas of the Segregationists." *Journal of American Studies* 32, no. 2 (1998).

———. *A Stone of Hope: Prophetic Religion and the Death of Jim Crow.* Chapel Hill: University of North Carolina Press, 2004.

Chernus, Ira. *Eisenhower's Atoms for Peace.* College Station: Texas A&M University Press, 2002.

Cosman, Bernard. "Republicanism in the Metropolitan South." PhD dissertation, University of Alabama, 1960.

Courtney, Kent, and Phoebe Courtney. *The Case of General Edwin A. Walker: The Muzzling of the Military Who Warn of the Communist Threat.* New Orleans: Conservative Society of America, 1961.

Cowan, Louise. *The Fugitive Group: A Literary History.* Baton Rouge: Louisiana State University Press, 1959.

Cravens, Chris. "Edwin A. Walker and the Right Wing in Dallas, 1960–1966." Master's thesis, Southwest Texas State University, 1991.

Crespino, Joseph. *In Search of Another Country: Mississippi and the Conservative Counterrevolution.* Princeton, NJ: Princeton University Press, 2007.

———. *Strom Thurmond's America.* New York: Hill and Wang, 2012.

Crichton, John A. *The Republican-Democrat Political Campaigns in Texas in 1964.* Author House, 2004.

Criswell, W. A. *Did Man Just Happen?* Grand Rapids, MI: Zondervan, 1957.

———. *Standing on the Promises: The Autobiography of W. A. Criswell.* Dallas: Word Publishing, 1990.

Critchlow, Donald T. *The Conservative Ascendancy: How the GOP Right Made Political History.* Cambridge, MA: Harvard University Press, 2007.

———. *Intended Consequences: Birth Control, Abortion, and the Federal Government in Modern America.* New York: Oxford University Press, 1999.

Critchlow, Donald T., John Korasick, and Matthew C. Sherman. *Political Conspiracies in America: A Reader.* Bloomington: Indiana University Press, 2008.

Critchlow, Donald T., and Nancy MacLean. *Debating the American Conservative Movement: 1945 to the Present.* Lanham, MD: Rowman & Littlefield, 2009.

Cronon, William. *Nature's Metropolis: Chicago and the Great West.* New York: W. W. Norton, 1991.

Cunningham, Sean P. *Cowboy Conservatism: Texas and the Rise of the Modern Right.* Lexington: University Press of Kentucky, 2010.

Dailey, Jane. "Sex, Segregation, and the Sacred after Brown." *Journal of American History* 91, no. 1 (June 2004): 119–44.

"The Dallas Rejoinder." *Nation,* May 25, 1964.

Dallek, Matthew. *The Right Moment: Ronald Reagan's First Victory and the Decisive Turning Point in American Politics.* New York: Free Press, 2000.

Dallek, Robert. *Lone Star Rising: Lyndon Johnson and His Times, 1908–1960.* New York: Oxford University Press, 1991.

Daniel, Carey. *God, the Original Segregationist.* Dallas: privately published, 1955.

Darden, Ida M. *The Best of "The Southern Conservative."* Fort Worth, TX: Author, 1963.

Davenport, Walter. "Savior from Texas." *Collier's,* August 18, 1945.

Davidson, Chandler. *Race and Class in Texas Politics.* Princeton, NJ: Princeton University Press, 1990.

Davis, Mike. *City of Quartz: Excavating the Future in Los Angeles.* London: Verso, 1990.

Degler, Carl. *Out of Our Past: The Forces That Shaped Modern America.* New York: Harper and Row, 1956.

Diamond, Sara. *Roads to Dominion: Right Wing Movements and Political Power in the United States.* New York: Guilford Press, 1994.

———. *Spiritual Warfare: The Politics of the Christian Right.* Boston, MA: South End Press, 1989.

Dies, Martin. *The Trojan Horse in America.* New York: Dodd, Mead & Company, 1940.

Dochuk, Darren. *From Bible Belt to Sunbelt: Plain-Folk Religion, Grassroots Politics, and the Rise of Evangelical Conservatism.* New York: W. W. Norton, 2011.

Dudman, Richard. *Men of the Far Right.* New York: Pyramid Books, 1962.

Dulaney, W. Marvin. "Whatever Happened to the Civil Rights Movement in Dallas Texas?" In *Essays on the American Civil Rights Movement,* edited by W. Marvin Dulaney and Kathleen Underwood. College Station: Texas A&M University Press, 1993.

Ebenstein, Alan O. *Friedrich Hayek: A Biography.* New York: Palgrave, 2001.

Edsall, Thomas Byrne, and Mary D. Edsall. *Chain Reaction: The Impact of Race, Rights, and Taxes on American Politics*. New York: Norton, 1991.

Elam, Leslie A. *Harry W. Bass: Memories of His Life*. American Numismatics Society, 1998.

Epstein, Benjamin R., and Arnold Forster. *Report on the John Birch Society*. New York: Vintage Books, 1966.

Eshleman, Paul, and Norman B. Rohrer. *The Explo Story: A Plan to Change the World*. Glendale, CA: G/L Regal Books, 1972.

Evans, Rowland, and Robert D. Novak. *Lyndon B. Johnson: The Exercise of Power; A Political Biography*. New York: New American Library, 1966.

Fairbanks, Robert B. "Dallas in the 1940s: The Challenges and Opportunities of Defense Mobilization." In *Urban Texas: Politics and Development*, edited by Char Miller and Heywood T. Sanders. College Station: Texas A & M University Press, 1990.

———. *For the City as a Whole: Planning, Politics, and the Public Interest in Dallas, Texas, 1900–1965*. Columbus: Ohio State University Press, 1998.

———. "From Consensus to Controversy: Public Housing in Dallas." In *Dallas Reconsidered: Essays in Local History*, edited by Michael Hazel. Dallas: Three Forks Press, 1995.

Farber, David. *The Rise and Fall of Modern American Conservatism*. Princeton, NJ: Princeton University Press, 2010.

Fenster, Mark. *Conspiracy Theories: Secrecy and Power in American Culture*. Minneapolis: University of Minnesota Press, 1999.

Feser, Edward. *The Cambridge Companion to Hayek*. New York: Cambridge University Press, 2006.

Flamm, Michael W. *Law and Order: Street Crime, Civil Unrest, and the Crisis of Liberalism in the 1960s*. New York: Columbia University Press, 2005.

Flynn, John T. *The Road Ahead: America's Creeping Revolution*. New York: Devin-Adair, 1949.

Foege, Alec. *The Empire God Built: Inside Pat Robertson's Media Machine*. New York: John Wiley & Sons, 1996.

Foley, Neil. *The White Scourge: Mexicans, Blacks, and Poor Whites in Texas Cotton Culture*. Berkeley: University of California Press, 1997.

Forster, Arnold, and Benjamin R. Epstein. *Danger on the Right: The Attitudes, Personnel, and Influence of the Radical Right and Extreme Conservatives*. New York: Random House, 1964.

Foucault, Michel. *Madness and Civilization: A History of Insanity in the Age of Reason*. New York: Pantheon, 1965.

Freeman, Curtis W. "'Never Had I Been So Blind': W. A. Criswell's 'Change' on Racial Segregation." *Journal of Southern Religion* 10 (2007): 1–12.

Friedman, Saul. "Tussle in Texas." *Nation*, February 3, 1964.

Fuller, Robert C. *Naming the Antichrist: The History of an American Obsession*. New York: Oxford University Press, 1995.

Garcia, Gilbert. *Reagan's Comeback: Four Weeks in Texas That Changed American Politics Forever*. San Antonio, TX: Trinity University Press, 2012.

Gifford, Laura Jane. "'Dixie Is No Longer in the Bag': South Carolina Republicans and the Election of 1960." *Journal of Policy History* 19, no. 2 (2007).

Gitlin, Todd. *The Sixties: Years of Hope, Days of Rage*. Toronto: Bantam Books, 1987.

Glass, William R. *Strangers in Zion: Fundamentalists in the South, 1900–1950*. Macon, GA: Mercer University Press, 2001.

Goldberg, Robert Alan. *Enemies Within: The Culture of Conspiracy in Modern America*. New Haven, CT: Yale University Press, 2001.

Goffman, Erving. *Asylums: Essays on the Social Situation of Mental Patients and Other Inmates*. Garden City, NY: Anchor Books, 1961.

Goldwater, Barry M. *The Conscience of a Conservative*. New York: MacFadden Books, 1960.

Graff, Harvey J. *The Dallas Myth: The Making and Unmaking of an American City*. Minneapolis, MN: University of Minnesota Press, 2008.

Green, George Norris. *The Establishment in Texas Politics: The Primitive Years, 1938–1957*. Norman: University of Oklahoma Press, 1979.

———. "The Far Right Wing in Texas Politics, 1930's–1960's." PhD dissertation, Florida State University, 1966.

———. "Some Aspects of the Far Right Wing in Texas Politics." In *Essays on Recent Southern Politics*, edited by Harold M. Hollingsworth. Austin: University of Texas Press, 1970.

Greenstein, Fred I. *The Hidden Hand Presidency: Eisenhower as Leader*. New York: Basic Books, 1982.

Gregory, Joel. *Too Great a Temptation: The Seductive Power of America's Super Church*. Fort Worth, TX: Summit Group, 1994.

Grier, Meg McKain. *Grassroots Women: A Memoir of the Texas Republican Party*. Boerne, TX: Wingscape Press, 2001.

Haley, J. Evetts. *A Texan Looks at Lyndon: A Study in Illegitimate Power*. Canyon, TX: Palo Duro Press, 1964.

Hamby, Alonzo. *Liberalism and Its Challengers*. New York: Oxford University Press, 1985.

Hamilton, Neil A. *The 1970s*. New York: Facts On File, 2006.

Hankins, Barry. *Uneasy in Babylon: Southern Baptist Conservatives and American Culture*. Tuscaloosa: University Of Alabama Press, 2004.

Hannah, John D. *An Uncommon Union: Dallas Theological Seminary and American Evangelicalism*. Grand Rapids, MI: Zondervan, 2009.

Hardeman, D. B. "Shivers of Texas: A Tragedy in Three Acts." *Harper's Magazine*, November 1956.

Harvey, Paul. *Freedom's Coming: Religious Culture and the Shaping of the South from the Civil War Through the Civil Rights Era*. Chapel Hill: University of North Carolina Press, 2005.

———. "God and Negroes and Jesus and Sin and Salvation." In *Religion in the American South: Protestants and Others in History and Culture*, edited by Beth Barton

Schweiger and Donald G. Mathews, 285–91. Chapel Hill: University of North Carolina Press, 2004.

———. "Religion, Race, and the Right in the South, 1945–1990." In *Politics and Religion in the White South*, edited by Glenn Feldman, 101–24. Lexington: University Press of Kentucky, 2005.

Harrell, David Edwin. *Pat Robertson: A Life and Legacy*. Grand Rapids, MI: William B. Eerdmans, 2010.

Hayek, Friedrich A. von. *Capitalism and the Historians*. Chicago: University of Chicago Press, 1954.

———. *The Constitution of Liberty*. Chicago: University of Chicago Press, 1960.

———. *The Road to Serfdom*. Chicago: University of Chicago Press, 1944.

Haynes, Stephen R. *Noah's Curse: The Biblical Justification of American Slavery*. Oxford: Oxford University Press, 2002.

Hazel, Michael. *Dallas: A History of "Big D."* Austin: Texas State Historical Association, 1997.

Heale, M. J. *American Anticommunism: Combating the Enemy Within, 1830–1970*. Baltimore: Johns Hopkins University Press, 1990.

Hendershot, Heather. *What's Fair On the Air: Cold War Right-Wing Broadcasting and the Public Interest*. Chicago: University of Chicago Press, 2011.

Hill, Patricia Evridge. *Dallas: The Making of a Modern City*. Austin: University of Texas Press, 1996.

Himmelstein, Jerome L. *To the Right: The Transformation of American Conservatism*. Berkeley: University of California, 1990.

Hixson, William B. *Search for the American Right Wing: An Analysis of the Social Science Record, 1955–1987*. Princeton, NJ: Princeton University Press, 1992.

Hofstadter, Richard. *The Age of Reform: From Bryan to FDR*. New York: Alfred A. Knopf, 1955.

———. *The Paranoid Style in American Politics, and Other Essays*. Chicago: University of Chicago Press, 1979.

Howard, James. *Big D Is for Dallas: Chapters in the Twentieth-Century History of Dallas*. Austin, TX, 1957.

Hunt, H. L. *Alpaca*. Dallas: H. L. Hunt Press, 1960.

———. *Early Days*. Dallas: Parade Press, 1973.

———. *Fabians Fight Freedom*. Dallas: H. L. Hunt Press.

———. *Hunt Heritage: The Republic and Our Families*. Dallas: Parade Press, 1973.

———. *Right of Average*. Dallas: HLH Products, 1960s.

Hurt, Harry. *Texas Rich: The Hunt Dynasty, from the Early Oil Days through the Silver Crash*. New York: W. W. Norton, 1981.

Janson, Donald, and Bernard Eismann. *The Far Right*. New York: McGraw-Hill, 1963.

Jensen, Richard J. *The Winning of the Midwest: Social and Political Conflict, 1888–1896*. Chicago: University of Chicago Press, 1971.

John Birch Society. *The Blue Book of the John Birch Society*. Boston: Western Islands, 1961.

Johnson, Ben F. *Arkansas in Modern America, 1930–1999*. Fayetteville: University of Arkansas Press, 2000.

Jones, Daniel Stedman. *Masters of the Universe: Hayek, Friedman, and the Birth of Neoliberal Politics*. Princeton, NJ: Princeton University Press, 2012.

Jones, Ted. *Dallas: Its History, Its Development, Its Beauty; Points of Interest and a Map of the City*. Dallas: Lamar & Barton, 1925.

Jordan, Winthrop D. *White Over Black: American Attitudes Toward the Negro, 1550–1812*. New York: W. W. Norton, 1968.

Jorstad, Erling. *The Politics of Doomsday; Fundamentalists of the Far Right*. Nashville, TN: Abingdon Press, 1970.

Judis, John B. *William F. Buckley, Jr., Patron Saint of the Conservatives*. New York: Simon & Schuster, 1988.

Kabaservice, Geoffrey M. *Rule and Ruin: The Downfall of Moderation and the Destruction of the Republican Party, from Eisenhower to the Tea Party*. New York: Oxford University Press, 2012.

Kaplowitz, Craig Allan. *LULAC, Mexican Americans, and National Policy*. College Station: Texas A&M University Press, 2005.

Keith, Billy. *W. A. Criswell: The Authorized Biography; the Story of a Courageous and Uncompromising Christian Leader*. Old Tappan, NJ: Revell, 1973.

Keller, Morton. *Affairs of State: Public Life in Late Nineteenth Century America*. Cambridge: Belknap Press/Harvard University Press, 1977.

Kennedy, David M. *Freedom from Fear: The American People in Depression and War, 1929–1945*. New York: Oxford University Press, 1999.

Kessel, John H. *The Goldwater Coalition: Republican Strategies in 1964*. Indianapolis: Bobbs-Merrill, 1968.

Key, V. O., Jr. *Southern Politics in State and Nation*. New York: A. A. Knopf, 1949.

Keyssar, Alexander. *The Right to Vote: The Contested History of Democracy in the United States*. New York: Basic Books, 2000.

Kingston, Mike, Sam Attlesey, and Mary G. Crawford. *The Texas Almanac's Political History of Texas*. Austin, TX: Eakin Press, 1992.

Kirby, Jack Temple. *Rural Worlds Lost: The American South, 1920–1960*. Baton Rouge: Louisiana State University Press, 1987.

Kirkendall, Richard. *A History of Missouri*. Vol. 5, *1919 to 1953*. Columbia: University of Missouri Press, 1986.

Klatch, Rebecca E. *Women of the New Right*. Philadelphia: Temple University Press, 1987.

Kleppner, Paul. *The Cross of Culture: A Social Analysis of Midwestern Politics, 1850–1900*. New York: Free Press, 1970.

Knepper, George W. *Ohio and Its People*. Kent, OH: Kent State University Press, 2003.

Kousser, J. Morgan. *Shaping of Southern Politics: Suffrage Restriction and the Establishment of the One-Party South, 1880–1910*. New Haven, CT: Yale University Press, 1974.

Kraemer, Richard, Ernest Crain, and William Earl Maxwell. *Understanding Texas Politics*. New York: West Publishing, 1975.

Kruse, Kevin Michael. *White Flight: Atlanta and the Making of Modern Conservatism*. Princeton, NJ: Princeton University Press, 2005.

Kusmer, Kenneth L. *A Ghetto Takes Shape: Black Cleveland, 1870–1930*. Urbana: University of Illinois Press, 1976.

Ladino, Robyn Duff. *Desegregating Texas Schools: Eisenhower, Shivers, and the Crisis at Mansfield High*. Austin: University of Texas Press, 1996.

Lahr, Angela M. *Millennial Dreams and Apocalyptic Nightmares: The Cold War Origins of Political Evangelicalism*. New York: Oxford University Press, 2007.

Laing, R. D. *The Politics of Experience*. New York: Pantheon, 1967.

Lamb, Karl A. "Civil Rights and the Republican Platform: Nixon Achieves Control." In *Inside Politics: The National Conventions, 1960*, edited by Paul Tillet. Dobbs Ferry, NY: Oceana Publications, 1962.

Lambert, Frank. *Religion in American Politics: A Short History*. Princeton, NJ: Princeton University Press, 2008.

Lamis, Alexander P. *The Two-Party South*. New York: Oxford University Press, 1984.

Lamis, Alexander P., and Mary Anne Sharkey. *Ohio Politics*. Kent, OH: Kent State University Press, 1994.

Larkin, Micaela Anne. "Southwestern Strategy: Mexican Americans and Republican Politics in the Arizona Borderlands. In *Barry Goldwater and the Remaking of the American Political Landscape*, edited by Elizabeth Tandy Shermer, 66–86. Tucson: University of Arizona Press, 2013.

Lassiter, Matthew D. *The Silent Majority: Suburban Politics in the Sunbelt South*. Princeton, NJ: Princeton University Press, 2006.

Leeston, Alfred M., John A. Crichton, and John C. Jacobs. *The Dynamic Natural Gas Industry: The Description of an American Industry from the Historical, Technical, Legal, Financial, and Economic Standpoints*. Norman: University of Oklahoma Press, 1963.

Leonard, Bill J. "A Theology for Racism: Southern Fundamentalists and the Civil Rights Movement." In *Southern Landscapes*, edited by Tony Badger et al, 165–81. Tubingen, Germany: Stauffenburg Verlag, 1996.

Leslie, Warren. *Dallas, Public and Private: Aspects of an American City*. New York: Grossman Publishers, 1964.

Leuchtenburg, William. *Franklin Roosevelt and the New Deal, 1932–1940*. New York: Harper and Row, 1963.

———. *The White House Looks South: Franklin D. Roosevelt, Harry S. Truman, Lyndon B. Johnson*. Baton Rouge: Louisiana State University Press, 2007.

Lewis, George. *Massive Resistance: The White Response to the Civil Rights Movement*. London: Hodder Arnold, 2006.

Lichtenstein, Nelson. *State of the Union: A Century of American Labor*. Princeton, NJ: Princeton University Press, 2002.

Lichtman, Allan J. *White Protestant Nation: The Rise of the American Conservative Movement*. New York: Atlantic Monthly Press, 2008.

Linden, Glenn M. *Desegregating Schools in Dallas: Four Decades in the Federal Courts*. Dallas: Three Forks Press, 1995.

Lindsley, Philip. *A History of Greater Dallas and Vicinity.* 2 vols. Chicago: Lewis Publishing, 1909.

Lipset, Seymour Martin, and Earl Raab. *The Politics of Unreason: Right-Wing Extremism in America, 1790–1977.* New York: Harper and Row, 1978.

Lowndes, Joseph E. *From the New Deal to the New Right: Race and the Southern Origins of Modern Conservatism.* New Haven, Conn: Yale University Press, 2008.

Lublin, David. *The Republican South: Democratization and Partisan Change.* Princeton, NJ: Princeton University Press, 2004.

"Lynn Landrum vs. the Modern World." *D Magazine,* September, 1987.

MacLean, Nancy. *Freedom Is Not Enough: The Opening of the American Work Place.* New York: R. Sage, 2006.

———. "Neo-Confederacy versus the New Deal: The Regional Utopia of the Modern American Right." In *The Myth of Southern Exceptionalism,* edited by Matthew D. Lassiter and Joseph Crespino, 308–30. New York: Oxford University Press, 2009.

Madison, James H. *The Indiana Way: A State History.* Bloomington: Indiana University Press, 1986.

Malvasi, Mark G. *The Unregenerate South: The Agrarian Thought of John Crowe Ransom, Allen Tate, and Donald Davidson.* Baton Rouge: Louisiana State University Press, 1997.

Manchester, William. *The Death of a President, November 20–November 25, 1963.* New York: Harper & Row, 1967.

Manis, Andrew W. *Southern Civil Religions in Conflict: Civil Rights and the Culture Wars.* Macon, GA: Mercer University Press, 2002.

Marley, David John. *Pat Robertson: An American Life.* Lanham, MD: Rowman & Littlefield, 2007.

Marsh, Charles. *God's Long Summer: Stories of Faith and Civil Rights.* Princeton, NJ: Princeton University Press, 1997.

———. *Wayward Christian Soldiers: Freeing the Gospel from Political Captivity.* Oxford: Oxford University Press, 2007.

Marcus, Stanley. *Minding the Store: A Memoir.* Boston: Little, Brown, 1974.

Marsden, George M. *Fundamentalism and American Culture.* New York: Oxford University Press, 2006.

Martin, William C. "God's Angry Man." *Texas Monthly,* April 1981.

———. *With God on Our Side: The Rise of the Religious Right in America.* New York: Broadway Books, 1996.

Mattson, Kevin. *Just Plain Dick: Richard Nixon's Checkers Speech and the "Rocking, Socking" Election of 1952.* New York: Bloomsbury, 2012.

McBeth, Leon. *The First Baptist Church of Dallas: Centennial History, 1868–1968.* Grand Rapids, MI: Zondervan, 1968.

"McCarthy, Hunt, and Facts Forum." *Reporter,* February 16, 1954.

McCleskey, Clifton. *The Government and Politics of Texas.* Boston: Little, Brown, 1972.

McCombs, Holland. "The Dynamic Men of Dallas." *Fortune,* February 1949.

McConnell, D. R. *A Different Gospel.* Peabody, Mass: Hendrickson Publishers, 1995.

McGirr, Lisa. *Suburban Warriors: Origins of the New American Right*. Princeton, NJ: Princeton University Press, 2001.

McKnight, Tom Lee. *Manufacturing in Dallas: A Study of Effects*. Austin, TX: Bureau of Business Research, University of Texas, 1956.

McMillen, Neil R. *The Citizens' Council: Organized Resistance to the Second Reconstruction, 1954–1964*. Chicago: University of Illinois Press, 1971.

Meinig, D. W. *Imperial Texas: An Interpretive Essay in Cultural Geography*. Austin: University of Texas Press, 1969.

Middendorf, J. William. *A Glorious Disaster*. New York: Basic Books, 2008.

Miller, Char, and Heywood T. Sanders, eds. *Urban Texas: Politics and Development*. College Station: Texas A & M University Press, 1990.

Miller, Merle. *Lyndon: An Oral Biography*. New York: Putnam, 1980.

Miller, Stephen P. *Billy Graham and the Rise of the Republican South*. Philadelphia: University of Pennsylvania Press, 2009.

Miller, Zane L. *Boss Cox's Cincinnati: Urban Politics in the Progressive Era*. New York: Oxford University Press, 1968.

Minutaglio, Bill, and Steven L. Davis. *Dallas 1963*. New York: Twelve, 2013.

Mises, Ludwig von. *Bureaucracy*. New Haven, CT: Yale University Press, 1944.

Moore, Leonard Joseph. *Citizen Klansmen: The Ku Klux Klan in Indiana, 1921–1928*. Chapel Hill: University of North Carolina Press, 1991.

Morris, Robert. *Disarmament: Weapon of Conquest*. New York: Bookmailer, 1963.

———. *No Wonder We Are Losing*. New York: The Bookmailer, 1958.

Morris, Willie. "What Makes Dallas Different?" *New Republic*, June 20, 1964.

Moser, John E. *Right Turn: John T. Flynn and the Transformation of American Liberalism*. New York: New York University Press, 2005.

Murley, John A., and John Alvis. *Willmoore Kendall: Maverick of American Conservatives*. Lanham, MD: Lexington Books, 2002.

Murphy, Paul V. *The Rebuke of History: The Southern Agrarians and American Conservative Thought*. Chapel Hill: University of North Carolina Press, 2001.

Nash, George H. *The Conservative Intellectual Movement in America Since 1945*. Wilmington, DE: ISI Books, 2006.

Nelson, Jack, and Gene Roberts. *The Censors and the Schools*. Boston: Little, Brown, 1963.

Newman, Mark. *Getting Right with God: Southern Baptists and Desegregation, 1945–1995*. Tuscaloosa: University of Alabama Press, 2001.

Nickerson, Michelle M. *Mothers of Conservatism: Women of the Postwar Right*. Princeton and Oxford: Princeton University Press, 2012.

———. "Politically Desperate Housewives: Women and Conservatism in Postwar Los Angeles." *California History* 86, no. 3 (June 2009): 4–21.

———. "Women, Domesticity, and Postwar Conservatism." *OAH Magazine of History*, 17 (January 2003): 17–21.

Nickerson, Michelle, and Darren Dochuk, eds., *Sunbelt Rising: The Places of Space, Place, and Region*. Philadelphia: University of Pennsylvania Press, 2011.

O'Brien, Michael, *Rethinking the South: Essays in Intellectual History*. Baltimore: Johns Hopkins University Press, 1988.

O'Leary, Stephen D. *Arguing the Apocalypse: A Theory of Millennial Rhetoric*. New York: Oxford University Press, 1998.

Olien, Roger M. *From Token to Triumph: The Texas Republicans Since 1920*. Dallas: Southern Methodist University Press, 1982.

Olmsted, Kathryn S. *Real Enemies: Conspiracy Theories and American Democracy, World War I to 9/11*. New York: Oxford University Press, 2009.

Olson, Ted. *Crossroads, A Southern Culture Annual 2006*. Macon, GA: Mercer University Press, 2007.

Oppenheimer, Evelyn, and Bill Porterfield. *The Book of Dallas*. Garden City, NY: Doubleday, 1976.

Oshinsky, David M. *A Conspiracy So Immense: The World of Joe McCarthy*. New York: Free Press, 1983.

"Out: Not with a Whimper but a Bang." *National Review*, November 18, 1961.

Parmet, Herbert S. *George Bush: The Life of a Lone Star Yankee*. New York: Scribner, 1997.

Paterson, Thomas G. *Kennedy's Quest for Victory: American Foreign Policy, 1961–1963*. New York: Oxford University Press, 1989.

Patterson, James T. *Mr. Republican: A Biography of Robert A. Taft*. Boston: Houghton Mifflin, 1972.

Pauly, Karl B. *Bricker of Ohio: The Man and His Record*. New York: G. P. Putnam's Sons, 1944.

Payne, Darwin. *Big D: Triumphs and Troubles of an American Supercity in the 20th Century*. Dallas: Three Forks Press, 1994.

———. *Initiative in Energy: Dresser Industries, Inc., 1880–1978*. New York: Simon & Schuster, 1979.

Pentecost, J. Dwight. *Things to Come: A Study in Biblical Eschatology*. Grand Rapids, MI: Zondervan, 1958.

———. *Prophecy for Today: An Exposition of Major Themes in Prophecy*. Grand Rapids, Mich: Zondervan, 1961.

Perlstein, Rick. *Before the Storm: Barry Goldwater and the Unmaking of the American Consensus*. New York: Hill and Wang, 2001.

Peters, Shawn Francis. "'Did You Say That Mr. Dean Acheson Is a Pink?': The Walker Case and the Cold War." *Viet Nam Generation* 6 (1995).

Phillips, Michael. *White Metropolis: Race, Ethnicity, and Religion in Dallas, 1841–2001*. Austin: University of Texas Press, 2006.

Phillips-Fein, Kim. "Conservatism: A State of the Field." *Journal of American History* 98 (December 2011): 723–43.

———. *Invisible Hands: The Making of the Conservative Movement from the New Deal to Reagan*. New York: W. W. Norton, 2009.

Pickett, William B. "The Capehart Cornfield Conference and the Election of 1938: Homer E. Capehart's Entry into Politics." *Indiana Magazine of History* 73 (December 1977): 251–75.

Poder, Michael Paul. "The Senatorial Career of William E. Jenner." PhD dissertation, University of Notre Dame, 1976.

Posner, Sarah. *God's Profits: Faith, Fraud, and the Republican Crusade for Values Voters.* Sausalito, CA: Polipoint Press, 2008.

Poucher, Wayne. "What Kind of Disarmament." *Life Line,* December 14, 1962.

Pyle, Hugh F. *The Truth about the Church of Christ.* Murfreesboro, TN: Sword of the Lord Publishers, 1977.

Quebedeaux, Richard. *The New Charismatics: The Origins, Development, and Significance of Neo-Pentecostalism.* Garden City, New York: Doubleday, 1976.

Reeves, Richard. *President Kennedy: Profile of Power.* New York: Simon & Schuster, 1993.

———. *President Nixon: Alone in the White House.* New York: Simon & Schuster, 2001.

Reinhard, David W. *The Republican Right since 1945.* Lexington: University Press of Kentucky, 1983.

Robertson, Pat, and Jamie Buckingham. *Shout It from the Housetops.* Plainfield, NJ: Logos International, 1972.

Ruegamer, Lana, and Emma Lou Thornbrough. *Indiana Blacks in the Twentieth Century.* Bloomington: Indiana University Press, 2000.

Rymph, Catherine E. *Republican Women.* Chapel Hill: University of North Carolina Press, 2006.

Salinger, Pierre. *With Kennedy.* Garden City, NY: Doubleday, 1966.

Schlesinger, Arthur M., Jr. *The Age of Roosevelt.* 3 vols. Boston: Houghton Mifflin, 1957–1960.

Schneider, Gregory L. *Cadres for Conservatism: Young Americans for Freedom and the Rise of the Contemporary Right.* New York, NY: New York Univ. Press, 1999.

Schoenwald, Jonathan. *A Time for Choosing: The Rise of Modern American Conservatism.* New York: Oxford University Press, 2001.

Shadegg, Stephen C. *What Happened to Goldwater? The Inside Story of the 1964 Republican Campaign.* New York: Holt, Rinehart and Winston, 1965.

Shafer, Byron E., and Richard Johnston. *The End of Southern Exceptionalism: Class, Race, and Partisan Change in the Postwar South.* Cambridge, MA: Harvard University Press, 2009.

"The Shame of Dallas." *Saturday Evening Post,* April 11, 1964.

Shermer, Elizabeth Tandy. *Sunbelt Capitalism: Phoenix and the Transformation of American Politics.* Philadelphia: University of Pennsylvania Press, 2013.

Sherrill, Robert G. "H. L. Hunt: Portrait of a Super-Patriot." *Nation,* February 24, 1964.

Sherwin, Mark. *The Extremists.* New York: St. Martin's Press, 1963.

Smith, Oran P. *The Rise of Baptist Republicanism.* New York: New York University Press, 1997.

Smith, Richard Austin. "How Business Failed Dallas." *Fortune,* July 1964.

Smoot, Dan. *The Dan Smoot Report.* Dallas: Dan Smoot Report, 1956–1969.

———. *The Hope of the World.* Dallas: Miller Publishing, 1958.

———. *The Invisible Government.* Boston: Western Islands, 1962.

———. *People along the Way: The Autobiography of Dan Smoot.* Tyler, TX: Tyler Press, 1996.

Sorenson, Dale R. "The Anticommunist Consensus in Indiana, 1945–1958." PhD dissertation, Indiana University, 1980.

Steinberg, Alfred. *Sam Johnson's Boy: A Close-Up of the President from Texas.* New York: Macmillan, 1968.

Sternsher, Bernard. "The Harding and Bricker Revolutions: Party Systems and Voter Behavior in Northwest Ohio, 1860–1982." *Northwest Ohio Quarterly* 50 (Summer 1987): 91–111.

Storey, John W. *Texas Baptist Leadership and Social Christianity, 1900–1980.* College Station: Texas A&M University Press, 1986.

Strickland, Kristi Throne. "The Significance and Impact of Women on the Rise of the Republican Party in Twentieth-Century Texas." PhD dissertation, University of North Texas, 2001.

Sugrue, Thomas J. *The Origins of the Urban Crisis: Race and Inequality in Postwar Detroit.* Princeton, NJ: Princeton University Press, 1996.

Synan, Vinson. *The Holiness-Pentecostal Tradition: Charismatic Movements in the Twentieth Century.* Grand Rapids, MI: William B. Eerdmans, 1997.

Szasz, Thomas S. *The Myth of Mental Illness: Foundations of a Theory of Personal Conduct.* New York: Hoeber, 1961.

———. "Psychiatry's Threat to Civil Liberties." *National Review,* March 12, 1963.

———. "The Shame of Medicine: The Case of General Edwin." *Freeman* 59, no. 8 (October 2009). http://www.thefreemanonline.org/columns/the-therapeutic -state/the-shame-of-medicine-the-case-of-general-edwin-walker/ (accessed July 27, 2012).

———. *Psychiatric Justice.* New York: Macmillan, 1965.

Thometz, Carol Estes. *The Decision-Makers: The Power Structure of Dallas.* Dallas: Southern Methodist University Press, 1963.

Thurber, Timothy N. *Republicans and Race: The GOP's Frayed Relationship with African-Americans, 1945–1974.* Lawrence: University Press of Kansas, 2013.

Tinkle, Lon. *Mr. De: A Biography of Everette Lee DeGolyer.* Boston: Little, Brown, 1970.

Tower, John G. *A Program for Conservatives.* New York: Macfadden Books, 1962.

Turner, John G. *Bill Bright and Campus Crusade for Christ: The Renewal of Evangelicalism in Postwar America.* Chapel Hill: University of North Carolina Press, 2008.

United Press International. *Four Days; The Historical Record of the Death of President Kennedy.* New York: American Heritage, 1964.

Voegeli, V. Jacque. *Free but Not Equal: The Midwest and the Negro during the Civil War.* Chicago: University of Chicago Press, 1967.

Walker, Edwin A. *Walker Speaks—Unmuzzled! Complete Text of Three Speeches.* Dallas: American Eagle, 1962.

Walvoord, John F. "The Crisis of This Present Hour." In *The Prophetic Word in Crisis Days.* Findlay, OH: Dunham Publishing, 1961.

———. *Israel in Prophecy.* Grand Rapids, MI: Zondervan, 1962.

———. *The Millennial Kingdom.* Findlay, OH: Dunham Publishing, 1959.

———. *The Revelation of Jesus Christ: A Commentary.* Chicago: Moody Press, 1966.

———. "Russia, King of the North—Part I." *Fundamentalist Journal*, January 1984, 37.

Weeks, O. Douglas. *Texas Presidential Politics in 1952*. Austin: Institute of Public Affairs, University of Texas, 1953.

Welch, Robert. *The Politician*. Belmont, MA: Belmont Publishing, 1964.

White, F. Clifton and William J. Gill. *Suite 3505: The Story of the Draft Goldwater Movement*. New Rochelle, NY: Arlington House, 1967.

White, Theodore H. *The Making of the President, 1964*. New York: Athenaeum, 1965.

———. "Texas: Land of Wealth and Fear." *Reporter*, June 8, 1954.

White, William Smith. *The Taft Story*. New York: Harper, 1954.

Whitlock, Brand. *Forty Years of It*. New York: D. Appleton and Company, 1925.

Wilentz, Sean. *The Age of Reagan: A History, 1974–2008*. New York, NY: Harper, 2008.

Williams, Daniel K. *God's Own Party: The Making of the Christian Right*. Oxford: Oxford University Press, 2010.

Woods, Jeff. *Black Struggle, Red Scare: Segregation and Communism in the South, 1948–1968*. Baton Rouge: Louisiana State University Press, 2004.

Woodward, C. Vann. *Origins of the New South: 1877–1913*. New Orleans: Louisiana State University Press, 1951.

Wright, Lawrence. "Why Do They Hate Us So Much?" *Texas Monthly*, November 1983.

Wuthnow, Robert. *Red State Religion: Faith and Politics in America's Heartland*. Princeton, NJ: Princeton University Press, 2011.

———. *Rough Country: How Texas Became America's Most Powerful Bible-Belt State*. Princeton, NJ: Princeton University Press, 2014.

Index

Agnew, Spiro T., 134
Agnich, Fred, 42, 141
AIDS, 150
Alford, Dale, 84
Alger, Bruce: 1954 elections and, 77–78,
178–79n44; 1956 elections and, 9,
79–82; 1964 elections and, 10, 130–34,
143; Adolphus Hotel incident and,
86–88, 93–94, 132; Alger model, 189n9;
antigovernment impulse and, 34,
37–38, 82; apocalypticism and, 132;
black vote and, 134; career of, 8–9;
Dwight Eisenhower and, 77–78, 82;
far-right institutions and, 113; federal
milk program and, 84, 88; Barry Goldwater and, 135; historians' dismissal
of, 9; John Birch Society and, 93–95,
113; legacy of, 134–35; as moderate,
4, 34, 113; National Indignation Convention and, 95; Billy Naughton and,
120; Richard Nixon and, 80; on *Plessy
v. Ferguson*, 82, 179–80n66; racial moderation and, 78–79, 81; Ayn Rand and,
35–36; resistance to *Brown v. Board
of Education*, 77; segregationist turn,
80–85, 150; Southern Manifesto and,
79; Southern Strategy and, 9, 85,
115–16, 143; supporters of, 44; television acumen, 78; ultraconservatism
and, 84, 93, 117, 131–32; Edwin Walker
and, 100, 101, 185n74; white supremacy and, 84, 85; women's support of,
48, 178–79n44
Allen, Robert, 66
Allitt, Patrick, 105
American Bookstore, 45–46
American Civil Liberties Union, 22, 102
American Opinion (John Birch Society
publication), 64
Anderson, Earl, 77
Anderson, Tom, 62
Antichrist, 1, 55, 155n2
anti-Communism: Communist tactics,
94; conservative bookstores and, 46;
Dallas Morning News and, 22; defense
industry and, 17; Eisenhower as Communist, 61, 89, 94, 99; Freedom Forum

and, 31–32; John Birch Society and,
89–90; literature of as required reading, 96; Midwestern migrants and, 31;
moderates versus ultraconservatives
and, 30–31, 32–33; Robert Morris and,
104; pinks versus reds and, 30–31;
preaching about, 26; Ronald Reagan
versus John F. Kennedy on, 29; rise
of Dallas GOP and, 27–28; school
textbooks and, 32; Southern Strategy
and, 125
antigovernment impulse: 1962 Ronald
Reagan speech and, 29–30; Bruce Alger and, 34, 82; color-blind discourse
and, 140; conservative populism and,
27–28; economic theories and, 148;
federal milk program and, 84, 88;
Friedrich Hayek and, 36–37; market-
based alternatives to government
programs and, 151; Ludwig von Mises
and, 36; opposition to centralized
planning and, 36; rejection of federal
funds and, 38, 124; in Southern Strategy, 115–16; state coercion and, 36–38;
welfare state and, 35
anti-intellectualism, 31, 44, 66–67
anti-Semitism, 63–64
apocalypticism: 80 Women from Dallas
and, 109–10; Bruce Alger and, 132;
apocalyptic rhetoric and, 52–56;
biblical prophecy and, 54–56; Dallas
Cowboys' Doomsday Defense and,
150; Explo '72 and, 145–46; Hal Lindsey and, 146; media propagation of,
52–53; secular doomsday scenarios
and, 147; of Robert Welch, 89–90; of
Edwin Walker, 98
Armageddon, 155n2
Armey, Richard (Dick), 148
Arms Control and Disarmament Act of
1961, 110
arms sales, 62
art, ultraconservatives' objections to,
65
Assemblies of God, 23–24, 141
atheism, 61, 67
Atwell, William H., 83

Lynch, W. W., 31
lynching, 70

MacArthur, Douglas, 97
Maddox, Lester, 10, 142
Mallon, Henry Neil, 2–4, 18, 109, 133
Manion, Clarence, 19, 61
Manion, Dean, 45
Manis, Andrew W., 180–81n80
Mansfield High School, 79, 81, 82, 85
Marcus, Stanley, 7, 21, 64, 86, 133
Marsh, Charles, 180–81n80
Marshall, George C., 89
MART. See Mexican-American Republicans of Texas (MART)
Martiniere, Joseph, 25
Massey, Homer, 80
Matthews, Homer, 74
Mattingly, Barak, 20
McCarran, Pat, 104
McCarthy, J. (John Birch Society member), 59
McCarthy, Joseph: Bruce Alger's imitation of, 132; critics of, 94; Dallas Morning News on, 22; Dwight Eisenhower and, 59; as Texas's third senator, 31; Edwin Walker and, 99
McComb, Hollis, 14
McCord, Bob, 44
McCord, Glenna, 44, 46, 50
McCready, Ellen, 39
McCullough, Robert, 17
McDaniel, George, 40
McDaniel, Katie, 44, 46
McGehee, Frank, 62, 95
McGirr, Lisa, 38
McIntyre, Carl, 46
McKenzie, George, 42
McKenzie, Sally, 130
McKone, John F., 184–85n69
McMann, Buck, 90
McNutt, Paul, 19
McWhorter, Charlie, 117
media, left-wing, 99
mental health and institutionalization of political enemies, 89, 102–4, 107, 186n94

Meredith, James, 102
Methodists, 24–25
Mexican-American Republicans of Texas (MART), 139
Meyer, Frank, 32, 34
military industrial complex. See defense industry
Milk, Harvey, 147
Miller, Giles, 45
Miller, Steven P., 180–81n80
Miller, William, 55, 131
Minute Women, 66
Mises, Ludwig von, 36, 38, 148
Mississippi Plan of 1875, 98
Missouri, Republican tradition in, 19–20
moderate Republicans: Barry Goldwater's racist rhetoric and, 129; civil rights and, 51, 137; color-blindness and, 137; conservatism as women's mission and, 46; Dallas moderates versus national GOP norm, 33–34; economic freedom as paramount issue, 38, 50–51; foreign policy positions, 33–34; Friedrich Hayek and, 36; institution building versus ideology, 50; mainline religious denominations and, 30; Midwestern influences and, 18, 38–39, 58, 167nn52–53; Ludwig von Mises and, 36; rapidly growing wealth of, 39; Ronald Reagan as, 30; reasons for appeal, 50–51; Southern Strategy and, 116; ultraconservatives and, 4–5, 30–31, 68; Edwin Walker and, 100–101; Western imperialism and, 34; women as backbone of GOP and, 46
Moncrief, W. A., 121
Moore, Walter, 77
Moral Majority, 147
Morris, Robert: 80 Women from Dallas and, 109, 187n115; 1964 Senate election and, 110; anti-Communism of, 104, 105–6; Rita Bass and, 109–10; on Mary Ann Collins, 91; far-right institutions and, 113–14; John F. Kennedy's disarmament proposal and, 109–10, 187n115; on one world government, 106, 109; radicalization of, 104–7, 109;

Morris, Robert (*continued*)
William Rusher and, 124; University
of Plano and, 148; Edwin Walker and,
101–2, 103, 106, 107, 109, 186n94
Moyers, Bill, 87
Munger Place Baptist Church, 77
Munich Conference of 1938, 111–13,
188n128
Murchison, Clint, 18
Murphy, David, 94
Muse, Vance, 56, 62
Mussolini, Benito, 55

NAACP, 62–63, 69–71, 80–81, 83, 117
Nash, George, 105
National Association of Manufacturers,
40
National Council of Churches, 69
National Education Association, 66
National Federation of Women's Republi-
can Clubs of America, 47, 169n101
National Indignation Convention, 62, 95
National Industrial Recovery Act, 121
National Review, 31, 103, 105
National Security Council, 95–96
Naughton, Billy, 120
Neiman Marcus, 160n9
New Deal, 22, 58–59, 71, 121, 140
New Frontier and, 140
NFWRCA. *See* National Federation of
Women's Republican Clubs of Amer-
ica
Nickerson, Michelle, 43–44, 173n57
Nixon, Richard: 1960 elections and, 87,
92, 123; black vote and, 130, 134;
China and, 112; color-blindness and,
138; fundraising and, 42, 134; NAACP
and, 80; Pact of Fifth Avenue and, 118;
as potential secretary of state, 104;
racial rhetoric and, 6; Southern Strat-
egy and, 5, 80, 116–17; umbrellas and,
112; white supremacy and, 85
Norman, Larry, 145
North American Aviation, 16–17
North Dallas–Park Cities News, 45
North Korea, 95
North Texas State University, 148

nullification. *See* states' rights
Nut Country, 7, 150

Obama, Barack, 1
O'Daniel, W. Lee, 159n3
O'Donnell, Peter: 1962 gubernatorial
elections and, 119; 1976 Republican
primary and, 194n11; Bruce Alger
and, 116; background of, 116; change
of heart on civil rights, 10; on Civil
Rights Act (1964), 127; Barry Goldwater and, 121–27, 130–31, 135, 191n55;
organizational strategies of, 133;
segregationism and, 9, 125; Southern Strategy and, 115–16, 119, 124,
143; tempering of Republicans' tone
and, 135, 136, 143; ultraconservative
stance on race and, 117; on women
as GOP backbone, 46, 49
Oglethorpe, James, 58
Ohio, as Republican stronghold, 19
oil industry: development of Dallas and,
15, 17–18, 39–40; Facts Forum and, 53;
as funder of evangelical initiatives,
146; Middle East and, 40; natural gas
and, 167n60; oil depletion allowance
and, 86, 87; political preferences in,
18
Oldham, Earl K., 73
Olien, Roger M., 178–79n44
Oliver, Revilo, 52
Olmstead, Freeman B., 184–85n69
Olmstead, Kathryn, 61
open housing, 137
Oswald, Lee Harvey, 42, 101, 111, 132

Pact of Fifth Avenue, 118
patronage, 12
Peabody, A. D., 38
Peale, Norman Vincent, 52
Pearl Harbor, 59
Pearson, Drew, 99
Pearson, Martha, 73–74
Pendergast, "Boss Tom," 19
Pentecost, J. Dwight, 55–56
Penter, John, 57
Perez, Marcos, 44

Perkins School of Theology, 45
Perot, H. Ross, 8
Perot, Margot, 8
Petroleum Engineers' Club, 132
Pharo, Gwen, 44, 46, 48–49, 194n11
Phillips, Michael, 14, 17
Phillips-Fein, Kim, 2
Planned Parenthood, 148
Plessy v. Ferguson, 82, 179–80n66
postmillenialism, 20
Poucher, Wayne, 54, 110
premillenialism. *See* dispensationalism
Presbyterians, 30, 141
property rights, Constitutional protec-
    tion of, 123
psychiatry. *See* mental health and insti-
    tutionalization of political enemies
Public Affairs Luncheon Club, 45, 56–57,
    65, 74–76, 83–85
public choice theory, 148
Public Works Administration, 71

Queeny, Edgar Monsanto, 20

race and racism: in 1954 elections,
    78–79, 179n47; black segregationists,
    73; "cheegros," 69–70; *Choice* (film)
    and, 127; coded racial language,
    129; criminal justice system and,
    70–71; curse of Ham and, 72, 73,
    176–77nn13–14; denial of, 63; Barry
    Goldwater and, 124–25; GOP softening
    on, 140–41; Billy Graham and, 141; as
    great Republican issue, 122–23; lack
    of opposition to racism in Dallas,
    73; lynching and, 70; market and
    religious solutions to, 141; minimi-
    zation of slavery, 63; miscegenation
    and, 63, 66, 70, 72–74, 77, 80–81; overt
    versus less overt rhetoric, 10, 81–82;
    Public Affairs Luncheon Club and,
    74–76; racism as mental illness,
    104, 186n94; religion and, 68, 141;
    in Southern Strategy rhetoric, 5, 6,
    142–43; stereotypes of black sexuality,
    72, 84; ultraconservatives' displays
    of prejudice, 62–63, 68; understated

advocacy of white superiority, 85;
    violent resistance to desegregation,
    76–77. *See also* color-blindness; Jim
    Crow; Ku Klux Klan; segregationism;
    white supremacy
race riots, 138
Radke, Dillard, 43
Rand, Ayn, 35–36, 38, 50
Rapture, 1, 155n2
Rayburn, Sam, 18, 44
Read, Leonard, 37
Reagan, Ronald: 1976 Republican primary
    and, 149, 194n11; 1980 elections and,
    147, 148, 149; 1984 elections and, 150;
    as moderate conservative, 30; racial
    rhetoric and, 6; Religious Roundtable
    and, 144, 149; Southern Strategy and,
    5; "What Price Freedom?" speech,
    29–30
Reconstruction, 12–13, 117, 120, 142
Red Ball Motor Freight, 29
Reed, James, 19
Reed-Dirksen amendment, 56
religion: charismatic movement, 2, 24,
    141–42; Cold War as religious conflict,
    31–32, 36, 50; condemnations of
    segregation in black churches, 180–
    81n80; denominational affiliations,
    23–24; free enterprise and, 36, 108;
    God banished from schools, 129,
    171n16; mainline denominations,
    24–25, 30, 38; megachurches, 25–26,
    145; parable of the talents, 24, 163n59;
    Pentecostal and Holiness groups,
    23–24; persecution of Christians,
    144; prayer in public schools, 146,
    147–48; racism and, 68; Ayn Rand
    and, 35–36; Religious Roundtable, 144;
    rise of Dallas GOP and, 27–28; social
    gospel, 59; support for segregation
    and, 6, 69–74, 77, 85, 176–77nn13–14,
    180–81n80; support for Ku Klux Klan
    and, 70; ultraconservative worldview
    and, 54, 57–58, 59. *See also specific
    denominations*
Religious Roundtable, 144, 147, 149
Republican Clubs, 108

Republican Party: 1962 gains in the South, 124; Bruce Alger and, 85, 189n9; Adolphus Hotel incident and, 87–88; appeal to affluent citizens, 21; black flight from, 134, 135–36; black vote and, 11, 125, 159n22; Catholics and Jews and, 143; civil rights and, 115, 118, 119–20, 136; conservative publishing and, 45; debt limit battles and, 151; Democratic-to-Republican conversions, 121; as dysfunctional, 151; evangelicals and culture wars and, 144–45; factors spurring growth in Dallas, 27–28; fiscal conservatism and, 148–49; Freedom in Action (FIA) and, 120; fundraising for, 40–41, 168n64; industry leaders and professionals active in, 39–40, 42; institutional framework of, 46–47; John Birch Society and, 113–14, 136; as lily-white in South, 125; Little Rock, Arkansas, school integration and, 117; Mexican-Americans and, 139; Midwestern strongholds of, 19; Operation Dixie and, 125; Pact of Fifth Avenue and, 118; as party of Lincoln and Reconstruction, 9, 12–13, 80, 115, 120, 127, 142–43; *Plessy v. Ferguson* and, 82; political socialization and, 43–44, 168n74, 168n77; poor pre-1950 performance of in Texas, 12–13; Public Affairs Luncheon Club and, 83; racialization of, 10–11; reasons for joining, 44, 45; segregationist discourse, 122–23; softening on race, 140–41; spectrum of beliefs and positions, 2, 155–56n6; tax policies, 18; tempering of tone, 135; ultraconservative and moderate overlap in, 110; voting restrictions' advantages for, 27; women active in, 39, 40, 46–51, 108, 189n9
Republican Women's Clubs, 44, 47–50, 120, 136, 169n101
Republican Women's Council, 47
Republic National Bank, 29
Reuther, Walter, 121

Richardson–Park Cities Digest, 45
Roberts, J. H., 174n69
Robertson, Pat, 142, 144, 146, 147
Robinson, Jackie, 127
Robison, James, 144, 147
Rockefeller, Nelson, 10, 118, 122–23, 128, 190n31
Rockefeller Foundation, 59
Rodgers, Florence, 65
Roe v. Wade, 145
Romney, Mitt, 11
Roosevelt, Eleanor, 83, 96
Roosevelt, Franklin Delano, and Roosevelt administration: activism of, 34–35; as Antichrist, 55; conspiratorial views on, 59; *Dallas Morning News* on, 21–22; defense industry and, 16; as leading sheep to slaughter, 62
Rove, Karl, 41, 42
Ruby, Jack, 29, 132
Rusher, William, 124–25
Russell, Richard, 119
Ryskind, Morris, 45

Savage, Michael, 151
Savage, Wallace, 78, 179n47, 179n49
Scaife, Richard Mellon, 149
Schaefer, Francis, 146, 147
Schlafly, Phyllis, 149
Schlesinger, Arthur, Jr., 96
school prayer, 104, 106, 146, 147–48
Schwarz, Fred, 31, 32, 50, 146
Scofield, Cyrus Ingerson, 54, 55, 71–72
Scofield Memorial Church, 54
Scofield Reference Bible, 71–72, 73, 170–71n15
Scranton, William, 10
secular humanism, 146
Seeger, Pete, 67
segregationism: 1954 elections and, 78; Bruce Alger's conversion to, 80–85; blacks alleged preference for, 81, 84; censorship of textbooks and, 67; coded racial language and, 129; condemnation of in black churches, 180–81n80; Dallas ordinances and, 70; Dallas school integration and, 83,

180n79; among Democrats, 142; discourse of on rise among Republicans, 122–23; fiscal conservatism and, 115, 116; language of miscegenation and, 72; merits of rhetoric of, 80; moderate republicans and, 2; popular support for, 180n79; Public Affairs Luncheon Club and, 74–76; religious defense of, 6, 69–74, 77, 85, 176–77nn13–14, 180–81n80; restrictionist view of the Constitution and, 64; as societal norm, 76, 178n33; in Southern Strategy, 116–17; violent resistance to desegregation, 76–77, 79; as welcome in GOP, 134. See also *Brown v. Board of Education*; race and racism; white supremacy

selfishness, Ayn Rand and, 35

Seven Days in May (film), 101

Sherman Anti-Trust Act, 57

Shivers, Allan, 13–14, 77, 159n3

Siebel, Eldon, 42

silver market, 147, 194–95n16

Simmons, William, 70

Sixteenth Amendment, 56

Skull and Bones, 2–3

slavery, 63, 64

Slay, Frank, 38, 80

Smith, Al, 13

Smith, Dick, 38

Smith, Donald W., 92

Smoot, Dan, 53–54, 56–59, 61, 63–64, 107, 151

Social Security, 82, 89

Sons of Thunder, 148

Southern Agrarian tradition, 105

Southern Aircraft Company, 17

Southern Baptists, 25, 73, 141, 146

Southern Baptist Theological Seminary, 26

Southern Conservative, 54, 59, 62

Southern Manifesto, 79

Southern Methodist University, 41–42, 45, 56, 63–64, 67, 75

Southern Presbyterians, 25

Southern Strategy: 1964 election results and, 130; announcement of to media, 124; anticipation of, 80; appearance of inclusiveness in, 143; birth of, 5, 85, 115–17; color-blind rhetoric and, 143; elements of, 5, 116–17; explicitly racial motivation for, 142–43; Barry Goldwater and, 127–28; megachurches and, 25–26; Richard Nixon and, 116–17; refinement of, 143; scholarship on, 5; segregationism and, 9–10, 115–16, 125; voting laws and economic factors, 157n12; writing off black vote, 123

Southwestern Baptist Theological Center, 25

Southwest Savings and Loan Association, 42

Soviet Union: apocalyptic rhetoric about, 52, 54; atheism of, 67; in biblical prophecy, 55–56; calls to break off diplomatic relations with, 57; coexistence with, 99; conspiratorial views on, 60; gun control in, 111; US merger with, 106–7, 110

Staples, Elizabeth, 65–66

states' rights: 1960 Democratic Party platform and, 92; Bruce Alger's conversion to, 80, 83; *Brown v. Board of Education* and, 174n68; Facts Forum and, 53; free enterprise and, 119; GOP prospects in the South and, 80; GOP's loss of black voters and, 136; interposition and, 62, 75, 84–85, 174n68, 179n54; Little Rock, Arkansas, school integration and, 119–20; nullification and, 85; property rights and, 123; in Southern Strategy, 115–16; Voting Rights Act (1965) and, 148; welcomed in GOP, 134; Edwin Walker and, 98; whistling Dixie and, 80

State Textbook Committee, 67

Staubach, Roger, 150

Steelman, Alan, 137

Stemmons, John M., 133

Stevens, Thaddeus, 80, 179n60

Stevenson, Adlai, 13–14, 112, 130, 133

Stevenson, Coke, 159n3

STOP ERA, 149

Communist positions of, 89; race and racism and, 62–63, 117; religion and worldview of, 6, 23, 54, 57–58; segregationism of, 9, 62; southern roots of, 58, 67; spreading influence of, 3; strangeness of, 2; umbrella protests and, 111–13, 188n128; unwillingness to compromise and, 57

Umbrella Man and umbrella protests, 111–13, 188n128

UNESCO, 46, 66

Unger, Merrill, 55

unions and union-busting: 1954 elections and, 78, 179n47; appeal to defense industry, 16; civil rights and, 165n17; *Dallas Morning News* on, 22, 33; Barry Goldwater and, 121, 124–25; GOP fundraising and, 40; right to work laws, 22, 125; Sherman Anti-Trust Act and, 57; union support for John F. Kennedy, 126

United Nations: in biblical prophecy, 55–56; calls for United States to leave, 57, 171n16; as controlled by Nikita Khrushchev, 60; John F. Kennedy's disarmament proposal and, 110; one world government and, 55–56, 57, 106–7, 109; in textbooks, 66, 67; as Tower of Babel, 73, 177n17; US military as controlled by, 99. *See also* UNESCO

University of Dallas, 91, 104–5, 148

University of Mississippi at Oxford, 102

University of Plano, 148

University of Texas, 66

urban renewal: opposition to, 38, 82; segregationist opposition to, 116

US Supreme Court: ban on school prayer and, 104; calls for impeachment and, 56, 74, 93, 95; Mary Ann Collins and, 91; as Communist, 89; *Dallas Morning News* on, 22; Democratic versus Republican decisions of, 82; of Gilded Age, 123–24; pro-Communism decisions of, 93. *See also Brown v. Board of Education*

Utt, James, 46, 56

Vietnam War, 131

voting laws and voting rights: Facts Forum and, 53; under Jim Crow, 70; Mississippi Plan of 1875 and, 98; Pact of Fifth Avenue and, 118; partisan effects of, 27; poll taxes and, 33, 40, 48–49, 120

Voting Rights Act (1965), 142, 148

Wade, Henry, 79–82, 115

Walker, Edwin: 1962 elections and, 120; apocalypticism of, 98; arrest and institutionalization of, 102–4, 107, 114, 186n94; conspiracy theories of, 99; controversies surrounding, 95–96; downfall of, 7; effect of on Dallas conservatives, 100–101; gubernatorial run, 100, 185n74; heroics, 97; influence of, 113; John Birch Society and, 7, 95, 96; John F. Kennedy and, 96–97, 101; on left-wing media, 99; Little Rock, Arkansas, school integration and, 98; military involvement in politics and, 96; Robert Morris and, 101–3, 106–7, 109, 186n94; Lee Harvey Oswald and, 101; Pro-Blue program and, 96; as prospective candidate, 99–100; public appearances of, 97–98, 100; relieved of command, 96, 97; resignation from Army, 97–98; ultra-conservatism and, 7, 101; University of Mississippi riot and, 102

Wallace, George, 81, 85, 136

Wallace, Lurleen, 10, 142

Wall Street Journal, 149

Walvoord, John, 55

Warren, Earl, 56, 59–60, 62–63, 93, 95, 99

Warren Commission, 42

Washington, George, 58

Wathen, L. J., 38

Wayne, John, 52

Weaver, Richard, 104

Welch, Robert: apocalyptic statements of, 89–90; background, 88; boycott of Communist nations and, 174n69; Bruce Alger and, 94; complaints about subversive intellectuals, 66; conspiratorial